4.4.03

To Stephanie

our love & wishes you
a great summer at
Leslie's.

Mom & Dad & Amber

BLESSED ARE THE FOALS

ALSO BY M. PHYLLIS LOSE, V.M.D.

No Job for a Lady
Keep Your Horse Healthy
Blessed Are the Brood Mares, Second Edition

BLESSED ARE THE FOALS

Second Edition

M. PHYLLIS LOSE, V.M.D.

HOWELL BOOK HOUSE
NEW YORK

Hungry Minds, Inc.
909 Third Avenue
New York, NY 10022

MACMILLAN is a registered trademark of Macmillan, Inc.

Library of Congress Cataloging-in-Publication Data

Lose, M. Phyllis
      Blessed are the foals / M. Phyllis Lose. -- 2nd ed.
            p. cm
         Includes index.
         ISBN 0-87605-286-3
         1. Foals--Diseases.   2. Foals.   3. Veterinary pediatrics.
I. Title
SF951.L67   1998
636.1'089892--dc21   98-12642
                                                 CIP

Manufactured in the United States of America

10 9 8 7 6 5 4

Book design by Scott Meola

To my sister NORMA

CONTENTS

ACKNOWLEDGMENTS

I gratefully acknowledge the tireless efforts, patience and understanding of my sister, Norma Virginia Lose; my dear nieces, Margaret Adams Vennell Vautard and Caroline Virginia Vennell; my precious nephew Richard Vennell; my lifelong friend, Suzanne Hineman Jenkins; and my loyal dogs, Sandy, Oscar, Rex, Tippy, Rosebud, Junior, Teddy, and Dee.

PREFACE

In the world of the Thoroughbred, pediatric problems start around mid-January of each year and continue on into autumn. The breeding season also coincides with the foaling season, so the equine veterinarian's schedule is indeed horrendously busy. I have found that the peak period for chronic foal sickness is about mid-June, around the time when most mares have foaled and the breeding season has come to a grinding halt.

This time window in the Thoroughbred breeding season is caused by the unnatural breeding season imposed upon the equine industry by the arbitrary birthdate of January 1 for all Thoroughbreds—as required by the Jockey Club. This creates unnatural breeding problems and is absolutely opposed to Nature's cycles.

Blessed Are the Foals will list and describe a foal's needs, care, and preventive measures, emphasizing the danger or warning areas where preventive action can be the answer; this can only be learned through knowledge. Many foals can and will be saved by these very simple yet vital suggestions.

I am convinced that we can reduce foal losses by 50 percent by involving conscientious people and continuing education.

For the newborn equine to survive and subsequently grow into a thrifty young adult, its life and prospects not only depend upon its stalwart mother, but also upon experienced and talented personnel. Care by dedicated professionals and conscientious amateurs decidedly shifts the odds in favor of the vulnerable foal. Skillful observation and early recognition of problems, followed by prompt attentive care, are vital to success, be it with one foal or one hundred.

There is an old adage that if the foal is not yet on the ground (or into the straw) by the time the veterinarian arrives, it is an ominous sign. Not all is lost, but time *is* of the essence. The brood mare, with her infamous explosive, dynamic delivery process, stands alone, unlike all other domestic animals.

If you are interested in breeding horses, I strongly suggest you read *Blessed Are the Brood Mares* and learn all about individual peculiarities and how they separate the equine from all other species. (*Cardinal rule:*

Never borrow information from any other species and apply it to your mare or foal.)

Each January, I am positive that I am mentally and physically ready for the annual siege of the combined breeding and foaling season, and each January, I find that I am often tried to the limit of my endurance. As most mares foal during the quiet of night, sleep for the veterinarian becomes a precious commodity at this time of year. A few hours of uninterrupted sleep are to be cherished.

One year, I had just snuggled down under my electric blanket and was luxuriating in the warmth when the ring of the telephone warned that the delicious comfort might be short-lived. It was. A mare was in labor and seemed to be in trouble. As I quickly dressed, I marveled at the insight of my equine patients. They seem to wait until my head touches the pillow, usually after a long and hard day, to present their problems. I have often said that when I turn on my electric blanket at night, it sends a message traveling out through the stars to my patients so that they can decide by lot who will be the one to prevent a reasonable night's rest.

My assistant had also heard the phone, and when I repeated the frightening phrase, "in labor for almost an hour!" she started dressing before I had even hung up. It was only a matter of minutes before we were both in the veterinary truck rushing to the farm.

The furious drive to the farm had somewhat unraveled my composure. When we arrived, I quickly got a few sketchy details from the shaken owner, then looked for my assistant through the steam steadily rising from the recumbent matron and filling the stall. The alert young woman had already set out pails of hot water, antiseptic, and a sterilized pack of obstetrical instruments. I asked the attendants to force the mare to her feet, as I scrubbed my hands and arms in readiness.

So many unanswered questions were racing through my mind—all related directly to the time versus the safety of the mare and the unborn foal. Had the placental sac encasing the foal separated prematurely from the mother's uterine lining, cutting off the maternal support system to the foal? How much natural lubricating fluid had already escaped? Was there enough fluid left to aid a delivery? How large was the foal's body in relation to the size of the mare's pelvic canal? Was the foal hopelessly locked in a malpresentation, or could the baby be repositioned to make delivery possible?

As I started to examine the mare, I was grateful she had been coaxed to rise and was up on her feet. With the mare in a standing position, gravity sometimes allows the foal to slide back into the mare's huge abdomen away from the boney, rigid pelvic birth canal (every inch is a blessing). This allows freer and easier positioning of the foal, and, in my opinion, automatically downgrades a critical situation to a less serious one.

My outstretched hand first touched a foot and coronary band, then a leg; were the long limbs displaced or twisted so as to prevent passage through the birth canal? I thought I felt a reaction when I touched the foot, but I couldn't be positive. I was relieved to find a pulse in the little leg. The foal was still alive, and there was an outside chance that it could be repositioned and delivered within the as yet unknown margin of time allotted. Did we have time to save this foal? How much? It was beyond determination. As quickly as possible, I sedated the mare, vigorously scrubbed my hands and arms, and proceeded with repositioning the foal. As I touched the foal's body, it actually moved! If we acted fast enough, the foal's life could be saved.

Much was involved, and all must function favorably in order for success. The mare must remain quiet and cooperative during the manipulation, yet she must work very hard to aid in the delivery. Corrective repositioning must be accurate and rapid, with the advantage of an adequate amount of placental fluid for smooth and easy movements to protect the mother's reproductive tract as well as the foal.

The foal responded to my efforts. It slipped into a good position, and I was able to align both forefeet with the head and long neck. Then small, sterile, stainless-steel chains were placed around the foal's tiny, soft, coronary bands. Now it was essential that the mare cooperate and help me with the delivery. A tug on the chains restarted the mare's contractions, and as she began to bear down, I applied respectful and careful traction, synchronized with the mother's powerful, muscular contractions. Our combined, rhythmic effort resulted in some progress of the foal through the birth canal. It seemed eons before the feet and then the head were fully presented to view. At this point the matron's active, productive contractions ceased and she rested momentarily. Within 60 seconds or so, the mare resumed labor, and the entire foal was delivered into the straw with relative ease.

The large bay colt was breathing. He lifted his head and blinked his eyes as if in amazement at being in the world and alive. With a glowing sense of pleasure, I turned to the owner to say, "Here is your foal."

Pediatrics is defined as that branch of medicine dealing with the care of infants and children and the treatment of their diseases. *Blessed Are the Foals* will deal with the care of the young equine from birth through the first year of life.

Just as the obstetrician hands the human infant to the awaiting pediatrician in the hospital delivery room, we hand you a live foal just arrived in the world.

Human babies are born in all extremes of environmental conditions, and many survive without much medical assistance or supervision. Many foals live and grow in the absence of preventive and protective veterinary medical practices. There are few records available comparing the survival rate of attended foalings versus those where the mare foals alone, but I am sure that if the data were compiled, the difference would be shocking.

I am not comparing the value of human life with that of an animal. But comparable hazards exist that, in many cases, can be prevented or overcome with recognition of the problem and conscientious care.

In the days before veterinary intervention, the American mustang escaped extinction through the process of natural selection, or the survival of the fittest. Bands of these small, rugged, and none-too-attractive animals exist today. We have no idea how many tragic and unnecessary deaths occurred during birth among mustang foals before medical help was made available to them. But survive they did, as did *Homo sapiens*.

Today's man-bred equine did not spring from natural selection and survival of the fittest; modern foals are much too precious to leave to chance. *Every* foal is important. Each individual equine represents generations of selective breeding for desired traits. Many times thousands, even hundreds of thousands, of dollars are invested in a single specimen. Whether a horse is a pet, a pleasure horse, a show horse, a hunter, a trail horse, a working cow pony, a harness horse, or a racehorse, it always requires an investment of time, energy, and money. These factors, aside from each owner's personal interest in his or her horse, must all be weighed. In addition, the unusually long period of gestation—11 months—of the equine, during which the owner waits in suspense, adds to the intrinsic value of the new foal to the owner.

Hereditary and congenital defects with associated complications are the result of intensive selective breeding efforts to modify the horse for specialized and/or limited purposes. The practice of indiscriminate inbreeding has only added to the dilemma.

Every breed of horse boasts a few outstanding horsemen who are conscientiously trying to produce and preserve the ultimate in conformation, suitable size, stamina, speed, ability, intelligence, and temperament. Unfortunately, a majority of breeders have only a single goal. They seek either the speed to win a race, conformation of the breed to win at horse shows, or ability to meet the requirements of various types of competition. They ignore or lose sight of the "whole" animal, of their responsibility to their breed and to future generations of horses and horsemen.

Although we have achieved well-made, sizable, capable individuals, we often gain one desirable characteristic at the expense of another. Thus each breed has acquired its own inherent problems. As man has required specimens to conform to breed standards and performance goals, desirable traits have been involuntarily forfeited.

It should also be recognized that our modern horse, no matter what its lineage, lives in an unnatural environment. By moving the equine, over a time span of hundreds of years, from its normal habitat into fenced fields and well-equipped barns with prepared stalls, we have produced an altered environment. The spin-off effects are horse-specific bacterial and viral diseases, each creating its own problems.

Multiple problems are created by concentrations of horse populations, especially where grazing land is limited. This self-perpetuating road to health hazards is most commonly found in suburban and urban areas, where the resurgence of the pleasure horse is most prevalent, as well as on large commercial farms with overgrazed, horse-poor land. Overcrowding should be cause for increased concern, as it produces an ideal environment for the spread and propagation of infection, disease, and parasitism.

Although it is always sad to lose a foal, the unavoidable loss can be better accepted with the knowledge that everything possible has been done. It is unforgivably tragic if a foal dies due to an attendant's inexperience, because of unawareness of proper treatment and medications, or through misguided use of any knowledge extrapolated from experience with other species. Quite unlike all other domestic animals, the equine has specific physiologic needs. If we hope to improve our foals' survival rates, we must burn this fact into our conscious minds and daily thinking.

Chapter One

THE NEWBORN FOAL

Your foal has just arrived into the bedding—wet and wooly, with water-logged feet, but, ideally, also with an intact and functioning umbilical cord still attached to its abdomen.

This exciting event may appear to be a spontaneous happening. Nothing is further from the truth. A foal is actually 11 months old before humans have the privilege of first laying eyes on it. Although you may be aware of these facts, let's go back 336 days—roughly 11 months—and review what occurs.

Life begins when a single spermatozoon, one and only one, out of millions present in the mare's oviduct, is permitted to enter the recently released and quite vulnerable ovum (egg). The remaining spermatozoa are rejected and die.

It has been documented that at the very second of penetration, a biological barrier is produced in the egg's outer cellular layers, accompanied by an ever-so-slight vibration. Pregnancy has thus been initiated, and life has begun. All this happens in the upper part of the mare's oviduct, very near the ovary that was responsible for the egg's development and subsequent release.

At this point, size, shape, sex, color, physical conformation, and disposition of your future foal have already been decided. Natural health, inherent resistance or vulnerability to disease, and even varied and questionable ability and talent have been predetermined. From this awesome moment on, all genetic traits and characteristics are fixed, determined for the horse's entire embryonic and extrauterine life. Quite an impressive moment.

The fertilized ovum, called a zygote, is a rounded cellular mass of microscopic size, encompassing all the detailed data and intriguing information that affect the life of the foal. Although I am an old practitioner, I cannot resist equating the embryonic zygote with the modern computer chip. If only we could peer through the abdomen and translate what the future holds.

The 11-month gestation period may seem a long wait to the anxious owner, but it is in fact a busy time of constant growth and development. (The brood mare requires two months longer than the cow and the human to produce an offspring, but their "time in waiting" is considerably shorter than the poor

1

elephant's 23 months.) My admiration and respect go to any and all brood mares who accomplish the feat of producing a dynamic and complete foal, fully capable of growing into a full-sized horse, within the given time. If all is healthy, the restless owner is rewarded with a soft, ever-so-clean, brand-new foal, intact, with all its essential parts. Well worth the wait. All is forgiven! Even though I've seen it time and again, the whole affair knocks my socks off.

The innate hardiness of a foal, and its ability to resist diseases, is often a reflection of the prenatal care the mare received during her 11 months' gestation. Proper nutrition and exercise, an effective parasite control program, and an environment that nurtures a relaxed and contented dam are contributing factors to the health and well-being of the newborn.

Still, all newborns are vulnerable to external environmental stress, and the equine infant not only appears but has proven to be quite fragile and unique in its needs. The evolutionary process has been kinder to other species of animals, providing a bonus of built-in protective means for survival and self-perpetuation. This has been well documented by improved survival rates of these species even with less efficient husbandry practices. Conversely, evolution has literally bypassed the equine species. I have observed in one short lifetime that the natural protective mechanisms against disease in some of our better-bred individuals appear weaker, and that there has been a steady decline in reproductive efficiency.

The typical delivery of the brood mare is rapid and explosive in nature, rarely requiring more than 30 minutes from the time that visible active labor begins until the whole production is completed and the foal is in the world. It is therefore unusual for a veterinarian to witness a normal foaling unless the person in attendance is exceptionally astute or the imminent mare is in close proximity to the veterinarian's office.

Once the foal has arrived, a thorough examination is in order. Although a few qualified horse people can evaluate a newborn in a worthy fashion, these same talented people often prefer to summon a "dyed-in-the-wool" horse doctor. It is important to have a veterinarian examine the foal as soon as possible in order to assess the newborn's immediate and future health and to rule out the chance of hidden physical or medical problems. The pertinent facts of parturition are always invaluable in this assessment. When an alert attendant is able to describe to the veterinarian what he or she observed during delivery and the foaling process (three stages), the conscientious horse doctor will listen carefully to the information and subsequently sort out what is significant, never disregarding what is offered.

Parturition can vary greatly in the brood mare, but it is an uncontested and truly dynamic event. A maiden mare's style and ability to deliver a foal can be sharply contrasted to a multipara mare of many foalings. Time involved during the actual act of giving birth has been reported to exert a direct bearing on the new arrival's vitality and energy, significantly affecting its capability to cope with the external environment. The various facets of parturition weigh heavily on the foal's need for early care and attention. Again, a valid judgment by your veterinarian is in order. (For further information, please refer to *Blessed Are the Brood Mares*, Second Edition.)

If left to nature, your foal will be subjected to the old survival rule "survival of the fittest." To me, this means that the fittest will live, but the best individual may not necessarily survive.

Through careful education, you can prepare to raise a foal properly and avoid losing it through ignorance. You may choose to pay the expense of placing the heavy mare into professional hands for delivery and foal care. (Be careful to select a conscientious and knowledgeable person, preferably one who has a rapport with a good equine obstetrician and pediatrician. Unfortunately, my experience has been that the bigger and greater the reputation, the smaller the knowledge and the less concern for details. A sad commentary indeed.)

The attendant who witnesses the parturition can be very helpful to the veterinarian, who undoubtedly will arrive late and spontaneously begin debriefing those present. The attendant should be able to answer questions such as: What position was the foal in at presentation? What position did the mare assume early and late in delivery—standing, walking, or recumbent—either sternal (on breastbone) or lateral (on side)? How long did each major progressive step require? Where were the placental membranes located early in the delivery?

In addition to asking these questions, the veterinarian and all others responsible should pay close attention to two other areas: first, the time required by the

Normal complete afterbirth membranes.

mare to pass *entirely* her afterbirth membranes; second, the reading of the placental membranes, which are usually spread out on a level, clean surface to enhance total assessment. In competent, knowledgeable hands, this information will point to the medical needs of both the brood mare and her newborn foal.

NORMAL DELIVERY/PARTURITION

Differences in strength and stamina of the newborn vary tremendously. Some individuals are so limp and weak that there is concern for their lives, while other foals literally squirm and twist with vitality. An exceptional foal may lift its head and even manage a whinny before it is completely delivered. The foal thus endowed will wiggle resentfully while being dried. The vigor of such an infant, whether a colt or a filly, will be felt as soon as you place your hands on it. Some foals are so determined to live that quite often they can overcome a weakness or even a mild handicap.

RESPIRATION

To describe a normal delivery would require many pages, so let us assume that the foal about to claim our attention has been delivered by means of an uncomplicated parturition and appears free from any serious problem.

During gestation, fetal lungs are virtually collapsed and fluid-filled. The circulating blood is responsible for all vital exchanges of gases and nourishment via the umbilical cord. An intact umbilical cord is essential to the foal's life during a normal delivery and is absolutely imperative during a delayed delivery. The cord is attached to the midline abdomen (belly button) and returns inside as a lifeline extension to the placenta still attached to the maternal uterine lining.

With the foal abruptly out of the protective uterus and into the outside world, its pulmonary tissue must make a major adjustment: that of exchanging accumulated fluid from fetal life for oxygen and atmospheric air. As the foal begins to breathe, a nerve center located in the brain stem is suddenly stimulated, and as a result, thousands of minute elastic lung-tissue compartments, called pulmonary alveoli, are stretched and activated as they are filled with inrushing air.

The normal foal will be breathing by the time its hind feet are free of the mare. As the hocks appear during birth, the foal should begin manifesting an effort in the form of a ragged and labored breathing. The foal is attempting to initiate and establish its own independent respiratory pattern. Do not be alarmed by this struggle; it is a reassuring sign to the experienced attendant that the neonate is quite alive!

With the head, neck, and forelegs presented, the head will drop to the side of the foreleg with the nose down. This position helps nasal fluids to escape, reduces the chance of pulmonary fluid retention, and enhances oxygenation by allowing the expansion of lung tissue. The nares (nostrils) should be unobstructed by the bedding or the fetal membranes. Prudent use of a small rubber bulb for aspiration of the nasal passages may be helpful.

As the newborn arrives onto the bedding, the remaining amnionic sac, a white glistening and slippery membrane encasing the foal during delivery, should be removed from its hind quarters and hind legs. The foal's entire body and extremities should then be promptly rubbed dry. Vigorous toweling stimulates both respiration and circulation and creates warmth while absorbing the moisture from the foal's sometimes dense and heavy coat. This reduces some of the initial stress to the foal and helps make its introduction into the world a little less traumatic.

FAILURE TO BREATHE

Rapid action should be taken when a foal is totally delivered but is not breathing. Be well prepared in advance for this possibility by arranging a detailed discussion with your on-call veterinarian, preferably an equine practitioner. Be prepared with knowledge. Some of the better brood mare farms equip the nursery with a small oxygen cylinder for just such an emergency.

Prompt effort should be made to clear the nasal passages of fluid and accumulated excretions. Once the nasal passages are clear and the foal is stimulated by vigorous toweling, the majority of foals begin to breathe on their own. It is not unusual to see a weak, deflated foal, totally delivered and showing no visible respirations, suddenly respond to zealous toweling with gasps and ragged respirations.

To stand by and watch your foal struggling to establish rhythmic independent breathing can indeed be an anxious moment. Great physical effort, producing deep thumping chest and heaving rib-cage movements, normally accompanies the final and concurrent surging of blood through the navel cord.

Years of experience have convinced me that the massaging action of energetic toweling of the foal's entire body and limbs serves as a complementary adjunct to all resuscitory efforts. (To read more about the dynamics of delivery in the brood mare, I refer you to my other book, *Blessed Are the Brood Mares*.)

UMBILICAL CORD

For several minutes after delivery of the foal, the equine's unusually long (24 to 30 inches) umbilical cord provides continued communication with the mother's uterine lining (endometrium) through the still-attached placenta. From 600 to 800 cc of oxygenated and enriched blood continue to be immediately available to the foal through the umbilical cord, even though the newborn is breathing independently. If the cord ruptures prematurely or fails to function for any reason, this added bonus blood transfusion remains in the placenta, serving no purpose at all.

To prevent this, the foaling attendant should support the newly arrived foal against the recumbent mare with one hand and hold the umbilical cord in the other hand to check the strong pulsations, which usually continue for a minute or two after delivery. Huge pulsations stretch the elastic cord with each surge of placental blood being delivered to the new foal. These pulsations may appear as large as pullet eggs passing through the cord and into the foal's circulatory system. Rupturing the cord before these pulsations subside deprives the newborn foal of the much-needed fortification provided by this placental blood. Please maintain a quiet environment for the benefit of the matron; she may then remain recumbent until the pulsations cease in the intact cord.

When the pulsations cease, the foal should be allowed to kick away from the mare, successfully rupturing the cord as nature intended and freeing the foal.

The average foal will arrive with an intact umbilical cord: One end is attached to the navel of the foal, while the other end, quite out of sight, is attached to the huge placenta, still firmly adhered to the inner surface of the uterine wall. The navel cord disappears inside the mare and fans out into a large umbrella-like shape becoming part of the placenta or afterbirth. Usually within an hour of delivery, this large and heavy membrane encompassing the umbilical cord is shed from its attachment under hormonal influence and passed by the matron into the bedding.

WARNING: With the foaling membranes trailing behind her, it is essential that the attendant tie a respectable knot in the slippery amnion. Tie the knot so that the sac is elevated above the bedding and the mare's feet, preferably at hock level, permitting its own weight and pressure to remain on the still-attached maternal placenta. This is not always as easy as it sounds, but it is vitally important to prevent the mare's hind feet from accidentally stepping on the amniotic sac, which would create enough undue pressure to result in severe injury to and bleeding in the uterine lining and cervical canal. Such trauma to the reproductive tract could cause scar-tissue formation, with subsequent inability to regenerate normal tissue, and possible resultant infertility. I must stress the importance of this simple attention as an invaluable service to preserve the mare's reproductive future. As the membranes slowly peel away from the maternal endometrium and descend into full view, it is often necessary to retie the knot in order to maintain its proper height.

One day I received an emergency call from an unfamiliar barn, stating that a foal was down in the stall, unable to rise. I quickly drove to the farm, a short five miles, and found the foal recumbent and quite unwilling to get up. A groom held the large mare over in the corner of the large stall, which enabled us to examine the very uncomfortable neonatal foal, approximately 24 hours old. Rapid respirations and a fever of 104 degrees indicated some form of septicemia. At that moment, the foal jumped to its feet, and I saw the umbilical stump—enlarged, swollen, moist, and very painful. To my utter surprise and disgust, my fingers located a piece of suture material snugly ligated around the base of the cord, obviously compromising drainage and blood circulation. After an emergency removal of the ligature, local cleansing of the navel stump, and injections of antibiotic, the foal expressed relief by showing an interest in nursing from his mother. The fever subsided two full degrees within the hour, and all was well within a few days of follow-up injections. Lack of specific equine knowledge existed in this barn!

There was no way to determine whether the primary cause had been infection trapped within the cord advancing into the abdomen or an incomplete or nonfunctional urethra, not yet ready to carry off the urine in the normal way. One of the many functions of the umbilical cord during fetal life is the passage of urine. If all goes well at birth, the urethra assumes this duty, and the cord simultaneously ceases to so function.

WARNING: *Never* allow the cord to be ruptured or severed in any fashion other than by the mare and foal, and *never* permit the cord to be tied by anyone for any reason.

Ideally, the navel stump should be treated as soon as the umbilical cord ruptures and before it comes in contact with any contaminants—i.e., straw, hay, feces, urine, etc.—so the importance of an alert attendant cannot be overemphasized. Be on the job! For many years, iodine, preferably in a concentration of 8 percent tincture or 5 percent aqueous iodine solution, has been a popular and relatively successful cauterizing agent for the navel stump. It is the method of choice for many practitioners, yet the subject remains controversial.

CAUTION: A fresh navel stump presents a major portal of entry for infection, warranting close observation for the first few days. And in some cases, if moisture persists, repeat treatment may be necessary.

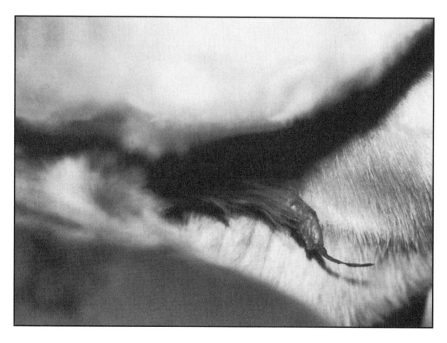

Navel stump.

NAVEL CORD TREATMENT

A small, wide-mouth jar should be sterilized and filled with the tincture of iodine. A baby-food jar is ideal. It should be prepared in advance of each expected foaling and kept nearby so that it can be used immediately after the rupture of the cord. An individual jar should be freshly prepared for each foal. The navel stump should be immersed in the jar and the wide mouth of the jar held against the foal's abdomen for several seconds. This will allow the stump to become thoroughly saturated and effectively cauterized, avoiding contamination.

Navel tissue is elastic in nature and retracts readily when stretched and naturally separated. This characteristic is aided by proper and prompt cauterization. While the recoil property is obviously advantageous, it can cause contaminants to be trapped and pathogenic bacteria to become sealed into a medium conducive to their rapid growth. Therefore the navel stump should be examined daily; if any moisture appears on the open end of the stump, or if any wet hairs, swelling, or discharge are seen in the adjacent tissue, the cauterization should be repeated with a fresh jar of iodine. Observe daily for any sign of stump enlargement. A daily reduction in size is a favorable sign.

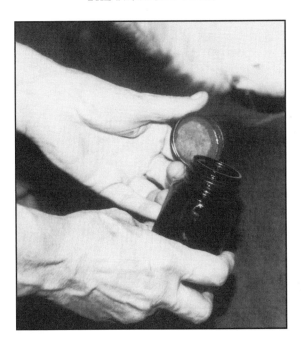

Proper-type jar.

The normal navel stump will dry within 24 hours and will shrink and ultimately disappear over a period of a few weeks. Some foals require several daily treatments of the stump before the moisture disappears, while others will require only the initial treatment at birth. Any navel stump that is larger than a man's little finger, remains moist for a protracted period of time, or exhibits swelling or tenderness in contiguous tissue, should receive prompt professional assessment.

WARNING: Moisture and slight enlargement of the navel stump within 24 hours or so are two salient clues to a possible leaky urachus. The urachus is a small tubular structure contained within the umbilical cord that carries the fluid waste from the fetal bladder to the placenta during gestation (prenatal life). After birth, when the umbilical cord ruptures, natural elastic closure of the urachus should occur. When the small tubular urachus is closed effectively, urine is then permitted to pass from the neonatal bladder out through the urethra. (See LEAKY NAVEL CORD, page 122; NAVEL ILL, page 67.)

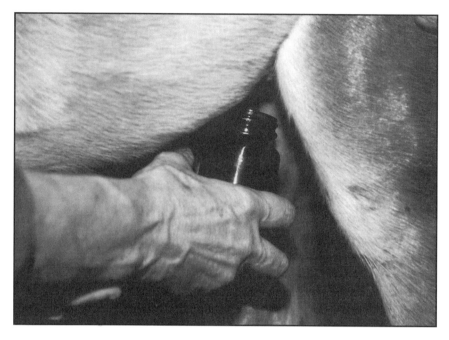

Application, standing foal.

ABILITY TO RISE

The equine neonate must cope with disproportionately long legs and a lengthy, slender neck that seems mismatched with his relatively compact torso. With this assortment of seemingly incongruent parts, the foal begins struggling to achieve an upright stance within minutes of birth.

At first, a newborn foal will stretch its legs and test its muscles, helping both its physiological and psychological forces to gather awareness, muscle tone, and—apparently most difficult—coordination. Many incomplete and sometimes traumatic attempts to stand are endured before balance is finally achieved.

The time needed for a foal to gain its feet and some semblance of balance varies tremendously not only from breed to breed but from individual to individual within a given breed. Conformation, built-in strength and vigor, health, and such intangibles as courage, will, and determination are all contributing factors.

Gaining control of the head and neck is the first order of business. Many foals arrive in the world with this faculty already mastered, and all but very weak or sickly foals use the head and neck for balance to roll up on the sternum (breast-bone) within seconds. This sternal position is advantageous for lung aeration and expansion, and seems to aid in all vital physiological functions.

Immediate application, recumbent foal.

From this position the foal may need as little as 10 minutes or as long as an hour to finally stand on all four feet and take its first few halting, stumbling steps. During this time, the average foal will struggle to rise, only to fall, then rest and try again. It seems that once the foal has managed a standing posture, however briefly, each subsequent attempt is easier. With each momentary success, a foal achieves phenomenal gains in motor skills, confidence, and overall ability.

After having become secure in this new erect position, some foals find getting down again to be almost as difficult a feat as learning to stand. Slow learners are pathetically near exhaustion as they try unsuccessfully to lie down for a much-needed rest. If these individuals lose their balance and fall down, they seem relieved to take the tumble and stretch out with a grateful sigh.

It is during these early floundering efforts that some foals sustain injury in spite of a stall especially prepared for their safety. The areas most commonly traumatized are the elbows, the hocks, the eyes, and the soft tissue around the mouth and nose. Injuries to these areas are usually superficial and appear more serious than they are in actuality.

The foal's beautiful, long, slender neck is a great help in getting to its feet, and it helps the foal maintain its balance once standing. But the length and flexibility that serves these purposes so well also increases the vulnerability of the neck to serious trauma. The protection of a properly bedded stall with straw banked against the walls, and a careful manual assist from the foaling attendant, minimize accidents.

Once the foal has achieved some degree of stability and control, it should locate a cooperative mare's teats with relative ease and ingest its first meal. The foal who cannot accomplish this feat within a reasonable time frame (one hour) is to be suspected of physiological malfunctions. I would suggest calling your veterinarian.

It is necessary for the foal to make many adjustments following its stormy, explosive, rapid delivery. Initiation of respiration by reflex action, clearing of the respiratory tract, the establishment and regulation of body temperature, and development of musculoskeletal tone must all synchronize to enable the foal to struggle, fall, rise, and eventually walk.

It seems to be an overwhelming task for the new foal not only to have to support its body weight in an upright position, but also to learn to bend and flex its long, slender neck in an effort to reach its mother's udder. It is fatiguing enough to master control of four unwieldy legs without coping with the problems of reaching and twisting its head and neck into the unusual position required for sucking from the poorly placed mammary gland. (In no other species do the young have to work so hard to nurse. The faltering hunt for the small, inaccessible, and seemingly inadequate teats suspended from above can be extremely tiring.) It is my contention that all newborn foals deserve a supportive hand or arm during their initial struggle for nourishment.

It never ceases to amaze me that after the hours, days, and weeks they devote to the foal watch, everyone runs off to rest as soon as the foal is born! No matter how exhausted a caretaker may be, the time spent *after* delivery to observe,

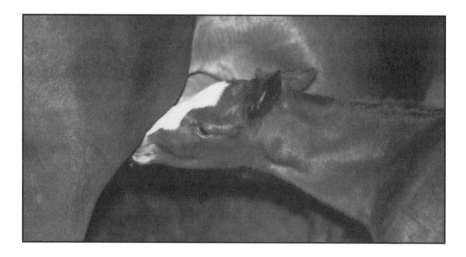

Essential first milk.

protect, and watch for red-alert symptoms far outweighs the temporary discomfort of lost sleep. Monitor the foal carefully during the post-partem period, ensuring the following:

1.   A well-bedded stall, especially the corners, walls, and doorways.

2.   Acceptance of the foal by the mare (especially maiden mares).

MATERNALLY PRODUCED ANTIBODIES

Because the placenta of the mare is unique and quite incapable of transporting the large molecular antibodies to the fetus during gestation and embryonic development, no antibodies are received by the foal during intrauterine life. In contrast to all other species, the equine baby is totally unprotected by preformed antibodies when it arrives in the world.

Maternally produced antibodies, however, are abundantly available from the colostrum, called "first milk." This single source of protection is found only in the mammary gland and only for a limited time. It is present for only 48 to 72 hours before the mare's regular milk, absent of beneficial antibodies, replaces the enriched colostrum. The udder then provides only natural, normal nourishment.

An additional disadvantage for the neonatal foal is the brief period of time that the foal's small intestine (duodenum) will permit passage of the essential antibodies, received from the colostrum, through the intestinal mucosa and into the circulatory system. This time of selective absorption has been documented as the first 48 hours of the foal's life. It is obvious that the critical early need for colostrum is of paramount importance. Other species receive preformed antibodies during gestation and arrive into the outside world with varying degrees of protection against infection. The equine is the exception to the rule!

Nature has provided all the necessary ingredients in colostrum for the new arrival. Protective antibodies, an abundance of glucose, and an essential laxative property are all available. It is unfortunate that such a stopwatch schedule for survival exists.

CAUTION: It is often difficult for some weaker foals to meet such a rigid schedule, especially those unattended or under the care of an attendant who is unaware of the life-or-death nature of this strictly limited time period. Be prepared to assist the weaker individual. A "911" assistance via a baby bottle can only be helpful.

ROUTINE ENEMA

Once the foal has located the teats and ingested its first meal, a warm, soapy enema should be routinely administered to assure the evacuation of meconium (fecal material that forms in the intestines during embryonic life) from the lower bowel and to stimulate peristalsis (progressive wavelike movement) in the intestines. Although an enema is not imperative for the average foal, the foal is more comfortable and relaxed once the lower bowel is evacuated. Comfortable, and with a warm meal in its stomach, the foal will drop down in the bedding for a peaceful, contented sleep.

An enema is a good routine practice for every foal, whether defecation has been observed or not. Do not be trapped into complacency by evidence of a bowel movement; the presence of fecal material, even following an enema, does not preclude subsequent constipation. The presence of impacted meconium can be manifest at a later time, usually 24 to 36 hours after birth, even after one or more fecal passages.

SIMPLE COLIC

Simple colic, which should not be confused with severe colic, can be remedied by a routine enema. (Severe colic will be discussed later.)

Early in life, many foals will become irritated and uncomfortable. When you see a foal with its tail elevated and switching, straining to defecate, restless and simulating colic, it is an indication that an additional enema is needed to aid in the removal of accumulated firm fecal balls (meconium) from the rectum. Once this is accomplished, the foal will nap comfortably.

The enema should not only be properly prepared but should also be given with proper equipment. Regardless of the choice of agents or equipment used, a soft rubber tube for insertion through the anus into the rectum is necessary for safety. Before the tube is inserted, allow the fluid to run out the end to ensure that the tube is free of air and filled with the enema mixture. Simply clamping the end of the tube shut with your fingers will keep it in readiness for insertion; this will prevent undesirable air from entering the rectum, where it can create discomfort to the newborn.

The soft rubber tubing should be inserted to a maximum of 4 to 5 inches, and great care should be taken to avoid irritation to the rectal mucosa. It is of utmost importance to allow for the escape of backflow pressure of fluids from the anus during the administration of the enema to prevent undue pressure on the thin, sensitive intestinal walls.

A number of safe, time-tested ingredients are available; each has a different action. No matter which agents are chosen, the maximum volume should not exceed 1 pint. Perhaps the solution most easily prepared and most often used is made with Ivory soap and warm water, but any unadulterated white soap is acceptable. Use only enough soap to form light suds. The temperature is of paramount importance. When the solution is administered to the foal, it should be lukewarm or tepid. Test the temperature in the same manner you would use to check a baby's bottle: A few drops of the solution on the inside of your wrist should feel just barely warm to your skin. This solution has a mild stimulating effect on the rectum and the lower bowel by virtue of warmth, volume, and the mild action of the soap.

Another popular mixture consists of equal parts of mineral oil and warm water. Given in much the same fashion as a soapy enema, its action is that of an emollient, although combined with its warmth and volume its action is also stimulating to the bowel. Equal parts of glycerine and warm water have the same desirable effects as mineral oil and water. When mixing either of these oily preparations, it is important to blend the two ingredients until the solution takes on a milky appearance. When possible, avoid the use of commercial enema preparations in the newborn.

Ideally, an enema should be given with the foal in a standing position. As the viscera are in the proper location in the abdominal cavity and free of external pressures, this allows for easy administration and reduced resistance to the required volume. When an enema is given to a recumbent foal, extra precautions must be taken. Abdominal pressure created by the weight of the foal on the ground can cause intestinal crowding and displacement of organs, with possible pressure on the colon or rectum.

As with many foal caretaking activities, administration of an enema is a two-person operation. One person should cradle the foal with one arm around its chest and one arm around its hind quarters. A foal may be held firmly and securely in this position to prevent injury to either the foal or the foal handler. For additional control and support and to maintain contact with the active foal, the person giving the enema should have a firm grip on the dock of the foal's tail to help prevent irritation or injury to the rectal mucosa caused by the quick moves that all foals are determined to make.

When the tip of the soft rubber tube is inserted, a mass of firm fecal material is often encountered. Introducing a small volume of the enema preparation will loosen and break down this mass, permitting the tube to be advanced to the allowable maximum.

A pint enema bag or can equipped with a half-inch-diameter, long, flexible tube, using gravity flow, is both safe and effective. The enema solution should be allowed to flow smoothly without force or pressure exerted. The secret of an atraumatic and productive enema is the determination that the flow is smooth and free from any but the mildest tissue resistance.

Enema equipment.

The rectal mucosa of a foal is delicate and fragile. Foals have been lost as a direct result of enemas administered by heavy-handed, insensitive persons. Hard rubber, Bakelite, or metal fittings on enema equipment have no place in an equine nursery; nor do impatient, rough, thoughtless foal attendants.

SEVERE COLIC

When colic does not respond to conservative treatment, and the abdominal pain increases in intensity, it then becomes a serious matter, one for the veterinarian to resolve. When meconium fails to evacuate the gastrointestinal tract of the neonatal foal, severe colic will become very evident and sometimes frightening. The foal will roll in the bedding, refuse to nurse, and exhibit constant intractable pain. If severe colic persists after all conservative efforts, such as enemas, antispasmodics, and sedatives, serious consideration should then be directed toward possible surgery. The patient should be moved as quickly as possible to the nearest veterinary medical facility, one equipped for abdominal surgery. Transportation of both the mare and the sometimes uncontrollable foal may present a problem, but one experienced horse people can handle. Unfortunately, urgency is of the essence. This is an agonizing decision for all horse owners and one that can be made easier by a dedicated equine practitioner who can make an accurate early diagnosis—a decision that can enhance the foal's prognosis. Call ahead, and be prepared.

Causes of meconium impaction (retention) are thought to be exercise- and diet-related in the dam during pregnancy. (See RETAINED MECONIUM, page 54.)

Back in my early childhood (I was 11 or 12 years old) the exciting news that a neighbor's mare had foaled quickly spread through the small community. The news reached our house just as we were finishing breakfast. Even though my parents humored many of my whims where horses were concerned, they turned deaf ears to my pleas to miss a day of school to see the result of my long wait. It had to have been an eternity since I had heard that Jenny was to have a foal, and the thought that I would now have to spend hours in a classroom without even a glimpse of the new foal was sheer torture. However, I somehow survived the long day and made record time covering the distance from school to home.

I hurriedly tacked up my pony and galloped across the big field to the nearby farm. As I reached the top of a small rise, I saw the veterinarian's truck parked by the barn that housed Jenny and her foal. Veterinarians, in those times, rarely made routine calls, so I knew there must be serious trouble. Urging my pony into a flat-out run, I flew the rest of the distance across the field. After hastily tying the pony, I slipped quietly into the barn through a side door.

The old bank barn was without electricity, and even on this sunny afternoon the light was subdued. When my eyes adjusted from the bright sunlight to the dim interior of the barn, I saw the groom holding the mare in a corner of the stall. I quietly inched my way closer and saw the still, flat form of a foal in the straw. Dr. Smith removed a rectal thermometer from the foal, and from the light coming in through the stall window, I could see that the thermometer was covered with blood. I heard him quietly tell the worried owners that nothing else could be done to help Jenny's new baby.

This somber statement upset those present, and I heard someone crying in the background. One by one the distressed people left the barn. I flattened myself against the wall next to the stall to make myself as small as possible so that I would blend with the shadows. Torn by fear and fascination, I still wanted to stay. The veterinarian slipped a needle into a vein in the motionless foal's neck and injected the contents of a syringe. The foal's irregular breathing stopped.

As the doctor prepared to perform a postmortem, I was very still and tried to take short shallow breaths so I wouldn't be discovered. I honestly didn't know whether I should be there or not. As he opened the abdomen, my stomach told me to leave, but my head said "Stay." I was as shocked and saddened by the loss of the foal as its owners were, but I was filled with curiosity and wanted to learn, with the veterinarian, what had caused the foal's death.

The meticulous search for information was under way, and I realized that this man was hoping to gain from this sad situation knowledge that would enable him to save other foals in the future. Even though this foal was dead, it was still useful. The veterinarian was so gentle and respectful of the body as he worked that even as a child I understood his purpose.

Suddenly the doctor gave a gasp and then, in his excitement, turned to me in the shadows. He pointed out a ragged tear in the foal's rectum. I will never forget his outrage as he accused the clumsy, heavy-handed person who, while giving an enema, had punctured the rectal wall and caused the death of the foal. I have carried this lesson with me all of my life, literally from foal to foal.

I think it is appropriate at this juncture to reemphasize the importance of proper enema equipment and the ever-so-gentle technique with which it should be administered. A productive enema, resulting in the visible passage of fecal material, is comforting to both the baby foal and to the owner. A nonproductive enema, however, is not cause for immediate concern. Lack of spontaneous results is not uncommon; in some cases, a longer period of time is required for the solution to effect a fecal passage. It is imperative, however, that the foal be kept under observation in order to be certain that this vital function takes place, ideally within a couple of hours.

The normal character of the feces of the newborn should duplicate in miniature that of the adult horse. The stool should be firmly formed into darkish brown, well-defined balls. The balls may vary in size from that of a large green pea to that of a large grape. Any variation from this color or consistency in the initial bowel movement may be an indication of an impending problem and should be considered as a warning. Subsequent movements may vary slightly without causing concern.

Approximately 12 to 18 hours after the foal's birth, the feces usually reflects the ingestion of colostrum in the upper bowel, resulting in a change in both its color and character. At this time, the stools become less firm and can vary from a dull mustard color to a bright yellow. If this change occurs within the proper time sequence, it is an indication that the bowel is patent and functioning.

If at any time a perceptibly unpleasant fecal odor is detected, it can signal the possible presence of a pathologic condition. Further, if either dry or hard light-colored stools are seen, or formless liquid feces observed, a problem may be brewing. Consult your veterinarian.

VETERINARY EXAMINATION

The average horse person will know within the first hour of the foal's life whether it is normal or should in fact be seen by a veterinarian as soon as possible. A good rule to remember: A healthy foal will *gain* strength and vigor with each hour; an unhealthy foal will *lose* strength and vigor with each hour.

If you have any qualms about the physical condition of your new foal or question your ability to evaluate the status of the newborn, your veterinarian should be called on an emergency basis. If you have no doubts or questions, then an early-morning veterinary inspection of your new foal is sufficient. A competent examination early in the life of your foal may be "a stitch in time," and at the very least you will have the satisfaction of knowing that you have given the newest member of your equine family every possible advantage.

PLACENTAL EVALUATION

If the foal has been on its feet, has nursed, defecated, and urinated, appears healthy and vigorous, and is comfortably napping, your veterinarian's attention undoubtedly will be directed to an examination of the placenta as the next order of business.

The story that the experienced veterinarian is able to read in the placenta sets the stage for medical care of the foal during the critical early time of its life. This story, coupled with a description of the actual delivery, is the most important source of information for assessment of both the mare and the foal. Color, size, and weight of the placental tissues are observed, but whether the membranes have been passed *in their entirety* is of utmost importance. Knowledge that the complete afterbirth membranes have passed is valuable to the brood mare owner. Retention of a small placental fragment within the uterus, usually found in the tip of the nonpregnant horn, if unrecognized and thus untreated, can cause very serious medical consequences.

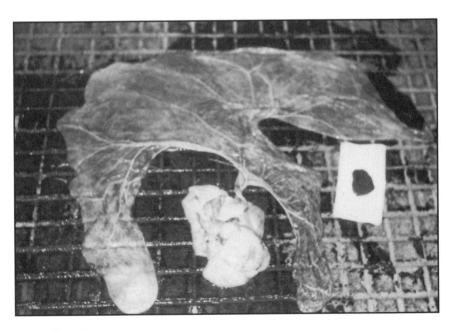

Excellent placental membranes.

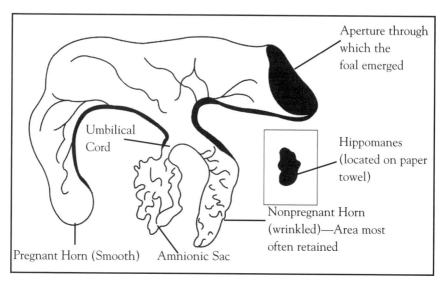

Complete and healthy afterbirth membranes.

By this time, the foal will probably have finished a brief nap and be back on its feet in search of another meal, affording the skilled observer an opportunity to gain an overall impression of the strength and vitality of the brand-new addition. Muscle tone, coordination, and skeletal structure can be evaluated; both attitude and responsiveness to stimuli are observable at this time. These are all important indices to the possibility of a hidden infection or the presence of disease or abnormality. (For further information please read *Blessed Are the Brood Mares*.)

PHYSICAL EXAMINATION

The physical examination should be brief but thorough. Eyes, nostrils, and mouth should be checked, and the color of the ocular, nasal, and oral membranes noted. Perceptive hands passed over the neck, shoulders, and rib cage can often locate either superficial injury or trauma or deep bruising sustained during delivery or shortly after birth. An unattended lengthy parturition can result in fractured ribs, ruptured diaphragm, or ruptured urinary bladder. These conditions are usually not diagnosed for the first 12 hours or so.

The navel stump should be checked to be certain that it has been properly cauterized, is firm in texture, and not enlarged. The urethral opening should be patent and the anal aperture appear complete and functional. Verification of the actual acts of urination and defecation is essential.

Your veterinarian should listen to the foal's heart and also confirm that the lungs are clear. By use of the stethoscope, the veterinarian can determine a clear lung field to preclude the existence of pulmonary disease or fluids accidentally aspirated during delivery. Heart rate and respiratory rate should be checked and recorded. The normal rate of the heart in the newborn foal is between 70 and 80 beats per minute at rest. With exercise, the heart rate can accelerate to as much as 150 beats per minute. Respiratory rates also vary greatly with rest and activity or discomfort; it is impossible to arrive at a norm. I have found the pattern and rhythm of respirations and the various types of rib and thorax excursions during respirations to be more revealing in foals than the rate. Any departure from the normal smooth breathing flow warrants attention.

BODY TEMPERATURE

The newborn's temperature is an important part of the initial physical examination and should be recorded.

At this time, I would like to emphasize the importance of a constant and stable body temperature in the foal. Normal body temperature is 101 degrees, and any variation of one-half degree, plus or minus, is significant and cause for concern.

Use your thermometer as often as you deem necessary, and if there is a question, keep a chart for reference until your veterinarian arrives.

I have found that a slight increase or, more importantly, a slight *decrease* in body temperature, has been a warning of an impending illness. Please take heed!

INJECTIONS FOR THE NEWBORN

For the average-size foal, 6cc of a Pen-Strep preparation and 1,500 IU of tetanus antitoxin can be combined for a single intramuscular injection. When the foal is down again for another nap, the required injections, quietly administered, usually go unnoticed except perhaps by a flick of the tail or the twitch of an ear, and the foal will continue to rest undisturbed. The injection of Pen-Strep should be repeated daily for three days to provide protection against infection and disease while the navel is closing and the foal is adjusting to the outside world. All injections should be administered in the gluteal or rump muscles of the foal. No injections should ever be given in the foal's neck muscles. The only exception to this rule is the use of the jugular vein (located in the neck area) for intravenous purposes. Some European countries have recently categorized the injection of medicine into a horse's neck muscles as an act of malpractice.

PROPER HANDLING OF THE NEWBORN AND RECOMMENDED METHODS FOR ROUTINE INJECTIONS

At this juncture, it is only proper to stop and stress the information that has been learned over the years and deserves respect and recognition. Along with someone to hold the mother, someone should secure and quietly cradle the neonate before the veterinarian enters the stall. It requires, in my opinion, some knowledge and experience in this field of endeavor to handle a 70-pound, high-strung, somewhat nervous neonate with some degree of safety to both foal and handler. The veterinarian can then proceed with the physical examination, navel assessment, and administration of needed injections plus drawing of blood for laboratory samples.

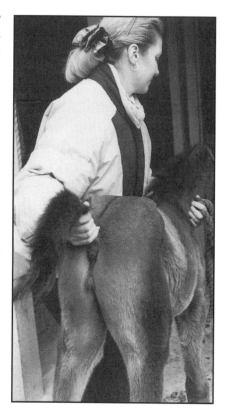

Cradling filly foal.

I have listed my tried-and-true rules along with some descriptive photographs for the reader's edification and some clarification. These factors are of critical importance, and as a foal owner, you have every right to insist that the rules be followed:

1. Restraint

   Have your assistant quietly cradle the newborn so as not to upset the mare. My small niece held innumerable foals by the chest and tail (up close to the dock) and would, if needed, use their stall wall for support, taking special caution to protect bruising the foal's eye. A strong man wrestling a foal is a recipe for disaster, and he should be asked to leave!

2. Site of Injections

   Never use an area other than the two gluteal (rump) muscles, alternating sides, for IM injections.

   To repeat, presently there is a strong movement in some foreign countries to ban the horse's neck (cervical) as a site for intramuscular injections. The multiple large yet thin muscles are arranged in various planes that predispose to problems—i.e., poor drainage, abscess formation, and, with any neck movement, great pain for the horse. The large and deep-seated rump muscles are well suited for injections and vaccinations.

To inject your foal the correct way: Carefully draw a line in the hair from the spinal column to the point of the hip, then determine the center of that line. The ideal point of injection is where the muscle appears the highest and thus deepest, making it the best location to receive the needle.

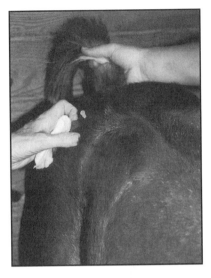

Precise injection site, gluteal muscle.

3. Method of Injection

If the foal's muscle appears super-soiled from parturition, scrub the gluteal area with Ivory soap and warm water. Rinse and dry well. Then, with cotton well soaked with isopropyl alcohol, proceed to cleanse the area. Insist upon the use of a 20-gauge, 1-inch needle. After the injection is prepared, separate the needle from the syringe, being certain to touch only the hub of the needle. Hold the needle in the fashion of a

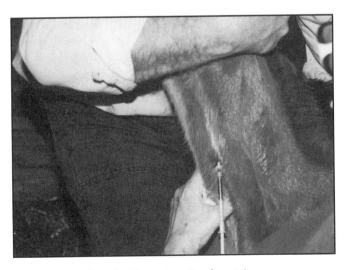

Restraint and site for IV injections (jugular vein).

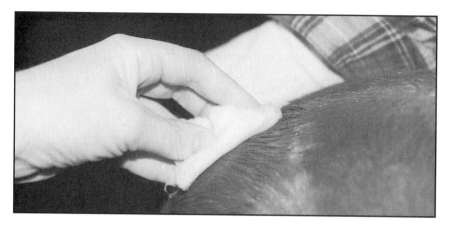

Cleanse area.

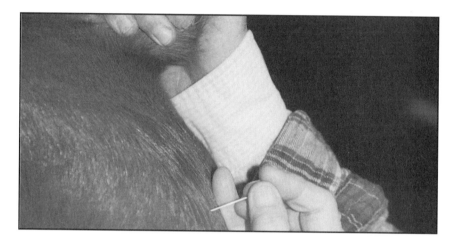

Slapping technique.

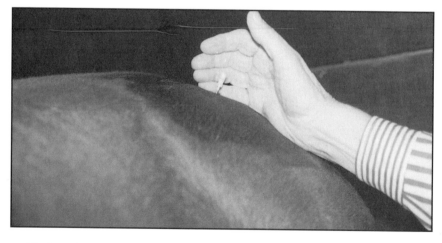

Needle in deep soft muscle.

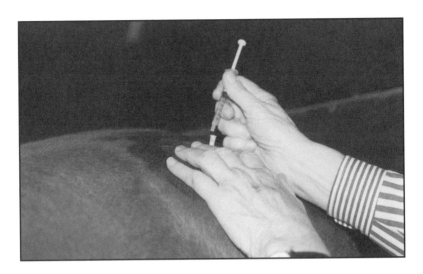

Attach syringe cautiously.

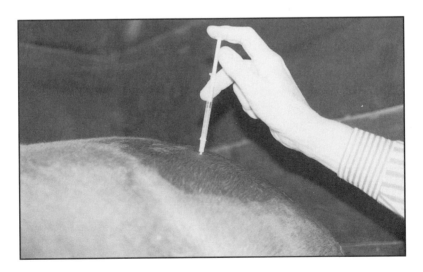

Inject contents slowly after slight withdrawal.

pen or pencil, and as the side of your hand deftly slaps the foal's gluteal muscle, the needle is simultaneously injected. The foal will feel no pain sensation—no response. Skillfully attach the syringe to the needle. Slightly withdraw the syringe plunger for evidence of blood, averting an accidental intravenous injection. With no visible blood upon withdrawal, gently proceed to inject the contents. Remove the needle and syringe from the muscle, then massage the area with cotton and alcohol, creating an atmosphere of kindness. Almost all foals stand quietly, as they feel only the slightest tap of your hand. This is the best method I have ever known, and I guarantee it is humane.

4. Intravenous Injections and Drawing Blood

> All this can be accomplished in the same quiet manner (see photographs).

It is your foal, so insist upon nothing less than the best.

ROUTINE LABORATORY TESTS

I strongly suggest subjecting every newborn to three invaluable tests shortly after delivery: a blood count, a compatibility test, and a serum test for immune bodies. Each test screens for the presence of or a warning sign of a common fatal malady in foals.

I advocate a blood count and a hemoglobin determination for every foal in my care. Some people feel that a red and white blood cell count and a determination of hemoglobin percentage for the newborn is unnecessary and an added expense, caused by overzealousness on the part of the attending veterinarian. Fortunately, most often it is! Although a complete blood count is not diagnostic in itself, it does serve as a baseline in the healthy individual and as a distinct warning in an asymptomatic diseased foal. Proper interpretation of the blood picture can alert the veterinarian to a potentially ill foal even before the onset of symptoms. For the foal with a developing blood poison (septicemia) or other insidious pathologic condition, it will give a few precious hours' advantage that often means the difference between life and death to the equine baby.

While it may seem that many unnecessary serology studies are done, I believe that there is no such thing as an unnecessary blood study.

A laboratory test for early recognition of incompatibility between the fetus's blood cells and the mare's milk (isoerythrolysis) should also be done. A sample of the foal's blood and a sample of the mother's milk can be sent to the laboratory for diagnosis.

A serum test for detection of immune deficiency in the foal is also necessary. A blood sample is drawn from the foal, and its serum is analyzed for immune-body content. The immune bodies, normally found in blood after ingesting the first milk, protect the foal from disease and stress.

If you have a strong and healthy-looking foal, I suggest for the sake of accuracy that you delay the serum test for a few hours to allow the foal to ingest the mare's colostrum, which is loaded with antibodies. A test taken too early results in false values.

HEALTHY FOAL CRITERIA

The value of time spent in observation of your foal should be apparent.

The behavior pattern of your normal foal can be judged by five criteria. Probably the most important of these guides is the act of nursing. The other four, not necessarily in the order of importance, are short regular napping, physical activity, frequent urination, and regular defecation.

A *brief nap.*

PREPARATION FOR NURSING

Immediately after foaling, quietly cleanse the mare's udder by rubbing and massaging it gently with a towel dipped in hot water and wrung thoroughly dry. Be certain that the towel is wrung dry and cooled slightly so that the mare will not be burned. Careful attention should be given to the space between the two mammary glands, for this is a prime location for accumulated dirt.

After this cleansing, it is wise to deftly expel a few streams of colostrum from each teat, then coat the teat generously with the advance milk. This diminishes the bacteria present and induces milk flow in the mare. This simple cleansing provides many advantages and is well worth the time and effort.

CAUTION: When dealing with a maiden or even a cranky older mare, please stand by, prepared if necessary to exert a little restraint or control over the mare. If she acts nervous, hold her until she either recognizes the foal as hers or until you are satisfied that the baby is suckling without resistance from either a super-sensitive udder or an exhausted and sometimes confused mare. I have been shocked to see some matrons lash out inexplicably!

NURSING

When questioning your foal's condition, the first rule is to examine the mare's udder. The condition of the udder can be an important clue to your foal's physical condition. Its size, texture, and amount of milk flow indicate the period of time since the last full meal was consumed. It takes a profuse milk producer to supply more than a hardy, vigorous foal demands. All healthy foals manage to keep the mammary gland drained of milk at all times.

A young foal afflicted by any problem, regardless of the etiology, first suffers with weakness and depression. This is immediately reflected in the nursing pattern. While nursing does not decrease in frequency, it appears that the amount consumed at each feeding is reduced, resulting in a slow buildup of milk in the

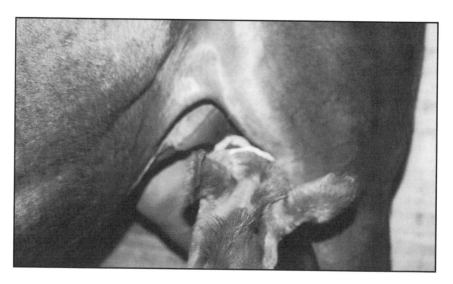

Hungry foal.

udder. This buildup of milk in the semi-filled mammary glands is usually indicated by drops of milk on the teat ends. In a very short while, the mare's udder will become large, firm, and even painful, with occasional streams of colostrum or milk seen. When a weak or depressed foal decreases its milk consumption ever so slightly, the resulting degree of physical deterioration in the foal seems grossly disproportionate to the small decrease in nourishment ingested.

Even a vigorous foal will quickly weaken and appear sick if smaller amounts of milk are ingested over but a few hours. Foals, like young children, can be active and healthy one minute and be found quite ill the next minute. The buffer zone between well and sick in the very young is small and easily breached.

It is important to ascertain that the foal is truly nursing and not just making appropriate noises in the vicinity of the udder. One should observe the foal with the teat securely in its mouth and with its tongue curled for proper suction. An unobtrusive hand gently cupped around the little neck just below the throat can feel the expansion of the esophagus and the gurgly swallow as the milk is, in fact, ingested.

If the foal appears with "milky nose"—that is, with milk all over from below the eyes down over the top of its nose, whether wet or dry—it is a clear sign of systemic weakness. Most weak foals are unable to cope with the mare's normal milk stream. The tentative approach of such a foal to the udder results in a strong

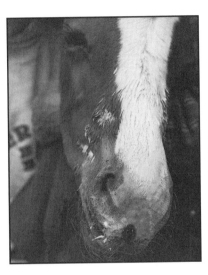

Milky nose.

release of milk from both teats, which then sprays over the foal's face. Milky nose should serve to alert a foal's caretakers to the presence of potential illness or a weak foal in the process of recovery.

URINATION

The subject of defecation has been fairly well covered; urination is of equal importance. New foals urinate frequently, and the volume of urine is very small. The urine of the new foal should be watery clear and should flow evenly with no evidence of straining. In the case of colts, note should be taken as to whether or not the penis extends from the prepuce during urination. If the penis remains retracted, the urine will dribble from the prepuce. This condition will not permit the navel to dry, causes irritation, and provides an ideal environment for bacterial growth. Suspect a systemic infection if your colt's penis does not descend during urination. Summon your veterinarian if the condition has not corrected itself within 24 hours.

If urination is not observed within the first few hours of birth, veterinary consultation is then in order.

ALERT: For the first few hours of life, please note the location at which urine is escaping. Each gender is different—under the tail for the filly and through a dropped penis near the navel stump in the colt. Then look closer at the colt during urination and determine whether the urine is coming from the penis or the adjacent navel stump. This rates a hurry-up call to your equine veterinarian. See LEAKY NAVEL CORD, page 122.

FOAL VISION VS. PHYSICAL ACTIVITY

The foal's first physical activity is usually limited to an exploration of the mother's huge body. Eventually, the foal will explore the entire stall. These early, tentative explorations are related to the newborn's limited visual proficiency. Foals will stumble over any obstacle not because of lack of coordination, but because of reduced visual acuity. All newborn foals function with a distinct visual disadvantage, causing some normal foals to appear somewhat awkward. Until the foal's vision becomes more acute, usually from 48 to 60 hours after birth, the foal must depend on blurry vision, its olfactory and auditory senses, and the all-important tactile hairs found scattered around the lower face and muzzle. Fortunately, this awkward transition period is short-lived.

Contrary to popular belief, a large eye does not confer better vision. The equine's relatively large ocular globe has in its back compartment an obtuse concave retina. This, coupled with a sluggish iris, contributes to the foal's peculiar lack of visual definition. However, with age and practice, the foal learns to bring objects into focus. Even the adult horse must use its head and neck position to enhance its ability to see clearly.

Some foals possess the faculty to adjust their vision rapidly and consequently appear quite agile and well coordinated. Other foals may give the appearance, at a very early age, of being blind. This peculiarity has needlessly upset many inexperienced owners. The variations in visual ability explain why some foals seem to glue themselves to their mothers' sides while other foals appear independent. Doesn't it make you wonder how any foals ever survived in nature, vulnerable to predators and natural hazards? Each foal should be protected and confined in a stall until it demonstrates a visual readiness to be turned out into a paddock or a field. Three days is the average recommended stall confinement time. See EYE LESIONS, page 119. For warnings on initial turnout time, see page 247.

SUGGESTED VETERINARY TREATMENT FOR THE HEALTHY NEWBORN FOAL

Physical examination—check for:

- Ability to stand.
- Vigor.
- Body temperature—alert: Be certain that it is precisely 101 degrees.
- Nursing ability.
- Straight legs—evaluate flexor and extensor tendons.
- Body weight.
- Body attitude and reflexes.

Navel medication:

- Examine for a healthy navel stump.
- Prevent infection from entering the open navel.

Ascertain ability to defecate:

- Color and consistency.
- Enema—check for retained meconium (pain).

Ascertain ability to urinate and location of urination

Injections:

- First day only—1,500 IU tetanus antitoxin.
- 6cc Penicillin/Strep IM.
- Repeat antibiotic for two additional days.

Laboratory tests:

- CBC and differential.
- Zinc sulfate turbidity test—immune status.
- Compatibility test—isoerythrolysis (foal's RBCs vs. mare's colostrum).

Chapter Two

NEONATAL EMERGENCIES

Ahealthy, normal foal is not a rarity, but should always be counted as a
blessing. Foals are subject to many disorders, deviations, and diseases,
even when cared for and supervised under the best-known conditions.
In spite of ongoing educational efforts to improve the plight of the pregnant
mare during embryonic development, gestation, and parturition, careless, ignorant, and thoughtless owners continue to neglect these heavy matrons and
"leave it to nature." This antiquated attitude accounts for the majority of losses
in both mothers and babies!

So often, early life in the equine neonate is quite precarious. Poor housing,
temperature and weather changes, uninterested or ignorant caretakers, and
absence of medical attention all directly contribute to increased incidences of
illness or even fatalities in the newborn.

Do not hesitate to read and increase your general knowledge about foals and
foaling when anticipating the arrival of a new foal. An informed owner—one
who expects and usually receives a higher standard of care and attention from
the veterinarian—is a good owner. Contrary to the adage, a little knowledge can
be helpful.

Over the last 20 years, I have witnessed appreciable progress in the field of
neonatal medicine and am proud to say that most pediatric problems are solv-
able today if recognized early and swiftly treated in a competent and professional manner. Yet some are insurmountable. Fortunately, scientific and
medical knowledge are curtailing the latter.

Foals that arrive in the world with a problem, whether chronic or acute,
depend upon their attendants for prompt recognition of the problem and rapid
application of appropriate measures to ensure survival. The presence of your veterinarian during parturition can be comforting to all concerned.

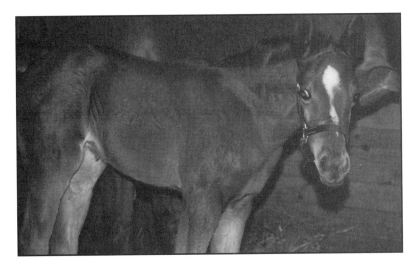

A healthy, handsome colt.

FAILURE TO BREATHE

One of the earliest causes of concern is the foal who fails to begin even a feeble effort to breathe during the latter part of its excursion through the birth canal and into the world. Most vigorous individuals will achieve a few ragged breaths toward the end of parturition. However, if the foal slips into the bedding and still fails to initiate respiration, then early concern quickly becomes an emergency. A normal foal should be breathing independently by this time.

Initiation of respiration is stimulated by reflex action in the brain stem. Many foals thought to be dead are only demonstrating a delayed respiratory reflex or an inefficient respiratory control center. The incidence of this condition seems to be on the increase and has been especially recognized in intensified, selective breeding programs and within certain breeds of horses. It is thought to be of congenital or hereditary origin.

In the absence of perceptible respiration, there are immediate and helpful procedures that can be beneficial without the use of sophisticated drugs and equipment. Three prudent procedures may aid in timely initiation of respiration and can be safely practiced by a conscientious attendant.

Merely allowing the foal's head to drop to the side of the forelegs during delivery—nose downward, but free of bedding—aids in the escape of nasal fluids, reduces the chance of pulmonary fluid retention, and enhances oxygenation with the expansion of lung tissue.

In the fully delivered foal, if there is even the slightest delay in initiation of respiration, the foal's thorax (chest) should be elevated promptly so that any

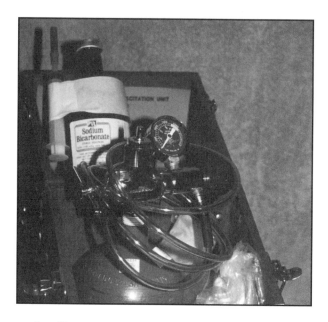

Portable oxygen cylinder.

fluids present in the respiratory tract can flow from the nares. If the foal is elevated and held suspended in this position for even a few seconds, drainage can take place. Vigorous toweling and massaging of the foal's entire body and limbs serve as a good assist to both respiration and circulation.

Very careful use of a small rubber bulb for aspiration of the nasal passages may be helpful. A small oxygen unit used to activate respiration is commonly found in large equine nurseries. Most equine practitioners carry an oxygen cylinder for just such emergencies. However, a word of caution: This popular practice absolutely requires trained personnel; improper percentage or sustained use of oxygen under pressure can be very harmful to newborn foals.

Since 95 percent of our foals arrive in remote barns well isolated from modern technology, let us not forget our God-given powers of resourcefulness. All able-bodied people carry with them a personal and readily portable supply of oxygen and carbon dioxide, with a capable mechanism for administering this physiologic mixture of gases at any given time or place. This mechanism is called mouth-to-nose artificial respiration. Such two-legged resuscitators have saved many lives, both human and animal, thanks to split-second availability.

Any delay in the birth process invariably causes metabolic acidosis in the body tissues and acidemia in the newborn's bloodstream. Acidosis and acidemia both mean a reduced bicarbonate reserve and thus an upset in the delicate and critical acid/base balance so necessary for life functions. Any disease process or deficient oxygen supply can quickly set up acidemia.

Newborn foals, whether septicemic or perfectly healthy and subjected to delay in delivery, notoriously suffer varying degrees of acidemia and acidosis. Equine obstetricians are always alert and cognizant of this common and threatening condition. Foals affected often exhibit a profound reluctance to begin breathing. Many such foals require immediate diagnosis and emergency treatment or assistance to trigger the respiratory center in the lower brain—or they are lost!

ALERT: In advance of parturition, discuss with your veterinarian what you can do if you are alone and your foal fails to breathe upon arrival. This is a critical situation. There is no time to lose. After schooling you well, your veterinarian may agree to leave a prepared dose of sodium bicarbonate in a syringe ready for IV use. This is to be used only in an emergency situation—specifically when respiration initiation is absent. Used properly, *sodium bicarbonate* (80–100 cc of 5 percent IV per 70-pound foal) can do no harm and can in some instances stimulate a ragged, gasping respiration. Inject the solution once; then, if there is no response, wait 60 seconds and repeat the injection. A small oxygen cylinder with an attached mask or endotracheal tube is a very useful adjunct to sodium bicarbonate injections. Oxygen can be safely administered to foals at the rate of 10 liters per minute so long as the expired air is permitted to escape freely. This is important, as expired air has a high content of carbon dioxide which, if re-inhaled, would compound the acidosis.

NOTE: The combined action of sodium bicarbonate and oxygen has been credited with saving many foals.

ARTIFICIAL RESPIRATION

When administering artificial respiration either to stimulate a breathing cycle or simply to augment feeble breathing, the same basic procedure applies.

Once it is established that the nasal passages are relatively clear of fluids, extend the head so that the mid-line of the head, when viewed from the side, forms a straight line with the mid-line of the neck. This adjustment will line up the nostrils and the nasal passages with the epiglottis and the trachea and achieve an open airway. Cover one nostril securely with one hand while supporting the head with the other hand. Take a deep breath and, with your mouth sealing the uncovered nostril to prevent the escape of air, blow with authority but without undue force. The amount of pressure or force required to elicit a slight movement of the rib cage is optimum. Excessive pressure will damage lung tissue, or may even rupture a lung. Continued repetitions of this action at two-second intervals will, in addition to providing the needed gases, serve to maintain the cleared airway and inflate the lung tissue. Whether using an oxygen cylinder with a tube or mask, or merely engaging in natural mouth-to-nose resuscitation, the same principles should be followed.

In summary, for the foal who does not begin breathing as nature intended, act immediately to:

1. Clear the airways.

2. Determine the presence of a heartbeat.

3. Check color of oral mucous membranes.

4. Position the head and neck in alignment.

5. Blow rhythmically into one nostril. (Remember, the equine is totally a nose breather.)

Any delay in following these steps could result in irreparable cerebral damage or cost the life of the foal.

HEARTBEAT

As quickly as possible following efforts to establish any pattern of breathing, the presence of a heartbeat should be determined. Without this vital function, further resuscitation efforts are futile. To determine the presence of a beating heart, place the fingers on the thorax, just behind and above the elbow on the left side directly over the heart.

The heartbeat in some foals is so strong, even in the absence of respiration, that movement of the rib cage with each beat can be observed from a distance of several feet. It is as if the heart is trying to escape through the chest wall. Other foals exhibit such weak or feeble heartbeats that detection is difficult. The prognosis for survival is the same whether the heartbeat is strong or feeble when respiration is absent. I have found it is impossible to predict the length of time the individual foal can survive with a heartbeat and without respiration and not sustain irreversible damage. The limits imposed by nature depend on the innate vitality of the foal, the length of labor, and the circumstances of delivery. Even if the mare foals unattended and there is no way to determine the length of time a foal has been in the world without breathing, the presence of a heartbeat warrants the effort to stimulate respiration.

Sophisticated methods of pinpointing trouble areas are available in equine hospitals but are not found in the foaling barn or equine nursery. Specialized equipment is available to monitor, record, and aid in the assessment of cardiac (heart) function. Blood gas machines can determine the exact amounts of vital blood gas contents, blood components, and relative percentages and concentrations. While this information is gratifying, the equipment is not available for a barn emergency, nullifying its practical usefulness.

Today's veterinarian concerned with obstetrics and pediatrics is prepared for cardiovascular failure with specific equipment and drugs. In large equine nurseries, mechanical aspirators and resuscitators, oxygen cylinders, proper-size endotracheal tubes suitable for foals, and an armamentarium of drugs for cardiopulmonary stimulation are available to the veterinarian. Although these numerous aids may be effective in skilled hands, be aware that their use by unskilled or untrained personnel may actually have disastrous results.

The fact that the modern breeding farm veterinarian is equipped in this manner is a commentary on the increased incidence of cardiopulmonary deficiency in the newborn equine.

In my opinion, injectable cardiopulmonary stimulants are of questionable value in foal pediatrics. I have failed to find any veterinary literature documenting either successful or safe usage of these drugs. It seems that negative results of any chemical interference with the natural mechanism have limited the use and popularity of this practice. In the established absence of a heartbeat, the use of intracardial injections is considered heroic and controversial. Personally, I have had no success with the current drugs and cannot find any valid statistical research to support their use.

ORAL MUCOUS MEMBRANES (GUMS)

When a foal experiences circulatory or respiratory imbalance, whether caused primarily by cardiovascular malfunction or a questionable respiratory system, the mucous membranes reflect the overall condition. Clinical observation of the foal by the attendant can be extremely helpful and revealing to the veterinarian in assessing the animal's condition. In addition, this observation is something that an alert owner can do to catch potential problems before they become serious. The color of the mucous membranes, for instance, directly reflects the status of and changes in systemic function.

If the foal's heart is beating, take the time—a split second—to flip up the foal's upper lip to check the color of the oral mucous membranes. A strong heartbeat will be circulating the blood through the foal's body, providing vital oxygen and thus producing a clear pink gum color. With the foal's placenta still attached inside the mare's uterine lining, the remaining maternal supply of oxygenated blood is surging through the navel cord to aid the newborn and augment its breathing efforts. A pretty pink gum color, accompanied by a viable beating heart, should encourage continued and sustained resuscitative efforts until it is deemed otherwise.

The color of gums will deepen quickly and darken unless supplemental oxygen is made available to the circulating blood. Any color change, especially a darker or deeper shade, should serve as a warning that help is needed. However, rhythmic breathing, regular heart sounds, and pink gums indicate that all is well, at least for the moment.

Color changes are both reliable and consistent mirrors of health or sickness. Simple assessment of the gums, coupled with easily monitored vital signs (heart rate, respiratory rate, body temperature, and blood pressure), provide a vivid picture of the young animal's cardiovascular and respiratory functions.

The following description of the mucous membrane color in the foal is somewhat oversimplified and allows for

This foal had pink, healthy gums.

some deviations and a broad interpretation of its significance. However, any appreciable or abrupt change in these parameters is a danger signal.

The gums of a normal foal should be a robust pink color, moist and warm; when pressed to blanch an area, they should refill to a normal pink color in one to two seconds. Refill time is a dependable barometer used and respected by the knowledgeable. Either a too rapid or a too sluggish refill time warrants noting or reporting.

A slight darkening in color with blue overtones indicates a reduction of oxygen content of the blood, usually with an increased carbon dioxide content and accompanying metabolic changes. The veterinarian must decide if this is a result of impairment, primarily of respiratory or cardiovascular function, or a by-product of another systemic problem, perhaps infection of intrauterine origin.

A darker, deeper red color indicates a serious imbalance in the oxygen and the carbon dioxide ratio and/or serious fluctuations in circulation. Disparities in pH, fluid, and electrolyte balance are frequently seen accompanying these changes.

Completely blue membranes indicate an emergency condition. The foal is not receiving oxygen, and death is imminent unless the inciting cause is corrected immediately.

Lightening of the usually pink membranes is not an indication of an immediate problem. Many animals normally look somewhat pale while resting or asleep, or after they just get up. However, if the membranes continue losing color, becoming increasingly pale, or if the foal seems weak, this is a signal that the peripheral circulation is collapsing. This may be due to a primary drop in blood pressure, blood loss, dehydration, shock, or infection, or it may be secondary to another serious systemic problem. Dry, cold membranes are further indicators of poor peripheral circulation.

Gum color changes continue to have significance even in the older foal, especially when seen with other clinical signs, such as depression, fever, etc. Sometimes an apparently healthy foal will manifest changing shades of mucous membranes. Although the implication is questionable, it should rate a physical examination.

A foal may arrive in the world with bluish-tinted or cyanotic membranes that ideally respond to oxygenation by turning pink in color. This specific occurrence is found most commonly in, and is diagnostic of, either premature placental separation or delayed parturition. It can be most often found in first-foal mares or in worn-out multipara mares who begin to foal and then, for whatever reason, cease all efforts, abandoning the foal still inside the reproductive tract. Unless the attendants rapidly recognize the situation, the cessation of labor by the mare will cost an otherwise healthy, strong foal its life. The majority of these foals are large, well-developed, and most often very close to the outside when the mothers stop. A quickly scrubbed hand slipped inside the mare's vagina readily finds a large foot and leg, and with a discreet tug can reinitiate labor and directly save the foal.

CAUTION: Be careful of naturally occurring pigmentation in gum tissue when evaluating the foal's mucous membranes. Some individuals, of no specific breed, have a wavy, somewhat wide, irregular band of colorful tissue running through the hard palate, the mucous membranes, and on into the gums. These perfectly normal darker areas could momentarily give an erroneous impression of cause for concern.

THE DEAD FOAL

Every year, unfortunately, some foals are born dead. It seems such a waste when a mare carries her foal to full term only to deliver a stillborn. What a tragedy!

Emotions run high, along with expenses, and in some cases the loss dictates a return to the drawing board for information and guidance for the next year's game plan.

The foal is dead! Why bother to seek answers? It should behoove all horse doctors and interested owners, when time and finances permit, to strongly pursue probable cause. The small facts, gathered by caring people, could serve as future tools toward defeating one of our major veterinary medical adversaries, and thus save many lives. If we continue the effort even in sadness or perhaps in the face of despair, we can turn a negative scene into a positive situation.

Veterinary examination of the carcass via a postmortem can and usually does provide answers as to the probable cause of death. This information can be more complete and somewhat more sophisticated when the service of a veterinary pathologist is engaged. However, even veterinary pathologists do occasionally strike out and are unable to advance satisfactory information to prevent a future loss.

When a foal is found "DOA," a barrage of questions undoubtedly will be forthcoming. When, where, and why did this foal die, and why so late in pregnancy?

Over many years and many losses, I learned through practice that a great deal of practical (basic) information concerning the plight of the emerging foal can be gleaned by reading the color, texture, and consistency of the oral and ocular membranes. Of course, the shorter the time span between delivery and examination, the more accurate the evaluation. Ideally, the postmortem should take place immediately after delivery.

Time is important, as after death, tissue destruction continues steadily and progressively until all evidence of what occurred is indefinable.

It is a matter of interest to note that the color of the membranes alone can denote approximately when, and where in the reproductive tract, death occurred, although this knowledge may be of small consolation.

When the membranes are a dark, muddy color, it is suggestive of intrauterine death from one of many causes. Regardless of cause, death assuredly ensued in the uterus well in advance of delivery, perhaps from 12 to 24 hours prior to parturition. This color signifies cellular damage, with decomposition of tissue. The dead foal has remained in the uterus long enough for the lack of circulation to create tissue changes causing a foreign-body reaction in the dam, and abortion or delivery of the dead foal.

An 18- to 22-day-old aborted embryo.

Determining the time lag from death to moment of delivery is better left to the educated.

Other color variations, from the extremes of very white to darker shades, tell us that most likely the foal perished very close to the time of parturition or actually during delivery. Darkened bluish or reddish membranes indicate a recent death by failure of the oxygen and nutritional support systems. These individuals perish in the uterus and are subsequently delivered post-haste, or have died in the reproductive canal, or advanced as far as the vagina and then expired.

In dead foals delivered with startling snow-white membranes, I have witnessed a shocking coincidence. The limbs of these foals are invariably icy cold. Other dead foals, following delivery, are normally warm from the mare's internal body temperature. This departure from the expected would appear to indicate a shock-like syndrome with visceral pooling of the foal's circulating blood volume. Snow-white membranes may cause speculation as to the cause of death, but undoubtedly the peripheral circulation was thoroughly drained.

Interestingly, in each documented case of snow-white membranes, I was able to establish from the attendant that the foal was unusually active in utero, kicking strongly or even violently just prior to delivery as if the intrauterine death was of a frantic, convulsive nature. This activity leads me to consider the possibility of sudden mechanical physiologic failure. Torsion of the umbilical cord or anything that could cause an abrupt cessation of oxygen supply and gaseous exchange could account for sudden death with shock symptoms.

Dead on arrival and *abortion* are common terms erroneously used interchangeably. They are two separate entities and should not be confused.

Brood mares are notorious for aborting at the slightest provocation and at any given time during gestation. Aborted material ranges widely in appearance. Gross characteristics, such as size, shape, texture, and color, all vary with the age and stage of embryonic development when expulsion from the uterus occurs. An early abortus usually appears as a small unidentifiable semi-fluid tissue mass, called an embryo. As pregnancy advances, the expelled material progressively takes the form of a minute horse, complete with head, neck, body, limbs, and feet, then termed a fetus.

In contrast, a stillborn individual is a fully grown and well-developed foal, carried to term and delivered on time in the fashion of a normal parturition—but born lifeless.

WEAK FOALS

A much more common problem in the newborn is that of the foal that does not have the strength, stamina, coordination, or know-how to get to its feet, find the mammary gland, and nurse. This physical deficiency can manifest itself in

"I'm feeling much better, thank you!"

varying degrees. Immediate recognition is of paramount importance to prevent a decline that would deplete the limited energy reserves of the foal and allow a desperate situation to develop. Prompt veterinary treatment may avert a serious condition.

Most frequently encountered is the foal who simply cannot manage to untangle four inordinately long legs and plant them firmly to achieve or maintain standing posture. These otherwise normal babies will suck on their mother's legs or any other convenient thing, expressing their hunger, their willingness to nurse, and the unmistakable presence of the sucking reflex. Quickly milk some colostrum into a sterilized baby bottle with a nipple—you will be startled to see the strength in the foal. Be certain to position the foal first on its sternum to prevent milk from entering the lungs.

SLIGHT ASSISTANCE

Usually even a weak foal manages to roll up on its sternum (breastbone) and extend its forelegs in an effort to rise. The hind legs tucked under the body must elevate the hind quarters and find purchase to support their share of the foal's weight. It is this maneuver that confounds many newborns. Their dilemma can be solved by "tailing" them to a standing position.

Be sure both forelegs are extended before beginning the stratagem. Grasp the foal's tail with your palm up and as close to the root of the tail as possible, and hoist the hindquarters up off the ground. Synchronize your efforts with those of the foal. Often, grasping a foal's tail will stimulate an effort to rise on the foal's part. Amazingly, the foal when given this help will align the forelegs and establish its balance. The hand not holding the tail may be used across the foal's chest to help steady the baby's first faltering progress toward its mother. Usually, once on its feet, the foal does remarkably well solo. More often than not, these foals will find the mare's udder, have their first meal, and drop down into the bedding for a nap. However, they should be carefully watched until you are certain they have acquired the faculty to get to their feet independently and nurse adequately and frequently.

Generally, one assist is all that is needed, although an occasional foal will require help for a few hours—some even for a day or two. Do not allow such a foal to exhaust itself with futile floundering. Give help as you see the need. Most new foals will nurse every 20 to 30 minutes, then nap. Attempt to emulate this time schedule with the foal who requires your special attention. One or two meals usually gives the foal the added strength and capability needed to become self-reliant.

NOTE: A foal should not be unfairly categorized as a lesser individual or prejudged as inferior because of an early physical weakness. If given a chance, a large percentage of these foals grow and develop normally.

SWOLLEN ANKLES

Some foals will remain up on their feet until they receive assistance to the ground, or fall in utter exhaustion. These individuals consistently develop swollen (edematous) fore and hind ankles. Rest periods in recumbency quickly resolve the swelling in the foal's extremities. Swollen legs are symptomatic of a very tired foal. Perhaps the foal is a slow learner who has somehow managed the intricacy of standing but cannot unravel the mystery of a descent back to the security of the warm bedding.

Another cause is the anxious psychotic mare who will not permit her foal to lie down to rest. Her exhausted foal always suffers swollen and stocked legs. Such a mare is worried or concerned when her foal is lying quietly. She is afraid that she will lose sight of the baby, or else she needs to be reassured that all is well by seeing the foal up on its feet and active. A mare will paw at her foal— and none too gently—to urge it to its feet; she may even nip the baby sharply. An occasional mare will actually lift the new foal off the ground with her teeth.

It is difficult to understand why these mares refuse to allow their foals to rest. Perhaps they either have lost a foal at one time or have a retained instinct that prods them to keep their precocious foal on the alert to escape some unknown dangers. I have seen some of these pathetic foals actually sleeping standing up by leaning against their huge mothers.

NON-NURSING FOALS

A further degree of physical weakness is exhibited by the foal that is unable to support its weight even when assisted to its feet. These individuals seem to possess legs made of rubber. In spite of support provided under the rib cage, and tailing for support to the hindquarters, these foals seem to melt, making it impossible to maintain them in a standing position.

It is a frustrating and impossible task to get foals who are unable to stand to nurse from their mothers. They flop around in their efforts to stand and are found in various changing positions. Their apparent weakness does not affect their strong sucking reflex, and with extended neck they will reach for the human attendant's hands, arms, and legs in search of sustenance.

With support to hold them, they are able to lift their heads momentarily while suspended in a standing position. The foal may be inches away from the life-sustaining mammary gland, but it might as well be miles for the foal who lacks the wherewithal to reach it. Here is where a human baby bottle can serve a great purpose.

The mare's udder should be prepared for the newborn by cleansing well with towels that have been dipped in hot water and wrung dry. It is then an easy matter for the foal to nurse, or for the attendant to milk the precious colostrum into a saucepan or large measuring cup. Being careful to maintain the natural warmth, transfer the milk meal into a baby bottle equipped with a nipple. If the holes in the nipple are slightly enlarged to provide a freer flow for the recipient, the meal is more handily ingested.

WARNING: Bottle feeding is not difficult to master and is safe if the foal is supported up on its sternum (breastbone) while being fed. Never bottle-feed a foal who is in a recumbent position. Kneel beside the foal and support the head by reaching your arm over the neck and placing your hand under the jaw. Extend the head forward and slightly upward. Supported in this natural posture, the foal is able to swallow comfortably and easily. Carefully adjust the rate of ingestion so that weak foals do not drink too rapidly. Once the nipple is placed in the hungry foal's mouth, the foal will readily swallow the prescribed 2 to 3 ounces for his initial feeding.

Repeatedly I have observed weak foals who, shortly after ingesting a single bottle feeding of the first milk, scramble to their feet, locate the udder on their own, and successfully nurse. I am astounded by the remarkable progress of the weak or "inferior" foal who responds to even a single bottle feeding, and, with the miraculous colostrum, assumes the expected behavior of a typical foal.

Some old-timers believe that bottle-feeding foals inhibits the instinct and desire of the foal to seek the udder and nurse naturally. To the contrary, a defective foal or any foal weakened by a difficult birth process, or shocked by extremes of exposure to the new environment, is fortified by this beneficial act, which enables it to gain the stamina and strength to become self-sufficient. Without the courtesy of this go-between service, many foals would perish only inches away from the life-sustaining nutritional substance they need.

As with the foal that must be "tailed" to get up, the bottle baby requires careful and diligent observation until you are completely satisfied that it has acquired all the capabilities needed to be self-sufficient.

One bottle will more often than not be the magic wand that transforms the feeble, uncoordinated, and helpless foal into an independent individual, able to meet the rigid requirements for survival. For other foals, additional bottles of 2 to 3 ounces at 30-minute intervals may be necessary before a favorable response and positive gains take place. Continuous observation of the individual's behavior is the single prerequisite and key to survival. Be positive of what the foal is able to accomplish independently before relaxing your vigilance.

NO NURSING REFLEX

By far the most serious and extreme category of non-nursing foals is composed of those foals who lack the nursing reflex. These foals may be prostrate and unable to rise, or may even be able to achieve an upright stance. In either case, this disorder is an indication for immediate veterinary assistance. Absence of this vital reflex is anticipated and more readily recognized in the laterally recumbent foal than in an ambulatory individual. Discrepancy in sucking can exist, nevertheless, whether a foal is up or down.

WARNING: We usually associate the absence of sucking with the inability to swallow. The inability to curl the front of the tongue to achieve the necessary suction for nursing is accompanied by a general lack of mobility of the tongue muscles, particularly the posterior muscles. Proper functioning of these muscles is essential to ensure swallowing. To offer a bottle to a foal afflicted in this manner would be useless. Attempting to pour or syringe liquid nutrients into the foal's mouth with the hope that it will be swallowed is dangerous and should never be attempted. If the swallowing mechanism is impaired, the liquids will either fall out of the mouth or flow unimpeded into the trachea and directly into the lungs, depending upon the position of the head and neck. If the liquid flows into the lungs, the result will be pneumonia, called aspiration pneumonia, which will compound an already difficult situation. I have seen foals die of induced mechanical pneumonia when the lungs were the accidental recipients of the milk intended for the stomach. The skillful use of a stomach tube is the answer.

Overzealousness in attempts to feed the foal contribute to deaths that occur before the original disorder is diagnosed. To reiterate: Do not lose one priceless moment in seeking professional services when a question or a doubt exists.

VETERINARY SERVICE–TUBE FEEDING

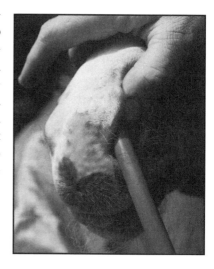

Tube-feeding the neonate.

Whether the initial problem is physiological or pathological in nature, the first step is identical. It is fundamental that a stomach tube be passed and that the critical need for nutrition be met. The experienced equine veterinarian will use a special foal tube for this purpose. A foal tube is small and smoothed, especially at the tip. The outside diameter should be no greater than three-eighths of an inch. The flexible tubing should be sparingly lubricated with a nonirritating, inert substance such as mineral oil or a sterile surgical lubricant. An excess of any lubricant can be accidentally aspirated and add unnecessary respiratory insult to an already weakened baby. In lieu of an infant foal tube, an equine male catheter, reserved solely for tubing a foal, is an ideal substitute.

The tube is gently and carefully introduced by way of the nostril along the floor of the nasal cavity, through the esophagus, and into the stomach. After 30 years of horse practice, I feel relatively confident in speaking for my friend and patient, the foal. Tubing is a painless and humane procedure. It may be unpleasant, since most foals are resentful of being tubed, but the displeasure the foal experiences is short-lived and is only a brief inconvenience.

NOTE: As the tube is being passed, the foal should be gently but firmly restrained to prevent self-injury. It is advantageous to both the veterinarian and the patient if the foal's head and neck are maintained in a normal flexed position. As when bottle feeding, it is mandatory that the prostrate foal be supported on its sternum while it is being tubed, and the position should be maintained for three to five minutes following tube feeding. This sternal position prevents backflow of the administered fluids in a weakened individual. Backflow can be caused by pressure created by a combination of reduced muscle tone and the foal's body weight in lateral recumbency. If the fluids are forced as high as the esophageal opening and the inefficient closure of the trachea, they may be fatally aspirated back into the lungs.

The veterinarian skilled in tubing newborn foals will exercise four of his or her five senses for this procedure. The senses of sight and touch are first used to insert the tube and direct it through the intricacies of delicate tissues in the nasopharyngeal space and into the esophagus.

The sense of touch becomes even more important to determine that the tube is properly placed in the esophagus and not the trachea.

Once the tube has entered the esophagus, it is permissible for the professional operator to blow a minute amount of air into the tube to expand the tiny, rubbery-textured esophagus. This structure in the newborn is only partially opened. It has permitted amniotic fluid to be ingested during embryonic life but will not become fully patent with normal tone until the foal has sucked and swallowed its first meal.

The small amount of air that emerges from the tip of the tube opens the lumen (the space within an artery, vein, intestine, or tube) of the esophagus and expands the adjacent soft tissue. The fleetingly expanded soft tissue reassures the veterinarian that the tube is indeed located in the esophagus and also eases the passage of the tube to preclude the possibility of irritation to the esophageal lining.

When the tube enters the stomach there is a characteristic release of gas. Although this stomach gas is small in volume in the newborn, it has a distinctive odor. The sense of smell plays an important role in identifying this odor, and it also verifies that the end of the tube has reached the stomach. At this time the peculiar stomach sounds are audible to confirm the proper placement of the tube. These sounds can only be heard if the free end of the tube is placed to the veterinarian's ear.

It is of interest to note that the esophagus is occasionally found on the right side of the neck in the young foal. In the older equine, I have yet to discover an esophagus on the right side of the neck. One must assume that during the growth process the esophagus relocates to the left side of the neck, which is the normal anatomical location.

Once the tube is safely in the foal's stomach, it provides an easy and efficient method of delivering the mare's milk where it is needed, overcoming the foal's reduced capacity to suck or swallow. The feeding schedule and the prescribed quantities of milk to be administered via the tube remain the same as for bottle feedings.

If the clinical findings indicate that the foal will require continued tube feeding, or if the foal's response to an initial tube feeding warrants the continued use of the stomach tube, a more permanent arrangement should be made. Such a decision should be based on the attending veterinarian's judgment. In this case, a simple but satisfactory solution is to secure the naso-gastric tube in place. A nylon suture can be looped around the exterior of the tube and fastened into place with a mattress stay suture through the soft tissue of the outer surface of the nares. Regular feedings can be dispensed by this route with ease, which obviates the need to remove and replace the tube with each frequent feeding the newborn demands.

This practice, proven to be satisfactory, serves a dual purpose. With a tube sutured in place, nonprofessional farm personnel will be able to adhere to the time schedule, and the necessity of passing a tube for each feeding will be avoided. The act of repeated and frequent tubing can cause irritation to the mucous membranes and subject an already weak foal to undue physical demands. In addition, a permanent tube provides a means of giving prescribed oral medication to a diseased foal. Medicines can be conveniently incorporated with any milk meal, can be given as frequently as prescribed by the veterinarian, and can be administered by laypeople.

CAUTION: The tube sutured in place offers many advantages, but there is a hazard that should be kept in mind. Unless the exposed end of the tube is securely plugged or clamped at all times except during the actual delivery of feedings, air will enter the stomach, causing abdominal distress, distension, and discomfort, robbing the uncomfortable foal of essential, uninterrupted rest. Do not fail to close the end of the tube immediately after each feeding.

It is a happy occasion, and not totally unrealistic, to find the foal with a naso-gastric tube sutured in place on its feet and successfully nursing. It is always a pleasure to remove a tube from a foal that has gained enough strength to obtain its meals independently.

DIAGNOSIS

When a foal is incapable of sucking or swallowing, and the emergency measure of the first tube feeding has been carried out, a differential diagnosis must be made without delay. Are you seeing a foal with a simple physical deterioration from birth stress and failure to meet critically timed nutritional requirements, or is there an insidious disease process (septicemia) of intrauterine origin at work?

ALERT: A high incidence of ill (septicemic) foals are delivered without the ability to suckle. This symptom should alert everyone and prompt a call to the veterinarian. It is therefore imperative that the veterinarian act promptly to make a clinical determination, institute interim treatment accordingly, and use laboratory procedures for confirmation and a definitive diagnosis. Time is of the essence, and this situation could prove fatal.

We have been discussing the foal who needs timely early assistance to survive. A foal who requires help to initiate respiration, needs a helping hand to control four unwieldy legs, or depends on a bottle or tube to provide basic nutrition to survive, is not necessarily a foal who is diseased or handicapped by a pathological condition. As serious as these problems seem when they occur, if promptly recognized and properly managed, they should not unfairly earmark a foal as an inferior individual who will not fulfill its genetic expectations. In my practice, I routinely treated these individuals and never doubted their ability to succeed.

Chapter Three

TRAUMA AND ILLNESS

Every newborn foal deserves a complete physical examination by a competent veterinarian as soon after birth as possible. This is a good sound rule to follow and will, I guarantee, produce gratifying results.

Any physical aberration of congenital or hereditary origin is ordinarily evident at birth or surely within the first 24 hours. Careful scrutiny of the head, mouth, jaws, eyes, eyelids, and particularly of the legs and feet should be made for malformation or any deviation from normal.

Of greater importance, however, are the body apertures so essential to life support. Their presence and completeness are vital for continuance of physiological processes such as the sucking and swallowing reflex, fecal passage, and urination. Carefully inspect the mouth, nostrils, eyes, and ears, then locate and inspect the navel cord under the abdomen. Next in order, but very important, are the anus, sheath and penis in the colt and vulva in the filly. Check to see that all orifices are present, then certify the fact that they are not blocked or obstructed.

The only exception is the navel cord stump, which (preferably) should be nonpatent, nonfunctional, and ideally in the process of drying up.

The foal should be examined for indications of physical trauma, usually sustained during parturition: facial or body bruises, fractured ribs, ruptured urinary bladder, crooked or strained limbs, and capped hocks and elbows. Most of these injuries occur when the mare is neglected and allowed to foal alone or unassisted.

During unattended deliveries, the foal's hocks and elbows principally sustain injury because of its floundering efforts to achieve a standing position and to seek nutrition without the helping hand of a caretaker.

Consequently, edematous swellings, with internal capillary bleeding, form over the foal's bony prominences. This condition is known as capped hock or elbow. Although a bruised head or eye, or capped elbows and hocks, can present a startling-looking foal, they are seldom cause for concern and soon subside. Abrasions can form on swellings and usually respond well to topical application of healing ointments. Large fluctuating swellings are frequently found shortly after birth, but, regardless of size, are of doubtful significance. Of great significance, however, are the infrequent occurrences of fractured ribs or ruptured urinary bladder, which should be carefully and conscientiously diagnosed and treated. These are caused by a prolonged or difficult parturition, either with too much traction or help, or, most often, with no assistance at all. Nature will prevail, but it can be quite costly.

Also of great significance are diaphragmatic rents. The diaphragm is a musculomembranous partition that separates the thoracic cavity (lungs) from the abdominal cavity (viscera). In shape it resembles an open umbrella. A ruptured diaphragm occurs infrequently through undue or excessive force and abdominal compression during the birth process.

I have learned that any suffering foal will make itself heard, either by overt symptoms unmistakable to anyone or by dying in short order. Watchfulness is the secret to a successful nursery and will increase the number of healthy foals and reduce the overall morbidity and mortality rates appreciably among newborns.

Before we embark on an in-depth discussion of various foal infections, I would like to describe four problems commonly encountered shortly after birth: constipation (either simple or severe), impaction, retained meconium, colic, and diarrhea (scours). There are two schools of thought regarding these so-called minor disorders. Some believe they are indeed minor. Others believe that a manifestation of any one of these conditions represents a harbinger of oncoming illness, and that rather than being a single and separate innocuous entity, each is a part of a generalized overall malady and should be treated as such. Most veterinarians share the latter sentiments and either proceed vigorously with prophylactic measures or probe deeper for a clear-cut diagnosis, leaving no stone unturned. Consequently, when constipation, diarrhea, or colicky signs appear, it's a good idea to summon the veterinarian for a differential diagnosis and an expert opinion of your foal. Time will then be on your side.

CONSTIPATION

Simple constipation is a relatively common ailment caused by the unnatural retention of fecal matter. It can be a problem at any time from the first half hour of life until the foal reaches its third day.

First symptoms are colicky signs of pain and discomfort, tail switching, straining, lying down, and rolling. This behavior is primarily caused by gastrointestinal pain created by a small, hard fecal mass in the rectum that cannot be passed easily. An ordinary soapy-water enema often solves the problem and gives immediate relief. If the foal does not respond favorably to the enema and continues to exhibit discomfort, consider placing a call for professional assistance. A fair-to-good prognosis is associated with mild constipation. Please avoid the commercial product Fleet enema unless no veterinary service is available.

If symptoms of constipation persist, then the next possibility, called impaction, should be given serious consideration. This is a more serious problem, located higher in the intestinal tract, yet producing symptoms identical to constipation.

SEVERE CONSTIPATION/IMPACTION

Serious constipation or impaction occurs in the newborn foal when the meconium—fecal material that forms in the intestines during gestation—fails to move along and pass out of the foal's body shortly after birth.

WARNING: Severe constipation is easily recognized by intractable GI pain, and specifically a very unnatural but reliable body position assumed by all stricken foals. A stricken foal is found on its back with its head and neck extended in a straight line with the body so that the lower jaw is uppermost and embraced by the outstretched front legs and feet. This unmistakable body position signals that there is serious constipation or impaction of the intestines; it also signals the immediate need of a veterinarian to begin treatment. Impaction requires a long course of treatments, averaging from one to four days, but with thorough medication and good fortune, many foals recover.

Initial medication consists of injectable painkillers to help relax the foal and permit passage of the naso-gastric (stomach) tube through which a laxative is delivered directly into the stomach. Some milk from the mare's udder may be included in the mixture if it has been ascertained that the foal has reduced its regular nursing pattern. This determination can be made only by evaluation of the mare's mammary gland, its size, shape, texture, and evidence of dripping white milk.

Injectable muscle relaxants, such as dipyrone (Novin), administered intravenously for immediate relief and intramuscularly for sustained action, is effective, ideal, and safe for use in young foals.

As soon as the foal appears somewhat more comfortable after receiving the injections, a routine enema is indicated, properly administered by a responsible person. This treatment will initially empty the rectal area and perhaps stimulate some peristalsis or fecal movement located farther up (higher) in the intestinal tract.

However, enemas given too frequently (more than once daily) or given with too much enthusiasm are contraindicated in the newborn.

Over the years, the use, frequency, and actual validity of enemas has continued to be controversial, since most impactions occur high in the intestinal tract. I prefer to keep my patient as comfortable as possible, constantly replace lost fluids and electrolytes (intravenous and subcutaneous), and relentlessly tube with nutrition and laxatives. Promiscuous and frequently administered enemas only serve to irritate the foal's rectal mucosa, causing swelling and pain, thus adding to the misery of the already sick foal.

Early in the course of impaction, foals discontinue nursing or nurse only intermittently; thus, dehydration and lowered blood-sugar levels set in rapidly. An emergency situation could easily develop by the time of recognition and subsequent diagnosis. Dehydration causes weakness and vulnerability to systemic disease and infection, and can be devastating to a small foal.

The importance of intravenous electrolyte, dextrose, and fluid loss replacement in cases of protracted constipation or impaction cannot be overemphasized, combined with nutrients delivered through a stomach tube. Dehydration in constipation equals that caused by diarrhea. In cases of diarrhea, the need for fluid and mineral replacement is obvious, but this same need is all too often overlooked or forgotten when the foal is constipated. The reasoning for this lapse escapes me. No constipation case is properly treated unless vigorous fluid therapy is included.

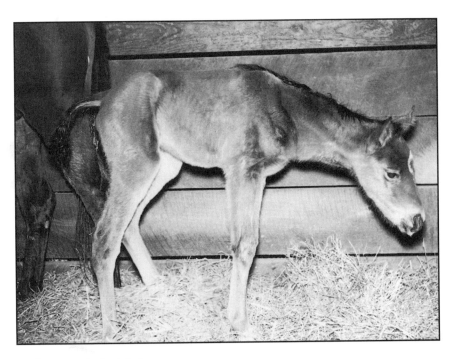

Gastrointestinal pain/colic.

A suffering foal will show irregular intervals of both pain and relief and will constantly change body position, appearing nearly dead one moment and somewhat relaxed the next. It is indeed not uncommon to find an afflicted foal on its back one minute and discover it up, feebly attempting to nurse, the next. This behavior is characteristic of impaction in the upper intestine, but new or uninitiated owners are frequently upset by this behavior.

Occasionally the mother will become restless or irritated by all the commotion and people moving in and out of the stall during the foal's illness. Additionally, her udder may become uncomfortable and teats sore due to the irregular pattern of nursing. If the mare is somewhat nervous or is a high-strung matron, I suggest a mild tranquilizer, preferably 1 to 2cc of acepromazine intramuscularly every 12 hours. This allows all personnel to concentrate on the needs of the sick foal more easily.

The foal should be kept as comfortable as possible during painful periods, when self-inflicted injury becomes a real possibility. Medication schedules should be followed closely; repeated treatments, administered every four to eight hours, coupled with the fluid therapy regime, should resolve the constipation. All efforts must continue until the discomfort level or pain episodes subside in severity and duration. Suddenly, the passage of fecal material will appear, and the problem will be solved. Once the bowels evacuate and begin true physiologic function, the afflicted individual seldom suffers a recurrence.

RETAINED MECONIUM

Retained meconium is a very serious form of total constipation found in the newborn foal and is diagnostically evident within the first 12 hours of life.

Meconium is the first intestinal discharge of the newborn. During the later period of gestation, a few fetal systems begin functioning independently while the fetus is still inside the uterus. Waste fluids are accumulated, stored in, and expelled with the placental tissue at the time of delivery. Although the brown (watery to lumpy) material staining the placental tissue at delivery is usually harmless, it tends to upset the inexperienced. In rare cases only has it been associated with weak or septicemic foals. However, semisolid waste materials that accumulate in the foal's gastrointestinal tract remain there until parturition has been completed. Then the necessary stimulation induces evacuation.

In some less fortunate foals, the meconium fails to mobilize as expected and remains in position.

WARNING: Any stubborn case of constipation that develops within the first few hours of life can almost always be attributed to various small amounts of meconium that have been partially or fully retained in the intestinal tract. An enema should stimulate evacuation of the rectum and promote some peristalsis in the intestines.

Unfortunately, enemas have little effect on retained meconium, which is usually located in the upper portion of the intestines. Retained meconium should be a number one suspect in early nonproductive enemas. Be alerted.

Pain is produced by the stasis of the fecal material. With stasis, the mass begins to lose moisture content and becomes progressively drier, and is thus less likely to move or respond to even heroic treatment. Concurrently, the intestinal mucosal lining that surrounds the meconium mass quickly dehydrates and subsequently loses its tissue integrity. This tissue change allows the absorption of toxic materials into the circulation, compounding the problems of an already sick and miserable foal. Time is of the essence now if the foal's life is to be saved.

Although retained meconium produces identical symptoms to those of simple impaction or constipation, the prognosis is indeed another story. Diagnosis can be based on the degree of discomfort, persistence of symptoms, and overall refractory nature of the illness to conventional conservative treatment.

SURGERY

Odds for the foal's survival are appreciably increased if a well-equipped surgical facility is within your reach. If surgical intervention is being considered, a more definitive diagnosis can be achieved by a series of successive blood tests, which can indicate, along with other values, the presence and progressive amounts of dehydration. With even an early systemic infection, an increased packed-red-cell volume and/or increased white-cell count reveal dehydration. However, blood tests can be helpful only if the results are quickly forthcoming.

It is sometimes better to present a case early for surgery and reserve an option than to second-guess, wait too long to act, and lose your right to decide. Hours are lost, and so are lives. If necessary, and at the proper time, your veterinarian will recommend this life-saving surgical procedure.

Upon admittance to the equine hospital, the foal's abdomen will be clipped, shaved, scrubbed, and receive an exhaustive pre-op preparation. After several tubes of blood are drawn and submitted to the laboratory, a sedative given intravenously will follow. An IV polyethylene catheter will be placed into the jugular vein, carefully taped into place, and retaped around the foal's neck for security. When all is ready, a pre-anesthetic is administered through the in-place catheter after which the long, easily accessible tubing will hang free for emergency use. Following a second injection of thiopental and a muscle relaxant, the patient will slump down onto mattresses. Then the foal is intubated orally with a small, uniquely designed red rubber endotracheal tube. This pediatric tube is introduced orally through a round, rigid mouthpiece held between and by the foal's incisors. This prevents collapse of the tube so it remains patent during surgery. It is then deftly slipped into the trachea (windpipe), thereby

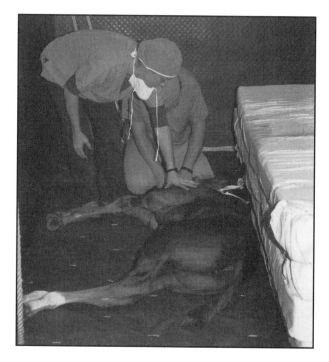

Recovering from surgery.

assuring that the foal has an open air passage at all times. A safe and effective general anesthetic is administered through the endotracheal tube in the form of an inhalation gas called Halothane or Fluothane. These modern gas anesthetics allow a surgical plane of anesthesia with great margin of safety to the patient. They are superior to the older injectable anesthetic agents.

RECOVERING FROM SURGERY

After sterile draping of the animal's body, the veterinary surgeon can prepare for a midline abdominal incision. Entering the abdomen, the surgeon skillfully locates the entrapped mass of meconium. A decision is then made, based on the experience and knowledge of the surgeon, whether to massage the fecal mass on through or to open the intestine and remove the offensive material surgically. If great tissue damage has occurred to the intestinal wall and circulation in the intestinal tissue has been compromised, the surgeon may choose to remove the intestinal section in toto and resuture the intestine end to end, a procedure called anastomosis.

It is astounding to see the size, length, and concrete consistency of some of the meconium masses removed from affected foals. Whichever procedure the surgeon elects to use, the foal has been given a chance to survive. And survive they do! I have known a good many such foals who have lived normal lives with no recurrence of any form of gastrointestinal problems.

DIARRHEA AND COLIC

The mere presence of either diarrhea or colic should signal the utmost need for a visit by an experienced equine veterinarian. Both diarrhea and colic are considered symptoms and not entities; in my opinion, their presence is an ominous sign of impending illness in the newborn. No healthy foal should evidence any degree or form of diarrhea or any type of gastrointestinal disturbance at any age. To ignore the symptoms is foolhardy; it is equally ignorant to administer home remedies prepared for humans. All this represents a costly delay. Do not be lulled into complacency by an active, alert, and vigorous foal; this same colt can quickly fade into a limp, sick individual. See SEPTICEMIA, page 63.

Body temperature; heart, pulse, and respiratory rates; gastrointestinal sounds; and the color of gums and ocular membranes are all significant and thus should be noted. A blood sample should be submitted to the laboratory for vital information that can confirm and guide the veterinarian. An increased count of white blood cells can indicate an infection; a reduced number may suggest an immune deficiency. Both conditions are insidious, serious, and life-threatening. A blood sample can play a paramount role in early detection of hidden problems and should be given first priority in the treatment of any foal suspected of illness.

Color, consistency, and odor of any diarrhea is significant and can also aid in the diagnosis, or reveal the cause of a gastrointestinal upset.

The one and only exception to the diarrhea rule occurs during the foal heat or so-called *nine-day scours*. To an astute foal owner, this is the only known form of scours acceptable.

FOAL HEAT SCOURS

Bear in mind that it is perfectly normal for a healthy foal to manifest diarrhea, slight or profuse, with the onset of the brood mare's nine-day heat cycle. The cause of this form of scours has been highly controversial for years, but today many agree that the foal while nursing swallows foreign matter along with milk, setting up irritation in the intestine. The foal ingests vaginal discharge that has drained down over the lactating udder and teats. This discharge is heavily laden with various forms of bacteria, and diarrhea quickly develops.

After an 11-month gestational period, the nine-day heat cycle is considered by many veterinarians to be a normal physiologic house-cleaning of the mare's reproductive tract. Semifluid vaginal discharges continue to flow throughout the average three- to four-day period and consequently steadily insult the foal's gastrointestinal tract for the duration.

The term nine-day scours is at times misleading and should be changed to foal heat scours. Onset of scours can actually be expected any time from the mare's sixth to the 12th postpartum day. Foal heat scours is normal and should end as quickly as it appears, in approximately four days. Healthy foals quickly return to normal. Weak foals, however, may become weaker and continue to scour, requiring treatment. Prevention of dreaded dehydration, lowered resistance, and increased susceptibility to systemic infection requires prompt attention. Diarrhea with electrolyte loss must be stopped abruptly. Initial treatment consists of penicillin and dihydrostreptomycin, preferably 5 to 6cc intramuscularly once daily for from three to five days. Replace electrolytes either intravenously or orally. A routine blood count as a barometer and guide should also be done at this time.

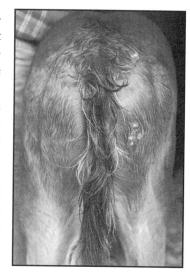

A scouring foal.

A conscientious foal owner can ease the intensity and even reduce the stress of this physiologic phenomenon called *foal heat scours*. Scrupulously cleanse the mare's vulva and perineal region, with special emphasis on the udder, simultaneously with the onset of estrus. A large towel, mild soap, and tepid water will serve well to clear away debris and bacteria; rinse it thoroughly, then dry it well. Repeat this daily for the duration of the cycle, approximately three to four days.

A thinking owner can provide another kindness. Intractable purging by the foal typically causes a soiled, wet bottom that eventually dries with loss of hair around the tail area. A bland soap-and-water scrub alleviates the physical discomfort and itching that assuredly occurs from several days of scouring. Generous daily applications of either mineral oil, glycerine, or Vaseline will soften and relieve the sore bottom and prevent hair loss.

COPROPHAGY

There is still another cause for diarrhea in the newborn foal. When scours develop and persist with no rhyme or reason, be suspicious of coprophagy (manure eating). The sneaky foal ingests irritants and parasitic larva and eggs, producing a self-perpetuating diarrhea that can be very distressing and perplexing to a conscientious owner. I classify coprophagy as a vice, one that requires careful attention and management to prevent an otherwise daily insult to the foal's gastrointestinal tract.

In my experience, the largest, strongest, and best-nourished foals are those found to develop this sneaky habit. The cause has eluded everyone to date, and treatment consists simply of prompt manure removal from the foal's area.

DISEASE

A foal is born free of parasites, totally lacking antibodies, but not necessarily free of infection. The mare's placentation is the source responsible for each of these facts. Her placenta is unique, not only in its physiologic selective functions and its anatomical structure, but also in its characteristic attachment to the inner surface of the mare's uterus. Thought by many to be antiquated and forgotten by evolutionary change, the ill-equipped placenta and copartner uterus continue to exert curious influences, perhaps good and possibly bad, on the encapsulated fetus.

No endoparasite (internal parasite) can cross the placental membranes and enter the fetus during the gestational period. The mare's own internal parasites inhabiting her gastrointestinal tract and bloodstream during pregnancy cannot gain entrance to her fetus, which is well surrounded by placental membranes inside the uterus. It is indeed a different story once the new arrival leaves its protective environment. At birth it automatically falls prey to a host of parasites waiting in the bedding on contaminated ground or soil surfaces.

Ascarid (roundworm) eggs abound in the foal's surroundings, ready to be ingested by the newborn. Thus begins the eternal parasitic infestation, a destructive cycle that lasts for the life of the foal.

Unlike other species, the foal receives no protective antibodies from the expectant mother during gestation. Again, the placenta is responsible. Equine antibodies cannot pass through the selectively impermeable placental barrier.

It is quite different in the case of infection. Infectious agents, whether viral or bacterial, quite easily penetrate and proceed to invade both the uterus and placental membranes. The customarily invincible placenta is quite vulnerable to infection, and, in fact, is selected as the target tissue by some infectious agents even as they enter the mare's body.

Viruses, fungi, and bacteria commonly live and regenerate inside the mare's reproductive tract, but principally flourish and grow deep down inside the pendulous uterine horn of a multipara brood mare. It is rare to see an infected maiden mare. Well-hidden infections often miss detection even with our modern means of gynecologic examinations, cervical and uterine swabs, cytologic, and bacteriological culturing. If undisturbed, these low-grade infections can engender flourishing growth and render a mare infertile or ultimately cause sterility. Perhaps the use of the ultrasound machine could help uncover and assess the uterine horns with well-established infections in the near future.

Although mares become infected in other ways, contamination and invasion by microorganisms capable of causing breeding problems occur most often during the breeding procedure. When a mare's genital tract is exposed to a venereal pathogen, several consequences can occur. Depending upon the mare's innate hardiness or resistance and the degree of virulence of the invading microorganism, three conditions can develop: infertility, requiring extensive antibiotic treatment; sterility, which is the end of the mare's reproductive life; or, surprisingly, a durable pregnancy. These problematic and worrisome pregnancies seem determined to survive by coexisting with the uterine venereal infection. Many mares become infected in the breeding shed through a breach in asepsis by careless personnel.

This coexistence is precisely why weak, diseased, or dead foals—all commonly called septicemic foals—are produced. The exceptional fetus that manages to survive (not aborted during embryonic development) usually arrives in a weakened and precarious condition. The foal may be comatose or never breathe independently, let alone rise and nurse.

An obviously sick foal, one diseased while in utero, is easily recognized by its gross appearance. This foal is profoundly weak and undersized and possesses a substandard musculoskeletal frame. Typically, it experiences difficulty even in rising and often will become exhausted long before it can reach nourishment or master the vital faculty of nursing.

Certain viruses, notably the notorious rhinopneumonitis virus, more recently referred to as equine herpes virus I, has a keen ability to invade the mare's body and expediently gain direct entrance to the pregnant uterus through its strong affinity for placental tissue. Here the virus establishes an infection between the placenta and uterine wall, causing primary patchy loosening of the membranes' attachment. The greater the separation, the less efficient the supply of gas and nutrients to the fetus. If a low-grade inefficiency occurs between the maternal uterine lining and the fetal membranes, the heavy brood mare may exhibit subtle symptoms. However, if the infection is extensive and destructive, most mares remain quiescent or symptomless until abortion is imminent and occurs spontaneously.

A spontaneous abortion of a full- or near-full-term foal with no mammary development, completely enveloped in its entire placental tissue, is considered diagnostic of rhinopneumonitis infection.

There are some specific bacteria capable of invading and eliciting similar symptoms with the same disastrous results. Some of these bacterial agents leave identifying lesions not only on the aborted fetus but also on and/or in the placental membranes. Again, examination of all afterbirth membranes, whether aborted or delivered normally, should be routine, even mandatory. Too much knowledge is lost forever when a placenta is discarded without professional evaluation.

To reiterate, all neonates are delivered parasite-free and immunologically deficient, but not all foals are born free from infection. Do not ever be fooled or misled by the healthy-looking, vigorous colt or filly: It could very well be harboring an infection. Any stress, even the rigors of a normal parturition, can in itself trigger a low-grade infection in an otherwise healthy individual. Unattended foalings may result in a stressful and prolonged delivery, delayed nursing, exposed and traumatized navel cord, dehydration, and exhaustion. The foal's resistance is thus lowered, and an infection can gain a foothold in a formerly healthy foal.

There really is no one consistent sign or valid symptom that can warn the person in charge to suspect an infection in a healthy-looking foal. When the newborn foal arrives, an in-depth physical examination is well worth the effort. An experienced equine veterinarian can determine the presence of or potential for development of a systemic infection.

Although some foals arrive with varying degrees of insidious infection contracted in utero and experience a lowered resistance during delivery, others become victims of hostile bacteria in the external environment.

THE SICK FOAL

Septicemia is a scary word, but after one has witnessed an afflicted foal literally fighting for its life, the term takes on a much greater meaning. Bacteremia, viremia, and blood poisoning are other names for this scourge, which is responsible for over one-half of all deaths in foals.

I can vividly recall intently listening to my professors at veterinary school at the University of Pennsylvania describe foal epidemics that they as young practitioners had experienced.

As these older gentlemen spoke, I could sense their emotion and despair. My upbringing in a dyed-in-the-wool horse family had sensitized me to better appreciate the agony suffered not only by the animals but also by caring owners, personnel, and attending veterinarians who shared and will carry the memories and emotional scars forever. Prior to the advent of sulfa drugs and then antibiotics, when epidemics occurred on large breeding farms, great losses were sustained in foal crops. The inevitable losses ran literally unrestrained in horse nurseries when an infection gained entrance to the premises.

High populations, or any degree of crowding, either in amount of pasture per head or stall space, invite disease and its propagation. With foals specifically bred and raised for their inherent abilities or genetic structure to compete or to be marketed for future generations, the needless loss of these superior individuals was almost sacrilegious.

With no truly effective drugs and with a mortality rate threatening well over 85 percent, the equine practitioner had little to offer other than control measures, such as quarantine and isolation efforts. Combined with nursing care and supportive therapy, every concerted attempt was made to contain the spread of the disease—and, needless to say, frustrations ran high.

Applicable knowledge is always slow to come and even slower to be accepted in some areas. However, I have found owners, managers, and farm personnel only too eager to listen to any information regarding the health of their foals. It seems only natural that they crave knowledge, as success can't be far behind.

Today, a potential epidemic is a horse of another color. We now have powerful antibiotics capable of not only containing but effectively eliminating the various pathogens that cause such deadly diseases. Consequently, the mortality rate is steadily being nudged lower, though at an agonizingly slow pace. Fewer and fewer foals are succumbing when specific antibiotics are combined with supportive electrolytic/fluid therapy, administered in a truly conscientious manner.

Careful surveillance and a watchful eye are key. Most farm personnel are truly aware of the axiom that a newborn foal can be well and happy one minute and ill enough to require emergency attention the next. I contend that the deciding factor of successful treatment in the neonate commonly lies with the dedicated person who religiously checks the baby foals at all hours, alertly looking for the slightest indication of weakness or depression.

WARNING: If a shadow of a doubt exists, a quick glance at the mare's udder is a reliable method of confirming the presence of a substandard foal. The condition of the mare's udder will reveal an impending foal illness. When a baby foal begins to feel ill, the first behavioral change is reflected in a reduced milk intake, not necessarily a reduced frequency of nursing. The delicate balance in the mare's mammary gland between milk production and the milk demands made by normal foals is extremely sensitive and easily disturbed by the slightest alteration in the amount of milk suckled. Basically, this disparity is manifested by an enlarged, tense, and sometimes sore udder. If not relieved, this will shortly produce milk drops on the teat ends. If the foal continues to fall behind on its nursing amounts or ceases nursing, the milk will then begin to stream independently down the mare's hind legs. Any udder change is a sure sign of a sick foal and should serve as a signal to call for emergency medical attention. While waiting for the arrival of the veterinarian, the foal's body temperature, respiratory rate, and mucous membrane coloring should be observed and recorded.

For some 25 years I had the privilege of being the farm veterinarian responsible for over 300 head of horses, including five breeding stallions, and over 150 foals per season. I fondly recall watching the owner, methodically making rounds while all hands were working, glancing into each stall and every paddock, and on occasion standing staring at a group of sucklings in a field. Great concern was placed on the foal's body position and overall attitude, followed by an astute glance, if needed, at the size and texture of the mare's udder. This regimen was repeated many times daily, but I learned that more emphasis was placed on the late-night bed check. All young, regardless of species, become more vulnerable as night approaches. On many occasions I was summoned after hours to examine foals thought to be sick; often they were only tired or exhausted from an active day of playing. And then, of course, on other late calls, a sick foal indeed was discovered early enough to allow successful treatment.

SEPTICEMIA/BLOOD POISONING

There are various types of microorganisms that have a special affinity for newborn foals and, if given the opportunity, seek not only to gain entrance to the foal's body but to literally destroy vital organs and body tissue. These bacteria then expeditiously establish a systemic infection called septicemia.

At this juncture I must emphasize the need for a definitive diagnosis by your veterinarian when faced with warning symptoms, even in a strong and apparently healthy foal. Constipation, diarrhea, or colicky distress have been described and discussed in detail, but let me remind you that all three can individually or collectively represent serious precursors to the dreaded disease septicemia. Whether to treat the symptom and lose valuable time waiting for lab results or to institute rigorous treatment for early septicemia is the awesome decision of the veterinarian.

A depressed foal.

Neonatal septicemia (blood poisoning) is defined as a systemic infection caused by the invasion of disease-producing bacteria or their lethal toxins into the foal's bloodstream. If attacked in utero, some foals die and are aborted. If delivered alive, most are comatose or very weak and quite debilitated.

Foal septicemia is a dreaded word denoting disaster in the equine nursery. Septicemia therefore heads the list of foal diseases most commonly responsible for abortions, the birth of sick foals, and well foals becoming sick. Those foals fortunate enough to recover from a protracted septicemia usually are easily identified by unthriftiness, retarded development, and various crippling skeletal deformities.

Septicemia is blood poisoning caused by bacteria that gain entrance to the blood system. When gram-negative bacteria leave their normal habitat, the intestinal tract, and enter the bloodstream, where they do not belong, blood poisoning develops. If the foal goes untreated or is under-treated, enterotoxemia develops. Blood poisoning, from any causative microorganism, is very dangerous and, if unrecognized, shock will undoubtedly ensue. See page 177.

Today we have a bacterin called Endobactoid, effective against enterotoxemia. Therefore, vaccinated brood mares can confer immunity to their foals through the colostrum. The thought of this great breakthrough is exciting.

Numerous types of septicemia currently are well-recognized, each with its distinct causative bacteria, clear-cut salient symptoms, and mode of attack. Occasionally, though, a foal will suffer from more than one infection simultaneously. When a combination of bacterial or viral infectious agents invades a foal, the diagnosis, treatments, and prognosis can become complex. The lungs, liver, kidneys, and gastrointestinal tract may be attacked, and each organ's functional efficiency compromised in varying degrees. Symptoms produced can be revealing to the astute veterinarian.

The severity and course of illness depends greatly upon the virulence of the causative microorganism and on the inherent health, natural resistance, and condition of the immune system. All these factors weigh heavily on susceptibility and/or resistance.

Septicemic infections strike in two distinct ways:

1. During embryonic and fetal life, resulting in (a) an abortion or (b) the delivery of a septicemic foal.

2. In a healthy foal that has (a) incubated or harbored an infection acquired in gestation or (b) developed septicemia from the external environment.

The aborted foal should be autopsied in an effort to determine cause of death. The mare should then receive a cervical swab, culture, and sensitivity tests to confirm the cause of abortion and so determine proper treatment in preparation for her next breeding season.

Surprisingly, in less severe cases, embryonic growth and fetal development persist, and life continues inside the infected uterus, although at a lower standard of proficiency; thus a sick and inferior foal is born alive. Foals who have contracted septicemia in utero, when delivered alive, are weak, depressed, underweight, and essentially substandard individuals, consistently undersized and poorly developed, with small bones and notoriously crooked legs.

Examination of the fetal fluids and the placental membranes usually reveals brownish stains, thickened areas, and discoloration indicative of intrauterine infection. With this knowledge, prompt action and rigorous treatment to the foal can in some cases result in success. This foal can receive early specific treatment and, it is hoped, survive.

A visibly healthy foal may be born harboring an infection that can gain strength if the foal is stressed during delivery or during its first few hours after birth. This foal can become weak and be septicemic within hours—with no warning.

The greatest shock, however, is the perfectly healthy, full-sized, vigorous, aggressive foal who becomes ill anytime from the first few hours to the first three days of life. This is caused by an extrauterine septicemia acquired from the external environment, i.e., a contaminated foaling stall.

WARNING: The major source of contamination on all horse farms is the brood mare who delivers an infected foal. The infection is spread by diseased placental tissue and accompanying fluids, which impregnate the ground surfaces of the foaling stall. If the mare foals outside, the soil or grass becomes contaminated but has a greater chance to be neutralized, destroyed, or diluted by sunlight and fresh air. Inside the foaling stall there is a different situation: In spite of sanitation and disinfectants, including, in some first-class breeding farms, the use of steam sterilization methods, the infected fluids enter and remain deep in the stall-floor crevices, seams, and cracks. Therefore, a community foaling stall can represent a reservoir of infection awaiting the arrival of the next newborn. Needless to say, the danger to other foals increases with the number of brood mares on the farm.

When a farm is experiencing some form of septicemia, all may be well advised to avoid the use of a common foaling stall. In this situation, it is almost better to let your mare foal elsewhere, perhaps in another stall or even outside under very strict privacy and, of course, supervision.

Pathenogenic or disease-producing bacteria are known to invade a normal foal's body via three routes:

1. Through the open navel stump.

2. During ingestion (orally).

3. During inhalation (respiration).

It is difficult to regulate completely what a foal ingests or inhales, but the navel cord is within the realm of control.

If the navel antiseptic is properly applied before exposure to contaminants occurs, this noted route of bacterial invasion can be at least partially closed. The accepted antiseptic contains an antibacterial agent, and its caustic properties stimulate tissue contraction, thus hastening closure of the umbilical tissue. An 8 percent tincture of iodine is an old standard navel antiseptic that has served well and withstood the test of time.

IMMUNE DEFICIENCY

When considering the causes of septicemia, one must be aware of a hazardous predisposing condition of newborn foals called immune deficiency.

Some authorities contend that septicemia per se cannot overwhelmingly invade and destroy a foal possessing a healthy functional immune system, and that only those victims of a failure of immune body transfer do in fact become ill, continue to remain ill, are commonly refractory to treatment, and usually perish.

Immune capabilities have great significance in the diagnosis and treatment of septicemias. A foal that appears to be healthy at birth may be predisposed to and become a victim of septicemia because vital immune bodies are lacking. Until just recently, we had no method to identify or confirm this dangerous condition, but now we are armed with a diagnostic blood test that can be used at stallside, with results determined within minutes: the zinc sulfate test, which is now part of every veterinary obstetrician or pediatrician's armamentarium. Specific treatment for immune deficiency is a prompt and safe serum transfusion. Immune deficiencies in the newborn foal are an interesting current topic and are discussed in detail in Chapter 4 (see IMMUNODEFICIENT FOALS).

Let us now address ourselves to the classic types of foal septicemia by probing more deeply and examining separately each known entity. For each infection, causes will be identified and symptoms described; we will also explore expected courses of illness, recovery rates, and anticipated prognoses.

To repeat: Every newborn deserves a complete physical examination performed by a competent equine veterinarian as soon after birth as possible, even when all vital signs appear fine. Ideally, blood tests should be obtained routinely. If, as an owner, you sense even the slightest deviation from normalcy, move the call to your veterinarian up to an emergency status—*do not wait!* This is a good insurance policy.

COMMON SEPTICEMIAS

1. Joint ill and navel ill.

2. Dummy, wanderer, or sleeper foal.

3. Foal pneumonia.

4. *E. coli* infection.

5. Ill-defined septicemias.

6. Primary foal pneumonia.

7. Strangles.

8. Barker foal.

9. Shaker foal vs. botulism.

10. Noninfectious foal pneumonia.

Following is a list and detailed description of the better-known septicemias facing the equine farms and all involved in the horse industry.

JOINT ILL AND NAVEL ILL

Causative agent: *Streptococcus pyogenes*.

Diagnosis: Septicemia.

Prognosis: Guarded to poor.

Treatment:

1. Complete blood count and differential.

2. Blood culture (requires time).

3. Zinc sulfate test (immune competence).

4. Tube feed.

5. Electrolyte and fluid replacement IV.

6. Antibiotic of choice (penicillin, ampicillin, oxytetracycline, sulfoamides).

SEPTICEMIAS

COMMON NAME	CAUSATIVE AGENT	SYMPTOMS	AGE GROUP AFFECTED
Joint Ill, Navel Ill	*Streptococcus pyogenes*	fever; depression; weakness; hot, swollen, painful joints; lameness	birth to 3 weeks; subsequent joint damage at 18 months; cause of abortions
Dummy (Sleeper, Wanderer) Foals	*Actinobacillus equuli* (*Shigella equuli*)	fetid diarrhea; subnormal temperature; refusal to nurse the udder; walking the wall; nursing the wall; mental confusion and weakness; excessive water intake	birth to 3 weeks; cause of abortions in mares
Foal Pneumonia	*Corynebacterium equi* (*Rhodococcus equi*)	high fever; depression; weakness; puffing respiration with flaring nostrils; persistence at nursing; thrifty body weight; pneumonia; lung abscesses; gastrointestinal distress abscesses	around 3–4 months; cause of abortions in mares

SEPTICEMIAS (CONTINUED)

COMMON NAME	CAUSATIVE AGENT	SYMPTOMS	AGE GROUP AFFECTED
Foal Pneumonia	Escherichia coli	fever; depression; weakness; equilibrium upset; head and neck pulled around to chest wall; spasms	around 10–21 days
Ill-Defined Septicemias	Pseudomonas aeruginosa, Salmonella abortus equi, Salmonella enteritis	mixture of symptoms; unexplained abortions; high fever; diarrhea; dehydration	no fixed age

7. Joint culture, lavage, and indicated injections.

8. Navel cord treatment assessment and treatment daily.

Streptococcus pyogenes is the cause of the infamous joint ill or navel ill infections of newborn foals.

Strep infections in foals can be contracted and spread by three different means: prior to birth, through the uterus of an infected mare; after birth, from a contaminated environment (foaling stall, stalls, barns, vans, etc.); and from other sick foals.

A brood mare can acquire a strep infection in the breeding shed either during coitus with an infected stallion or through physical contamination, as might be caused by a breach in aseptic techniques. Many mares, once infected, continue to harbor the infection deep inside the uterus for years.

Streptococcus is notoriously refractory to treatment. This microorganism appears to coexist with some more serious infections; not until the strep is cleared up will the underlying culprit infection become identifiable. Strep will notoriously mask deeper-located, more destructive infections in the uterine wall such as Pseudomonas or *Shigella* microorganisms. Uterine swabs will continue to produce strep culture growths until medications clear the infection; then and only then will the Pseudomonas or *Shigella* or other resistant infectious organisms, all slow growers, manifest their presence.

Once the strep has been eliminated from mares who have been barren for several years, the true cause of the infertility is in evidence. Inadvertent overtreatment with intrauterine antibiotics can create an imbalance of normal flora and allow the unnatural and devastating growth of fungi or molds, which can render the mare infertile or even sterile.

A cervical or uterine swab obtained from the mare and submitted to the laboratory for culturing can produce inconsistent results. A negative culture report is usually not worth the price of the paper it is printed on unless precisely taken by an equine practitioner experienced in obstetrics and gynecology. When evaluating a mare's fertility status, some practitioners prefer to include a uterine biopsy. When carried out properly, a uterine biopsy can reveal the cellular status of the uterine endometrium, which is directly responsible for successful pregnancy. Proper evaluation through a gynecological examination, preferably performed during estrus, is by far the superior method of determining the reproductive health and overall fertility of a mare being prepared for breeding.

However, if a strep mare with a false negative culture certificate inadvertently slips through the vanguard and is ultimately covered, the stallion, if not already infected, has now been exposed and is in jeopardy. Traditional breeding-shed protocol includes, along with a prebreeding wash, a postcover antiseptic scrub and rinse of the stallion. This affords surface cleansing only, and while these efforts do provide a hygienic approach, in the presence of pathogenic bacteria, the effectiveness is highly questionable.

Most intrauterine infections produce an environment hostile not only to the stallion's semen and its normal functions, but also to any subsequent fertilized egg that, by chance, might endure and arrive in the body of the uterus. If a pregnancy does ensue and persists against all odds for survival, the somewhat hardy fetus and its placental membranes are in constant contact with the streptococcal microorganism and its by-products. This virulent microorganism will readily invade and destroy embryonic tissue, causing, in most cases, the termination of pregnancy. In those cases with less severe involvement, pregnancy may continue but surely developmental retardation is extensive. Abortion is highly probable.

It has been my finding that, if not aborted, the foal determined to coexist with the infection will either be delivered prematurely or long past the due date, but rarely ever on time. Early arrival is prompted by the strength and ability of the infection to destroy and fragment the life-supporting attachments to the uterus. Strep infection also invades the fetus and all of its critical organs.

If sufficient placental separation and damage occurs before 10 months into gestation, spontaneous abortion results in either a dead foal or a diseased, short-lived, inadequate foal. If destruction of placental efficiency develops after 10 months into gestation, then a premature delivery becomes imminent.

It is considered a major feat for any premature foal to survive, even the healthiest. Consider the odds against a diseased premature foal in its fight for life. These foals require around-the-clock attention, and few survive even with intensive care units and supportive therapy. But a few do survive. (For further details on prematurity, see Chapter 5.)

It seems diabolical, when one considers the destructive impact on the maternal placental attachment, that a mare will continue to carry an infected foal beyond her due date. This contrary process is a consistent finding. However, every matron I have known who carried past the due date by two to three weeks or more, was in fact housing a foal with a major problem. (Many mares are thought to be overdue, but when the calculation is completed, they are usually on target. Be sure to confirm the last breeding date.) Foals carried overtime are not ready to cope with the external environment, nor are some of them fully developed. Perhaps the mechanism that triggers parturition is affected by the presence of the intrauterine infection, thus preventing an on-time delivery.

Known causes for a protracted gestation period are infections, either fetal or placental, fetal contraction, uterine inertia, and uterine rupture.

Streptococcus pyogenes also has the ability to attack, invade, and cause disease in a perfectly healthy foal either immediately or well after its birth. Usually this is the result of a contaminated external environment. These bacteria can be found everywhere in the horse's environment and habitat. Entering through the open navel stump, or ingested or inhaled, this microorganism can cause a full-blown septicemia within 24 hours. This is the main reason for insisting upon well-scrubbed and disinfected foaling quarters, walls and floors included, prior to each and every parturition. Care should also be taken to separate healthy foals from sick foals who might transmit the infection.

When the mare carries a strep-ridden fetus, the placental membranes have a diagnostic brownish stain color with patchy areas of discoloration. An astute caretaker will usually note the color and summon the veterinarian. This stained afterbirth is thought to occur from excessive fetal feces or foal diarrhea during the gestation period.

Symptoms in a diseased foal are weakness, inability or decreased capability to rise, difficulty in standing erect, and reduced ability to nurse unassisted. Often, the sucking reflex is absent, and the foal is unable or too weak to curl its tongue around the assistant's finger. Most of these foals are skinny, underweight, under-sized, crooked-legged, light-boned individuals. No one has trouble identifying this type of foal.

The birth of such a foal represents an emergency. Prompt and intensive treatment to replace lost fluids and electrolytes, and antibiotics to combat the responsible pathogen, are imperative. In spite of all modern treatment, the prognosis is poor for those foals delivered from a diseased uterus and placental tissues.

More typically, a foal appears normal at birth and then, within the first few days of its life, develops a fever, depression, and either constipation or diarrhea. Hot, swollen, painful joints (called joint ill) complete the picture of positive evidence of the justly dreaded *Streptococcus pyogenes* septicemia. Swelling of the joints can be transitory and inconstant in location from day to day, but very persistent. Bacteriological cultures of the joint fluid should be obtained and sent to the laboratory for identification of the microorganism so that the most effective drug may be selected for local joint flushing and instillation.

Blood studies are indispensable in evaluating septicemia and indicating the effectiveness of the drug being used. Frequent blood counts help the veterinarian to assess the response of the foal's defense mechanism to determine the course and prognosis of the disease.

Infection of the navel stump (umbilicus) is a consistent finding associated with streptococcal infections and is called navel ill. The navel stump is hot and swollen, with evidence of intermittent discharges. Other bacteria can enter the infected area and compound the problem. Stiffness and pain are always evident, and the foal characteristically shows a reluctance to move about.

The greatest danger stems from the fact that the navel cord provides the bacteria a direct route to the vulnerable abdominal cavity, especially to the urogenital system. When the streptococcal infection becomes septicemic, following its entrance into the circulatory system, multiple secondary sites of

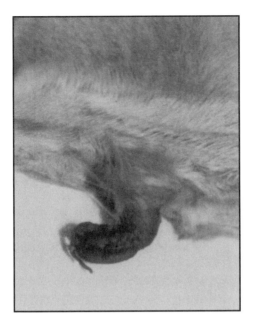

Infected navel stump.

infection can develop in the form of pulmonary liver and kidney abscesses, and various types of pneumonia. As a result of pain, depression, and fever, the foal may be unable to stand and nurse. Such foals become progressively weaker and are commonly found prostrate in the straw.

Unlike all other known septicemias, *Streptococcus pyogenes* is notoriously resistant to treatment, and invariably a residue remains. If the young foal survives, it usually remains symptomless, despite harboring a dormant residue of infection, until around eight to 18 months—when the illness suddenly reappears. The foal appeared to have recovered because the infection had become quiescent, only to cruelly reappear just as the foal becomes a young adult. Gradual or sudden joint enlargements that are occasionally painful and stiff, grossly infected joints, and/or generalized arthritis are the conditions most commonly encountered with the chronic form of this disease. These symptoms seem to develop for no accountable reason but actually are predictable by veterinarians who are cognizant of the ways of the strep bugs. It is most often misdiagnosed.

Such latent infections can be treated but not cured, and unless the situation is an exceptional one, they may result in irreversible chronic joint damage.

The prevalence of systemic streptococcal infections in the newborn is not as common as it was before the advent of antibiotics. Through identification and frequent culturing combined with specific chemotherapeutic drugs, not only our foals but also our entire horse population undoubtedly suffer less from pathogenic bacteria and so enjoy a better fertility rate.

Foal losses from strep were enormous prior to the advent of modern miracle drugs. Today's foals with streptococcal infections have a better chance for survival, as do foals with other formidable systemic infections. Appropriate and effective drugs are available, and a better understanding of these overwhelming foal infections has improved survival statistics.

It is difficult to be specific as to how long a sick foal should be supported, tube-fed, and treated. As long as the foal's condition does not deteriorate, it is safe to say there is hope for survival and justification for continuation of the exhausting and sometimes costly treatment. Your veterinarian is best equipped to weigh all factors, utilize laboratory tests, and then render a decision based on all data.

DUMMY, WANDERER, OR SLEEPER FOAL

Causative agent: *Actinobacillus equuli* (*Shigella equuli*).

Diagnosis: Septicemia.

Prognosis: Guarded to fair.

Treatment:

1. Complete blood count and differential (expect white blood cell elevation with slight decrease in red blood cell count).

2. Blood culture (laboratory required).

3. Zinc sulfate test (immune competence).

4. Chloromycetin IV 3 times daily.

5. Chloramphenicol capsules 3 times daily.

6. Electrolytic solution including dextrose or glucose 10 percent solution.

7. Tube feed with mare's milk 3 to 6 times daily or as indicated; include 1 ounce of milk of magnesia once daily.

8. Repeat blood count every 12 hours.

9. Repeat zinc sulfate test every 24 hours.

10. Serum transfusion (prepare and administer if zinc sulfate test indicates the need for preformed antibodies).

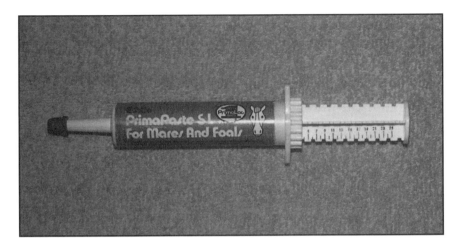

Replenishes beneficial bacteria.

11. *Lactobacillus* oral paste (a commercial preparation containing beneficial intestinal bacteria that may be depleted when oral antibiotics are administered over several days); administer on the advice of your veterinarian.

Lactobacillus acidophilus, *Lactobacillus bifidus*, and *Lactobacillus casei* are the three major bacteria used to replace or restore the essential gut bacteria absent either through disease or protracted oral antibiotic therapy. Probiotics (Probiosin and Startbac) are commercially prepared beneficial bacteria that are normally found in and required by the GI tract of foals for good health. This product is sold in syringe form with prescribed weight dosages on the label. It is a good product and is indicated for use in weak, premature, or ill foals.

Before the advent of these convenient syringes it was necessary to purchase Acidophilus milk and yogurt at the local grocery store. Acidophilus milk has helped many unthrifty foals in the past.

A LITTLE HISTORY

In spring 1986, a number of newborn foals, many of them especially valuable foals, all certified as receiving Probiotics shortly after birth, died unexpectedly. Research confirmed that an iron compound, called ferrous fumarate, had been added to Probiotics to counteract the short-term anemia that affects almost all equine babies in varying degrees because of the iron deficit in mare's milk. Ferrous fumarate, it was discovered, is incompatible with the neonate's liver and caused many deaths with fulminating hepatic necrosis. In short order, the iron was removed and the good name of the beneficial *Lactobacillus* restored. See pages 75 and 79.

Actinobacillus equuli, originally known as *Shigella equuli* infection, causes a deadly septicemia in foals. This microorganism is the source of the well-known syndrome variously referred to as "sleeper," "wanderer," or "dummy" foal.

If the foal is infected in utero, it may be aborted or delivered dead. When these foals arrive in the world alive, they are very weak, semi-comatose, and unable to stand. Regardless of all efforts to help, their survival is rare. As with other septicemias, perfectly healthy foals can contract this highly infectious microorganism from the normal horse environment, and they are highly susceptible from the time of birth to three weeks of age. Although it is believed by some that the bacterium abounds in normal horse surroundings and habitats, I contend that it must be freshly introduced to the premises, and that it must maintain its strength by passing through young horses, if it is to cause foal illness.

An epidemic at a breeding farm is most commonly initiated by the delivery of one very sick *Shigella* foal. I have watched subsequent foals delivered in the same foaling stall area consistently and assuredly contract the same disease. A less likely source is the infected foal that accompanies its dam to be bred.

Steam sterilization of the foaling area and adjacent stalls seems to help reduce the morbidity rate, yet with all hygienic efforts, susceptible foals continue to become ill and manifest the well-known symptoms. If strong enough to stand, foals suffering this debilitating disease characteristically wander aimlessly around the perimeter of the stall, habitually circle in one direction only, and ceaselessly nurse on the boards of the stall, on the feed tub, or on anything within reach except their mothers. They seem oblivious to normal surroundings and definitely ignore their mothers. A trail of moist spots is often visible on the walls of the stall as evidence of the continuous, unreasoning sucking. Such foals appear driven from within and, when exhausted, will stand as though in a stupor, ignoring the presence of their mother, or in a state of mental confusion. They will not nurse from their mothers, but will take milk from a bottle when interrupted in their endless treadmill-like circling of the stall.

Subnormal temperature with normal heart and respiratory rate, severe dehydration, prominent bluish white nictitating membranes (third eyelid), and a yellowish, fetid, distressing diarrhea are all classic symptoms of a *Shigella* infection. In a well-developed case, the peculiar fecal odor in the stall is a valid diagnostic clue. One can actually smell the diagnosis!

Pathonomonic symptoms of a *Shigella* infection are:

- subnormal temperature
- diarrhea and characteristic odor
- head pressing

Dummy foal rejects its mother. In the upper left corner of the photograph you can see the concerned mother as she watches her foal display abnormal behavior (head pressing).

- no interest in mother nor her milk
- walking perimeter of stall

A few years back, 90 percent of these foals were lost. With increased knowledge and the advent of broad-spectrum drugs and supportive therapy, the majority now survive with no known detectable aftereffects.

The specific drug for dummy foals, called Chloromycetin or chloramphenicol, is truly a miracle drug. When this drug is coupled with the necessary intensive regime of around-the-clock care, a foal often responds within hours.

If the foal responds favorably, it will stop its aimless wandering and walk across the stall—perhaps for the first time. The insistent need to stay near the wall gradually weakens. The foal approaches its mother as if it had been previously unaware of her existence. As progress continues, the foal touches and explores the mare with his outstretched nose. First attempts at nursing are usually misdirected, and the foal may suck on the mare's front legs. Finally, it seems to be able to locate the udder and actually nurses properly. The initial confusion and disorientation caused by the *Actinobacillus* disappears as the drug blood level establishes itself.

This initial response is not a signal to discontinue treatment. Oral and IV injections should continue daily for a minimum of from seven to 10 days. Subsequent blood studies will guide the veterinarian and owner in determining the procedures necessary for complete recovery.

It is unfortunate that occasionally a foal, surviving the acute stage of *Actinobacillus*, will suddenly develop a grayish-white area in both eyes. *Shigella* infection has the awesome ability to invade and destroy the chamber of the foal's eye globe by depositing purulent and fibrinous material. Treatment is unsatisfactory, and blindness soon results. I have seen cases where the infection prompted the cornea to weaken and prolapse. Euthanasia is the only alternative in these uncommon cases.

FOAL PNEUMONIA

Causative agent: *Corynebacterium equi* (*Rhodococcus equi*).

Diagnosis: Septicemia.

Prognosis: Guarded to poor.

Treatment:

1. Complete blood count and differential (expect high white cell count).

2. Blood culture (laboratory required).

3. Zinc sulfate test (immune competence).

4. Serum transfusion (to supply preformed antibodies).

5. Antibiotic of choice: ampicillin IV twice daily or neomycin or erythromycin combined with Rifampin once daily.

6. Electrolytic solution IV if indicated.

7. Tube feed once daily with 5 ounces milk of magnesia and 3 ounces castor oil (based on average foal weight at 3 months of age).

8. Repeat CBC every 24 hours.

9. Repeat zinc sulfate test as required.

Corynebacterium equi, also classified as *Rhodococcus equi,* is another micro-organism capable of causing a fatal infection during intrauterine life or in young foals. Contrary to other septicemias previously discussed, it does not attack the very young but is most prevalent and destructive in foals that are three or four months of age. This is the age group caught in between on the immune status time frame and therefore highly vulnerable to illness.

Under ideal circumstances, the mare's colostrum provides preformed protective antibodies that protect the foal through four to eight weeks of age. Not until 12 to 16 weeks does the foal's own reticuloendothelial system begin to mature and develop antibodies. The interim period, when maternal antibodies are waning and the foal's own efficiency is just beginning, is one of great vulnerability. *C. equi* operates best in this time span; any foal with this infection should receive special consideration in addition to drugs and supportive therapy. These foals should receive an immune status (zinc sulfate) test followed by a serum transfusion to provide a broad spectrum of protective antibodies.

Until just recently, the synthetic antibiotic ampicillin was the antibiotic of choice for this septicemia. Of late, however, the combination of either neomycin or erythromycin with rifampin has proven more effective. If your veterinarian is using ampicillin and the foal's fever does not subside within the first 24 hours, the ampicillin should be stopped and treatment with neomycin or erythromycin combined with rifampin should begin immediately. The drug rifampin is quite costly but very effective in penetrating the notorious abscesses caused by this dreaded foal pneumonia and generalized septicemia. In assessing the degree of infection, thoracic radiographs are very helpful in evaluating the antibiotic regime effectiveness.

When the foal begins to recuperate (shows appreciable improvement and has gained strength and comfort) your veterinarian may then suggest the oral use of *Lactobacillus* paste to restore the normal flora of the intestinal contents, as use of oral antibiotics can disturb nature's balance of good and bad bacteria, all so important for digestion and good health.

In the absence of effective medication, the foal's defense mechanism can no longer combat the rapid multiplication and advance of the pathogenic micro-organisms, and an overwhelming suppurating infection is released throughout the entire body, causing death. This phenomenon occurs with the rupture of a huge internal abscess. Lung radiographs are helpful in the diagnosis of pulmonary abscesses and varying degrees of lung congestion. Progressive radiographs, along with ultrasound, can monitor the effect of treatment and the pace of convalescence.

Pulmonary pneumonia is the primary manifestation; however, the infection also has an affinity for intestinal and mesenteric lymph nodes and kidney tissue. The lungs, kidneys, lymph glands, and intestines are literally covered with abscesses, and destructive tissue changes are evident throughout the body.

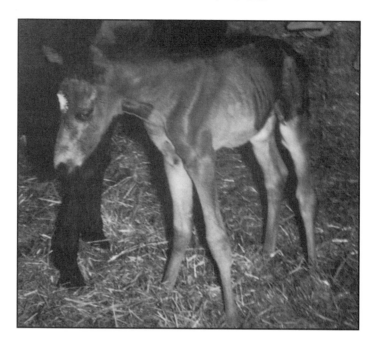

A foal with pneumonia.

NOTE: Sporadic in nature, this insidious disease may affect only one or two foals in a large group. It is therefore not highly contagious, but it is infectious, and believed to be transmitted primarily by inhalation.

C. *equi* is most often associated with refractory foal pneumonia, yet has been isolated as coming from many other hosts, including humans. It is a soil contaminant that can inhabit a farm and then reappear annually, causing foal losses and frustration among the farm owners, managers, and veterinarians.

An older veterinarian once told me of one specific farm that had a strong strain of C. *equi* in its soil that attacked and infected every crop of sucklings and weanlings. He treated vigorously and continued to lose many every year. Finally he submitted a sample to the laboratory and requested them to develop an autobacterin specific for this infection. It worked!

I have observed a characteristic respiratory pattern found in refractory cases of foal pneumonia with a systemic infection of unknown etiology to be quite diagnostic of C. *equi*. I call this condition the "puffing pattern." Quite diagnostic! These foals show an abdominal thump or pump at the end of expiration, which is synchronized with a flaring out of each nostril, identical with the stressful breathing pattern of adult horses suffering with heaves (alveolar emphysema). Foals with C. *equi* have spike fevers from 102 to 107 degrees and actually pant and thump with each respiration; they seem to become fatigued just from the effort required to breathe. These are the salient symptoms of a C. *equi* infection in the foal.

ALERT: I also regularly find a distressed fixed stare, high fever, and constipation. With the use of a stethoscope, one can readily hear increased alveolar lung sounds with dry or moist rales peculiar to this infection. Although pneumonia is primary, constipation is one constant symptom of C. *equi* that is curiously overlooked and thus neglected. In severe cases, constipation must be recognized and properly treated before high fevers will even begin to subside, even under massive antibiotic therapy. Experience has taught me that the best course is correct constipation first, while administering the antibiotic of choice, and then to give continuous supportive therapy. This combination has worked very well.

Once inside the foal's body, *Corynebacterium* can be misleading at times. Diagnosis of this disease has been difficult and somewhat elusive because of the absence of a specific test or means of identification. In the past, serology studies and routine cultures were inconsistent and sometimes unrevealing. Nasal swabs and laboratory cultures also produced inconsistent results. The only helpful tool the practitioner had for years was astute observation. Large, overcrowded farms and age of affected foals alerted farm veterinarians to this scourge.

There is no clear-cut symptom or precise combination of symptoms that permits a definitive diagnosis. Depression, coughing, elevated body temperature—with intermittent spiking fevers—and some degree of respiratory distress (panting respirations) can produce lung and intestinal lymph node abscesses quite often well in advance of any outward clinical signs of illness.

Diagnosis today has been improved by a method of transtracheal culture. This transtracheal washing technique provides an accurate method of culturing and identifying the insidious microorganism.

Other newer procedures have been very helpful as diagnostic aids in recognition and treatment of this frustrating foal disease.

Isolated cases are frequently lost because neither the course of the disease nor its severity are reflected externally nor shown by the foal's physical condition until it is too late. It is sad but interesting to note that these foals continue to nurse regardless of high fevers and difficulty in breathing, and thus maintain exceptionally good body weight until just before death. As a young, inexperienced practitioner, I was puzzled and perplexed when I saw a fat baby foal on its side in a stall, very dead of fulminating *Corynebacterium* infection.

With early recognition, keen perception, and effective treatment, some foals survive. If the foal lives, the internal tissue changes seem to heal, for no functional or external residual damage has been detectable in the cases which I have followed.

ESCHERICHIA COLI INFECTION

Causative agent: *Escherichia coli.*

Diagnosis: Septicemia.

Prognosis: Guarded to good.

Treatment:

1. Complete blood count and differential.

2. Blood culture (laboratory required).

3. Zinc sulfate test (immune competence).

4. Chloromycetin IV 3 times daily; or trimethoprim (sulfa); or Aminoglycosides (kanamycin, gentamicin, or Amikacin).

5. Supportive therapy (electrolytic fluids and tube feedings).

6. Serum transfusion (if zinc sulfate test indicates need).

Escherichia coli is a harmless microorganism when in its normal habitat, the intestines, but when this feared bacteria gains entrance to the rest of the body it becomes a potent pathogen, capable of causing severe illness, including septicemia in foals, usually occurring around 10 to 21 days of age. The identifying symptom in this septicemia is an equilibrium upset in the unstable sick foal, recognizable by an intermittent head and neck spasm. Symptomatically, the head and neck are involuntarily pulled spasmodically around to the side of the rib cage in a shaky but determined rigid movement and held there momentarily. When this salient symptom is observed in a depressed, weak, and febrile foal, the diagnosis is *Escherichia coli* infection. I classified this action as some form of seizure. See page 165.

Escherichia coli inadvertently leaves the gastrointestinal tract and enters the bloodstream quickly when even the slightest tissue change occurs in the intestinal lining or mucosa. Normally, the mucosa serves as a barrier to contain all poisons, toxins, debris, and fecal material inside the gastrointestinal tract—and away from the bloodstream—while allowing the passage of nutrients—fluids, minerals, etc.—needed for health. When the efficiency of the mucosa becomes altered through disease, toxins, and irritants, *Escherichia coli*, along with other pathogens, quickly gains entrance to the circulation and establishes a septicemia (blood poisoning).

Enterotoxemia is the term used for any condition or pathogen that can cause the breakdown of the intestinal barrier and thus allow entrance to the body.

In the very young foal, *Escherichia coli* can gain entrance through the open navel stump. In the mare, it is often inspired through the vulvar lips and subsequently causes an annoying and resistant cervicitis and endometritis, resulting in degrees of infertility.

The cases I have diagnosed and treated all responded well, recovered, and never recurred.

ILL-DEFINED AND LESS PREVALENT SEPTICEMIAS

Salmonella typhimurium, *Salmonella enteritis*, *Salmonella abortus equi*, and *Pseudomonas aeruginosa* are four additional offenders known to cause abortion and various unidentified infections and septicemias. Fortunately, all are seen with much less frequency today.

None of the four has characteristic symptoms to differentiate, so the diagnosis usually takes place in the laboratory or during the postmortem procedure.

Salmonellosis is a deadly infection associated with severe diarrhea, devastating purging, and electrolytic imbalances. Immediate, massive, sustained electrolytic and fluid replacement is essential! Dehydration and hypoglycemia are the foal's major enemies.

S. *Abortus equi* is noted as the cause of abortion in mares and S. *typhimurium* as the cause of generalized systemic infections, usually in the form of intractable diarrhea.

In foals, however, *Salmonella enteritis* notoriously attacks the four- to six-week-olds, causing profuse diarrhea, high fevers, and life-threatening dehydration. In spite of the severe scouring, symptoms of colic are rare and inconsistent. Mortality can reach 50 percent in untreated or poorly managed cases. This infection is known to be rodent-related and is spread by rat feces that inadvertently gain entry into horse feed and is subsequently eaten. Salmonella infection is both highly refractive to treatment and highly infectious; once established on the premises, it is almost

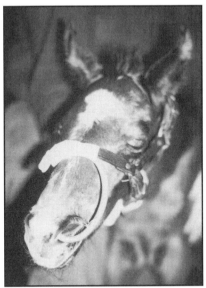

Septicemic foal tube sutured into place.

impossible to eradicate. This resistant infection has forced closure of equine medical facilities for weeks at a time. Sunlight and steam sterilization have effectively cleansed the premises.

Thanks to many dedicated people, to education, and to the enlightened and prudent use of drugs, vaccines, and bacterins, prevalence of these dangerous microorganisms has been dramatically reduced during the last 20 years.

PRIMARY FOAL PNEUMONIA

Although most neonatal septicemias are complicated by various forms of pulmonary infection and degrees of pneumonia, primary foal pneumonia commonly attacks older foals ranging from four to 12 weeks of age, when the maternally derived antibody levels are perhaps waning and the foal's own immune system is still inefficient (dangerous age period). Foals in this age group warrant special surveillance as they are supervulnerable to all infections.

Causes are variable and many. In addition to the infamous and previously discussed *C. equi*, *Streptococcus zooepidemicus* is an elusive and frequent cause of pneumonia, producing nondescript symptoms. *Streptococcus equi*, however, is readily recognized by the revealing swollen lymph glands under the jaws and around the head which often accompany lung infections, indicative of the infection strangles.

STRANGLES

Strangles is the lay term for the dreaded disease caused by *Streptococcus equi*. Similar to *C. equi*, it predictably attacks older foals—from eight to 12 weeks of age and older. This is the age when the foal has the lowest blood titre of maternal immune bodies; this is also before the foal's own immune system has begun to function efficiently. With little or no defense it is not surprising that almost all foals experience some form of *Strep. equi* infection. Symptoms are fever with depression and a mildly depressed appetite, mucopurulent nasal discharge, and the characteristic swollen glands. An occasional cough or sneeze is not uncommon.

Fortunately, the strep microorganism that most often affects the younger population is milder and less virulent; if watched carefully, it may subside without treatment. The enlarged glands found under and around the mandible (lower jaw) may require several weeks to reduce in size and firmness and then quietly disappear. This form of infection serves well to confer protective immunity to future exposure and causes only a small inconvenience in farm routine.

It is another story, however, when the virulent form of *Strep. equi* invades the premises and foal crop. Very sick foals with enlarged, sore glands, high fevers (104 to 105 degrees), poor appetites, respiratory infections, and, if treatment is delayed, pneumonia, are commonplace. Veterinary care is needed *immediately*. In cases of severe infection, no member of the farm escapes the illness.

Without proper treatment, and in the absence of normal protective antibodies, the Strep. equi readily escapes from the swollen lymph glands and ultimately spreads, causing abscesses throughout the body and establishing a chronic illness sometimes referred to as bastard strangles.

A word of caution regarding treatment: Penicillin is a common antibiotic, easily available and quite reasonable in cost; it is also very effective in the control of these high fevers. But its use in this disease is contraindicated. While it helps to reduce the fever, it also attacks and thus destroys the Strep. equi cell wall precisely where the antibody response occurs. Consequently, the infection, in essence, is unabated. Thus avoid penicillin.

Drugs of choice are ampicillin, Polyflex, Amp-Equine, oxytetracycline, and trimethoprim plus sulfonamides.

Veterinary treatment and supervision can help to contain the disease, treat the ill members, supervise nursing care, and, when necessary, surgically lance the sometimes huge, painful abscesses near the jaw area to relieve pressure.

When Strep. equi strikes, all personnel should be on a red alert against spreading the disease. The purulent material escaping from an abscessed gland is literally loaded with virulent Strep. equi, and through carelessness of barn personnel and the movement of pets and rodents, the diseased and contaminated material can spread readily.

CAUTION: A Strep. equi bacterin is produced by Fort Dodge Laboratories; it has merit when used with discretion by your veterinarian. It is very useful when an outbreak threatens, especially when you are dealing with large numbers of horses all housed together. When using the commercial Strangles Bacterin, dosage determination is critical, along with site of injection. Use only gluteal muscles.

ALERT: Fort Dodge Laboratories announced the availability of the first intranasal vaccine against strangles. Although this should be an improvement, be cautious.

Do not confuse strangles with tympanitis. One simulates the other initially until you are able to touch or palpate the swellings.

OTHER PULMONARY INFECTIONS

Although much less prevalent, Klebsiella pneumoniae, Actinobacillus equuli, and Salmonella typhimurium have all been isolated as offenders, especially in chronic and refractory cases of foal pneumonia.

Viral agents such as equine herpes virus I (rhinopneumonitis) and the influenza viruses are noted for upper respiratory infections and are thought to weaken and predispose the lung tissue for bacterial invasion. These viruses, therefore, are not primary causes, but accomplices.

Extraneous irritants and predisposing causes of foal pneumonia are parasites, namely larval migration of ascarids; polluted air (poor ventilation); and a dirty or contaminated environment.

Symptoms of foal pneumonia are labored breathing, fever, depression, weakness, nasal discharge, and usually a cough.

The physical examination should include auscultation of the chest area with a stethoscope to ascertain that air is in fact moving into and out of the pulmonary area. Evidence of dead areas and moist rales are indications of pneumonia. Labored breathing, with peculiar chest wall and abdominal assistance in respiratory patterns, is proof of stress, indicating that lung congestion is present.

A blood count can be an invaluable diagnostic tool and treatment guide. In cases of foal pneumonia, a CBC (complete blood count) may reveal an increase in the number of leukocytes (WBC, or white blood cells) called a leukocytosis, caused by a bacterial infection. A decrease in WBC, a condition called lymphopenia, is found in cases caused primarily by a virus. However, a profound lymphopenia can indicate a failure in the foal's immune system. This finding should also be addressed immediately by your veterinarian.

To guess at the causative microorganism and the effective drug is foolhardy—precious time can be lost this way. Cultures, either nasal or

Chronic septicemic foal, blind; infection ultimately entered eye globes.

transtracheal, can isolate and identify the culprit, and determine the drug to which the microorganism is most sensitive. By use of cultures one can avoid the trap of drug-resistant infections.

Since lung congestion in some foals can easily be missed or misinterpreted with the use of the clinical stethoscope, other diagnostic aids are available if symptoms are suggestive of congestion.

Radiographs of the young foal's chest can reveal areas of congestion and indicate the degree of lung tissue involvement. Progressive chest films, combined with ultrasound films, serve well to monitor and guide the therapy used in resolution of pulmonary congestion.

Ultrasound can be used synergistically applied with radiographs. Lung abscesses and fluid levels can be detected by scanning the chest walls.

Early intensive drug therapy combined with electrolytic support can successfully resolve even a severe case of pneumonia. Treatments should be continued a full week after the fever has subsided and returned to normal. At this time, a blood study can act as a barometer and assure a normal white blood cell count.

Antipyretic agents such as phenylbutazone, aspirin, and Dipyrone can comfort and calm foals with pneumonia. (My little rule of thumb that has been tried and true for many years is "Reduce pain and enhance healing!" Comfort level plus treatment!) Appetite and rest can be encouraged by their use in combination with regular antibiotic treatments. The drugs isoniazid and Lasix administered IM (intramuscularly) have been helpful in treating both lung congestion and lung abscesses.

BARKER FOAL

The neonatal foal is known to suffer yet another systemic infection, commonly called barker syndrome or convulsive syndrome of the newborn. Barker foal derives its name from the unmistakable diagnostic sounds made by the foal shortly after delivery. It usually arrives on its side in the bedding and is unable to rise. This syndrome is most commonly observed in foals not yet dry, but other foals thought to be normal may, after a few hours of life, suddenly convulse and bark ceaselessly until exhausted. Convulsions consist of involuntary head-jerking and spasms of the limbs and body. Since mares usually foal in the middle of the night, the eerie, primitive cry emitted by a small wet body convulsing in the straw is such a departure from the norm that, once heard, it is never forgotten.

It has been reported that if a barker foal can survive repeated convulsions and be tube-fed, kept slightly sedated, and given intensive antibiotics and supportive therapy, it may live. According to some authorities, it requires four to five days for symptoms to slowly subside, a weak sucking reflex to gradually appear, and the foal's other faculties to return. Perhaps this is true, but I personally have never witnessed a recovery of any barker foal.

The cause of this distressing entity is not known. At one time it was thought that human intervention during delivery was a factor since the incidence of barker foals was higher in well-run, possibly heated, and poorly ventilated barns with astutely assisted deliveries. A new and popular theory is that deprivation of oxygen to the brain is the cause of convulsions and seizures. Any factor, no matter how insignificant, that can cause a prolonged or delayed delivery greatly increases the likelihood of oxygen reduction to the foal's brain cells.

We know of three specifics in the so-called normal process of parturition that might cause an oxygen deficiency: premature placental separation; early rupture of umbilical cord; and compression of the cord during delivery, especially during a breech presentation.

An untimely separation of the fetal placenta from the maternal endometrium—known as placenta previa or abruptia placenta—creates a premature shutdown of the foal's life-support system.

WARNING: Rupture of the umbilical cord immediately after birth and before the foal receives its essential 500–700cc of placental blood can cause a dramatic drop in blood pressure, reduce aeration of lung tissue, and result in diminished available oxygen in the circulating blood. Early, untimely umbilical rupture can occur if a high-strung matron suddenly rises just as the neonate lands in the straw. I have seen mares who apparently cannot wait to greet their foals jump to their feet, spin, and rush back to nuzzle and inspect them. On countless occasions I have administered a small amount of tranquilizer to a known nervous mare just prior to parturition. This practice has consistently averted traumatic foaling tragedies.

Another cause of premature umbilical cord rupture is the ignorant act of a well-meaning, overly conscientious attendant. In an attempt to show the mare her foal, the attendant snatches the newborn from the recumbent mare and briskly drags the neonate around to her head. This abrupt movement breaks the navel cord, allowing the escape of precious placental blood, and may produce a devastating drop in the foal's blood pressure and oxygen content.

Since the umbilical cord serves as the lifeline to the unborn foal, a breech presentation can be hazardous to the oxygen supply during birth of the foal. The foal's backward position inevitably causes protracted pressure on the intact umbilicus as it is forced against the mare's bony pelvis. When a breech delivery is discovered, every effort should be made to prevent unnecessary delays and every attempt made to hasten the delivery *slowly*.

The barker foal can be helped by treatment, but it is indeed complex and usually a fatiguing and frustrating experience. I have stood in a stall with a syringe and needle ready to sedate a barker foal when it suddenly had a seizure. The violence of the convulsion literally threw me off my feet and sent the syringe flying. Personnel must be in attendance around the clock to prevent the

Shaker foal.

self-inflicted injury frequently sustained during the foal's violent seizures. Without constant care, death is inevitable.

Perhaps a definitive cause for barker syndrome will be uncovered by research in the near future and may provide answers to these disturbing questions.

SHAKER FOAL SYNDROME/ BOTULISM IN THE ADULT

Another foal scourge, until just recently with a questionable cause, is the shaker foal syndrome. Shaker foal is a highly fatal neuromuscular disease found in suckling foals approximately three to eight weeks of age. The incidence of shaker foal syndrome appears to be increasing both geographically and numerically.

Typical symptoms are inability to rise, weakness, and profound muscle tremors with flaccidity. With assistance the foal can perhaps gain its feet and nurse feebly, yet generalized muscular trembling and shaking makes it difficult to stand, so the foal drops limply back into the straw.

Although onset of symptoms seem abrupt, they most likely are insidious and develop unobserved.

Intense muscular trembling progresses to uncontrollable shaking, which then prevents the foal from standing or even nursing. Prostration soon ensues and death occurs by respiratory paralysis. With conservative and conventional treatment, most foals are lost approximately three days after stricken.

Recent information has revealed that the deadly *Clostridium botulinum* microorganism is related to the mysterious shaker syndrome in foals. (In adult horses, *C. botulinum* is the cause of a fatal disease called botulism or forage poisoning.)

As a result of research and new information, a new bacterin is available for use in pregnant brood mares called *Clostridium botulinum* Type B toxoid. This bacterin can prevent shaker foal syndrome in foals if pregnant brood mares are vaccinated 30 or so days prior to due date. Antibodies are thus produced and are ready for foal ingestion from the udder.

Foals suffer muscle tremors and weaknesses from reduced amounts or absence of cholinesterase at the nerve synapses in the muscle masses. Thus, avoid cholinesterase inhibitors: aminoglycosides, tetracyclines, and procaine penicillin. *Warning:* If the diagnosis is shaker syndrome, do not use these drugs. Their use can be lethal.

The following is recommended:

1. Potassium penicillin is safe, and its use is thus recommended.

2. Neostigmine is a cholinesterase enhancer and its use is indicated. The dose should be 20mg of neostigmine in 500cc of 5 percent dextrose administered intravenously over a period of 30 minutes. Please administer slowly!

3. Epsom salts (MgSO4), administered via stomach tube (one teacup in one quart water), will hasten the removal of ingested material from the gastrointestinal tract, and hopefully the use of a laxative will cause removal of any previously ingested toxic element.

4. Administer oxygen via a mask or small endotracheal tube to relieve any indication of respiratory complications.

5. Supportive fluid therapy, either maintenance or replacement level, should be considered. For the average anorexic foal at three to eight weeks of age, administer around 3,500cc per day, including a balanced electrolytic preparation, glucose, Ringer's lactate, and sodium bicarbonate. Foals become hypoglycemic notoriously easily. Administration of glucose is essential to protect the liver from toxins and imbalances in the very young foal. Acidosis can be combated by Ringer's lactate and sodium bicarbonate. If untreated, both hypoglycemia (low blood sugar) and acidosis (low bicarbonate) can contribute directly to deterioration of the foal's condition, and to ultimate death.

6. A serum transfusion is a valid adjunct to the other treatments and fortifies the foal's immune-body level.

7. *Clostridium botulinum* (polyvalent equine origin botulism antitoxin) has received high marks in the treatment of shaker foal disease. This hyperimmune serum, loaded with lifesaving antibodies, is difficult to obtain and is quite expensive. When available, administer 70,000 to 80,000 IU intravenously at the earliest possible time. Early initial treatment is essential for any hope of recovery from this devastating disease.

It is sobering to report that all information to date indicates few successfully treated cases. The FDA, however, has cleared a marvelous bacterin for botulism, one capable of conferring protective immunization (Clostridium botulinum Type B toxoid), mentioned above. This toxiod should be added to the other boosters given to the expectant brood mare one month prior to due date, or at the tenth month of gestation. These critical boosters enhance the production of protective passive antibodies and increase the level of stored immune bodies in the colostrum ready for ingestion by the newborn.

Botulism in the adult is caused by ingestion of preformed exotoxin produced by clostridium botulinum microorganisms, most commonly found in a dirty stall or spoiled grain or hay. When this normal soil inhabitant is found in horses' intestines it produces no harmful effects; but when found in spoiled feed or under a water pail in a neglected stall, it produces exotoxins that, if ingested, become a lethal threat to the life of the animal. Less than one teaspoonful can kill a 1,000-pound horse! One can readily understand why equine practitioners and horsemen alike celebrated the advent of the bacterin.

In conclusion, botulism cannot be treated well, but it can be well prevented!

NONINFECTIOUS FOAL PNEUMONIA

Causative agent: Accidental aspiration.

Diagnosis: Aspiration pneumonia.

Prognosis: Good if treated promptly.

Treatment:

1. Antibiotic of choice (ampicillin or oxytetracycline).

2. Chest X-ray.

3. Ultrasound scan.

4. Oxygen therapy (use either a tube or a mask; recommended dosage 5 liters per minute).

5. Diuretics.

6. Routine blood counts to monitor progress.

7. Constant observation for indication of secondary bacterial invaders.

Noninfectious foal pneumonia can originate from several causes, but mechanical means far outstrip the others. Mechanical pneumonia results from accidental (inadvertent) aspiration of a foreign substance and occurs most often in ill foals.

Aspiration of fetal fluids during a difficult or prolonged delivery, accidental aspiration of milk by a weak foal, or the aspiration of oral medications administered by inexperienced persons are three examples of how mechanical pneumonia can develop. (Many an unsuspecting person has half-drowned a foal through accidental aspiration while administering oral medication or a forced milk meal.) Any thoracic trauma sustained during or immediately after foaling can also contribute to pulmonary congestion.

Symptoms of pneumonia due to infectious and noninfectious causes are identical and constant: Common signs are depression, poor appetite, fever and, most important, respiratory distress and/or limited and painful rib cage movement.

Pneumonia from mechanical causes quickly opens the door to infectious agents, so early treatment must be decisive here.

TYZZER'S DISEASE

Tyzzer's disease is an acute and highly fatal liver disease affecting foals during the first month of life. Little is known about its symptoms, as the course of the disease is so rapid that most foals are found dead. Diagnosis therefore is usually at autopsy. Caused by *Bacillus piliformis*, it is thought to be spread by ingestion and perhaps carried by rodents who may also serve as a possible reservoir for the fulminating infection.

There are presently no known treatments and no known control measures. Although I have never diagnosed Tyzzer's disease, I would be greatly surprised if these foals proved to be immune-competent. However, when Tyzzer's disease is suspected, I would heartily recommend vigorous cleansing and improved hygienic measures with emphasis on rodent assessment, identification, and control procedures.

RABIES

Rabies (hydrophobia, Lyssa) is an age-old, worldwide, and highly fatal viral disease. With all mammals susceptible, rabies represents an important public health problem.

Rabies virus is carried in the salivary glands of infected animals and is spread exclusively through bite wounds. Reservoirs of the virus may be carried by skunks, foxes, raccoons and quite commonly bats, and transmission is chiefly through dogs, cats, and wild species.

The horse can be classified as a dead-end host for the rabies virus. Because of its non-penetrating bite and its preference for kicking rather than biting when it attacks, the horse is less likely than other species to spread the disease. The veterinarian, while attempting to diagnose, should be very aware of the oral cavity and thus avoid contact with saliva.

Symptoms are extreme restlessness, irritability, excitability, and expressions of aggressive meanness. Tremors, rigidity, and muscle spasms occur initially, together with increased heart and respiration rates. Violent chewing on foreign objects, out of character for the animal, is a behavioral symptom strongly suggestive of a rabies infection. Keep in mind, however, that these symptoms simulate those of lockjaw (tetanus); a differential diagnosis is needed.

The presence of microscopic Negri bodies in the brain tissue is the only post-mortem finding diagnostic of the viral disease rabies.

Commercial vaccines for horse immunization against rabies are available, but the advisability of their use is a decision for your veterinarian.

Both tetanus and rabies can be prevented but not successfully treated.

WATER-DRINKING SYNDROME (SELF-COINED TERM)

Every foal's natural environment includes availability and free access to water. But it is the rare individual or most likely sick foal who will be seen actually drinking water; even more serious is the foal who drinks and is *not* seen.

Careful watching may be required to catch some of these purging wet-tailed foals at the water pail, but the telltale results in the form of a fetid, watery diarrhea are undeniable evidence. Water-drinking in the young foal is an indication of illness. Corrective measures are imperative. Quickly summon your veterinarian.

Do not lose valuable time confusing a water-drinking, wet-bottomed, sick foal with a healthy foal with foal heat scours. The sick foal will quickly reveal its illness and will be found lying down on its side in the bedding or on the ground.

I have found that water drinking, disinterest in mother's milk (evidenced by a full udder or dripping milk), and peculiar behavior are the first signs of some forms of septicemia.

Neonatal foals cannot endure diarrhea for any short period, as the electrolyte loss is excessive and damaging. Your veterinarian will draw blood for laboratory analysis and immediately place the foal on antibiotics and replacement therapy for electrolytic loss.

For years this condition was not diagnosed. Fortunately, it is now being recognized as a legitimate warning of a serious impending illness.

NONINFECTIOUS DIARRHEA

Infectious diarrheas are classified under septicemias and considered dangerous. Noninfectious diarrhea, too, can cause dangerous dehydration and electrolytic imbalance, rapidly predisposing the foal to an infection. This so-called innocuous form of scours presents a threat equal to that of infectious diarrhea and should be handled appropriately.

Inform your veterinarian. While awaiting his or her arrival, do not hesitate to institute first-aid measures to relieve your distressed foal. Most respond well to intestinal astringents and antidiarrhetics such as Kaopectate, milk of magnesia, activated charcoal, paregoric, or mineral oil (heavy grade).

Your veterinary adviser will undoubtedly check body temperature and run a quick blood count (CBC) to rule out early signs of septicemia.

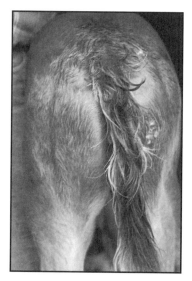

Foal diarrhea.

Known causes of noninfectious diarrhea are: coprophagy, pica, improper diet, parasites, antibiotics, and foal heat scours.

COPROPHAGY

Coprophagy is the practice of manure eating, and it is considered a vice. This sometimes becomes a sneaky habit and may not be detected until a puzzling intractable diarrhea develops. If you suspect coprophagy, wait around for the mare to defecate. As a fresh amount of feces falls, the foal will quickly devour some. Intestinal irritation promptly ensues as the gastrointestinal tract fills with debris and foreign matter. The worst insult to the foal's system is that ingested manure is literally loaded with internal parasites and irritating debris. Untold ill effects are suffered by manure-eating foals.

Perplexingly, I consistently find coprophagy present in large, well-bred, and well-fed foals on well-managed farms. Coprophagy is literally nonexistent in poorly managed and undernourished foals. Perhaps future research will provide an answer to this paradox.

With no known cause and certainly no cure, frustrated caretakers can only do the obvious. Religiously remove all droppings as promptly as possible and hope to break the obnoxious habit. I have found that early weaning (around three months of age), especially in precocious foals, has stopped this behavior.

PICA

Pica refers to the practice of eating unnatural substances. Also considered a vice, pica has been substantially incriminated in subclinical or low-grade systemic infections. Some authorities believe the cause to be an unidentified deficiency; however, some cases appear as a behavioral aberration or a basic neurosis. Unlike those with coprophagy, foals manifesting pica openly consume unnatural substances, such as sand, gravel, or soil, in an almost obsessive manner. Irritation of the foal's intestinal lining caused by ingestion of foreign material soon produces diarrhea.

Treatment for pica consists of mild laxatives and intestinal lubricants to remove the unnatural sediment. Bran mashes aid well in the removal of sand from the gastrointestinal tract. Mineral oil is very effective if used therapeutically—that is, until desired effects are obtained. Then its use should be discontinued. Low daily doses should be avoided as mineral oil notoriously interferes with the intestinal absorption of the much-needed fat-soluble vitamins A, D, E, and C. Daily doses of mineral oil over a period of time can therefore produce a vitamin deficiency, among other things.

The foals that I have treated for pica range in age from one to three weeks and have predominantly been suffering from an ambiguous chronic infection that was identified at a later date as *Shigella equuli* or, as some prefer, *Actinobacillus equuli*. Along with peculiar eating preferences, they develop an insatiable thirst for large quantities of water, not mare's milk. If left uninhibited, they can literally kill themselves through water ingestion.

These water-drinking foals are found prostrate in the bedding, literally in shock, severely dehydrated, and scouring profusely. If rapid electrolytic and sodium bicarbonate replacement is available, some foals recover. A definitive diagnosis of *Shigella* with appropriate treatment is then essential to sustain life. See page 76.

Prevention dictates that all suspected foals must be placed in areas free of running water and kept under close supervision during the treatment period. The mare's water pail should either be elevated well above the foal's reach or removed from the stall entirely. An independent source of water for the nursing mare must then be provided.

Chloromycetin IV is the drug of choice for *Shigella* infections and should be discontinued only after a blood count indicates normal parameters for three days.

The foal's behavior is a reliable indication that the infection has been cleared. A well foal will nurse from its mother, totally ignoring all available water—just as it should. A normal suckling foal will seldom drink any quantity of water; a few small sips suffices. This fact was highly controversial and rejected for years by the word of academia. It is now accepted by the experienced.

DIET-RELATED DIARRHEA

This condition readily develops in some foals, usually precocious ones with a great capacity to gulp milk rapidly and thus overindulge. More often than not, this foal has a superb milk-producing mother, so the condition is compounded. The veterinarian must be very astute when searching for causes and solutions to foal scours, especially when the cause is from overeating.

Another circumstance that may induce scours of this type is the separation of mare and foal when the mare is taken to the breeding shed. She will return to her hungry and emotionally upset foal with a full udder; hence, scours may quickly result.

Diet-related diarrhea is also found when foals ingest some types of hay. The young foal's immature digestive tract experiences difficulty in digesting fibrous material found in some particular hays.

PARASITIC DIARRHEA

This can be caused by a variety of internal parasites. *Strongylus vulgaris*, *Strongylus edentatus*, and *Parascaris equorum* are major offenders, but *Strongyloides westeri* is by far the most common parasite in the very young.

Strongyloides westeri are found in the dam's milk, and thus neonatal nursing foals ingest large numbers of infective larvae. These larvae proceed to damage the small-intestinal lining and inhibit digestive enzymes. The result is scouring. To diagnose *S. westeri*, obtain a sample of the mare's milk and a fecal sample from the foal and submit them to the laboratory for examination and identification.

Cambendazole and thiabendanzole are effective drugs against *S. westeri*.

For the health and well-being of all animals, but especially foals, prevention of parasitic infestation is of paramount importance. See Chapter 6.

ANTIBIOTIC-CAUSED DIARRHEA

Antibiotics are easily administered orally, so this type of diarrhea is not uncommon. Orally administered antibiotics, especially when given over protracted periods, are well-known causes of intractable diarrhea.

For this basic reason, I prefer treating foals by injections if at all possible, to prevent upsetting the delicate balance of intestinal flora so vital for proper digestion. But some illnesses require oral treatment using antibiotics; in these cases, a strict vigilance of the stool's consistency, color, and character is essential. Limited daily doses over short periods are strongly recommended, followed by reevaluation prior to administration of additional drugs.

Rapidly absorbed drugs are less likely to interfere with the beneficial bacteria and digestive processes by virtue of their rapid departure from the gut. Obviously, the poorly absorbed antibiotics, such as neomycin and gentamicin, are more offensive because of their prolonged presence in the intestinal tract. However, even some injectable antibiotics such as tetracyclines and erythromycin can cause diarrhea in some sensitive foals.

In suspect foals, discontinue the antibiotic therapy. Then give *Lactobacillus* culture orally, either in a commercial preparation (Probiotics) or in acidophillus milk or yogurt purchased at the grocery store. These beneficial bacterial cultures help to reestablish a normal intestinal flora in the young foal recovering from antibiotic abuse.

FOAL HEAT SCOURS

This form of noninfectious diarrhea was discussed on pages 57 and 58.

Recommended agents in the treatment of noninfectious diarrhea:

Kaopectate is a protectant of the intestinal lining readily accepted orally by the young patient.

Milk of magnesia is a dependable, reliable antacid and intestinal emollient.

Bismuth subsalicylate protects the intestinal lining, reduces toxicity, and is known to combat bacterial infection.

Bran mash provides intestinal bulk and therefore eases diarrhea. It is most natural, safe, and nourishing.

Mineral oil (heavy grade) helps remove toxins, bacteria, or other fibrous offenders, and soothes the intestinal lining.

Paregoric soothes intestinal discomfort and cramps, and reduces motility.

Activated charcoal neutralizes toxins and poisons.

CAUTION: The use of atropine, antihistamine, or any anticholinergic drug is strongly contraindicated, and their use ill-advised in any young foal. I have known four scouring foals to die shortly after receiving an injection of Diathal, an anticholinergic drug. Diathal's label recommends its use to prevent diarrhea. It should be abolished.

ROTAVIRUS DIARRHEA

The etiology of foal diarrhea outbreaks in Kentucky has been poorly understood for many years. It was thought that the virus (Rotavirus) was secondary to pathogenic bacteria, such as *Salmonella* and *Campylobacter* and possibly the parasite *Eimeria*. But today, through research, the rotavirus has been determined the causative agent of these protracted foal diarrhea illnesses. Fort Dodge Laboratories is developing a killed rotavirus vaccine (H-2 strain). With the use of this vaccine in brood mares, the young foal will receive protection from the maternal antibodies via the colostrum. No other treatment was effective against this insidious virus.

NEONATAL MALADJUSTMENT SYNDROME

Neonatal maladjustment syndrome is seen immediately after birth and characterized by bizarre behavioral disturbances. Brain hemorrhage, edematous swelling, and even lack of blood supply (hypoxia) are known findings in these foals. Because of their strange actions, convulsions, shaking, and sometimes violent thrashing, victims of this poorly understood and very frustrating condition have been given all sorts of incorrect names, such as wanderers, dummies, barkers, shakers, and epileptic convulsive foals. Also, various forms of seizures have been reported and described in the neonatal foal. See page 165.

There are some who believe that sustained cerebral compression, occurring during a dystocia or protracted unassisted delivery or during a vigorously assisted birth (too much traction), is the cause of brain damage suffered by these foals. Hypoxia (less than the physiologically normal amount of oxygen in the brain tissue) is a normal sequel resulting in abnormal behavior. Time and research will, it is hoped, provide a true answer.

Highly selective, distinct sedation, avoiding lowering blood pressure, and tube feeding should be first on the agenda. Sodium bicarbonate, both IV and orally, have been tried with some degree of success, while combined with fluid and electrolyte support.

A warm and comfortable bed, noise- and draft-free but with adequate ventilation, should be provided.

The few cases that I have seen survive this curious and puzzling condition were recipients of great effort and dedication from outstanding and courageous horse people.

The prognosis remains poor.

LYME DISEASE

Although this disease is classified as new, it can now be traced back to 1909. At present, Lyme disease has not been identified in foals.

The causative agents (spirochete/protozoa) or the telltale antibody titres have been isolated in dogs, adult horses, some wild and domestic animals, and humans. Lyme disease, therefore, is categorized as a public health threat. It has been steadily increasing in incidence, so it deserves close observation and constant research.

Lyme disease is caused by a protozoa or spirochete microorganisms carried by deer ticks, *Ixodes scapularis*. Deer, in all geographic areas, are infected with ticks, posing a hazard to all animals exposed to grass and wooded areas.

Early symptoms of dermatitis with flu-like symptoms, followed by arthritis, are the early salient signs of this malady. A red circle in the skin surrounding the tick bite, easily found in hairless areas, is diagnostic.

Although diagnosis is a challenge, it is imperative to institute early antibiotic treatment (oxytetracycline, ampicillin, and procaine penicillin). These antibiotics can control, but not necessarily cure, the infection. A blood test can confirm the diagnosis.

A vaccination has been developed and recently released for use in animals. Prognosis—guarded.

OMPHALITIS OR NAVEL-STUMP (URACHAL) ABSCESSES

Omphalitis or navel-stump abscesses develop in and around the navel-stump tissue. Navel-stump abscesses generally develop at two to three weeks of age and are detected by the pain, swelling, moisture, and discomfort that it creates. Purulent material trapped in focal areas in the tissue frequently exude a puslike discharge and can, if not properly treated, advance inward, causing either septicemia or peritonitis. Again, prompt attention is advantageous.

Quite unlike navel ill and septicemia, omphalitis is a localized infection of the navel-cord stump, and unless badly neglected, it remains confined to the navel area. Omphalitis and navel ill symptoms simulate one another in appearances, as both produce an enlarged and somewhat hot and painful navel, but the two conditions should not be confused.

Prevention consists of proper care and observation of the umbilical stump for the first six or seven days. To assure dryness and shrinkage of the stump tissue, use repeated daily cauterization with a strong Iodine tincture or equal parts of 7 percent Iodine tincture with glycerine.

Surgical intervention to remove the abscesses and thickened or fibrous navel tissue may be necessary if the cauterized tissue does not adequately drain and respond after approximately one week of treatment. Supportive therapy and antibiotics are in order for a few days after surgery. In this day and age, a foal suffering with omphalitis is a distinct sign of carelessness and neglect.

Always check the bedding in advance of foaling and conscientiously avoid the use of shavings, sawdust, or any dirty, dusty type of bedding. Clean rye straw is preferred. Environmental cleanliness and good hygiene are the least we should provide for our long-awaited foals.

Foals are subject to a variety of ills and diseases. However, many foal illnesses can be prevented by:

- Advance preparation.

- A clean environment.

- Good personal hygiene.

- A sound parasite control program designed by a veterinarian.

- Adherence to a vaccination schedule.

- Nutrition management.

- Avoidance of stress caused by exciting or traumatic handling.

- Quiet, timely routine and schedule.

TRANSPORTATION OF AN ILL FOAL

No sick foal should be subjected to the stress and rigors of a van ride unless life-saving treatment cannot be provided on location, and then only when the foal can be properly prepared for the stressful ride. If you abide by these two rules, you will greatly increase your foal's chances of survival; if these cardinal rules cannot be followed, it may be better to leave the foal at home.

Following are a few general words of advice for treating a critically ill newborn foal that the attending veterinarian has determined requires hospitalization and intensive care.

Most sick foals are both hypoglycemic (having low levels of sugar) and acidemic (having low levels of blood carbonate), so priority should be given to IV correction of the acidemia and the replacement of the blood sugar both prior to and during transport. Ask your veterinarian to place an indwelling catheter IV in the jugular vein; it should be secured by taping it around the foal's neck. Then provide a slow and constant IV drip of 10 percent dextrose and saline.

WARNING: Avoid the common mistake of administering intravenously one large vial or overdose 50 percent dextrose/saline. This solution is often given in haste and always in error. It provides a short-lived effect and can cause a fatal response through the excessive release of insulin, resulting in shock and, most likely, death.

Secondly, if the attending veterinarian approves, give a small milk meal via the naso-gastric tube prior to and during the trip to the hospital. This will provide much-needed strength to the weak foal. *Warning:* Exception to this rule is the premature foal with an immature GI tract, not yet ready for milk. Only the veterinarian can determine the G.I. status.

Keep the foal as warm and comfortable as possible. See that the van is draft-free, well padded with pillows or preferably air mattresses, and most importantly, supervised by a thoughtful attendant. A phone call to the hospital before departure can save precious time upon arrival.

It is heartbreaking to see foals carried into the hospital with no support, blue gums, and ice-cold limbs. If you van a critically ill foal without taking these vitally essential steps, it will more often than not arrive in a state of shock and die despite heroic treatment.

WARNING: Vulnerable Age Group   Over the years I have learned to predict a time period or calendar-related increase in foal sicknesses. Curiously, they correlate with the normal decrease in the nutritional content of mare's milk. The average age of affected foals ranges from 3–6 months.

All neonates ingest colostrum (first milk) loaded with preformed protective antibodies that serve well for approximately 8–10 weeks of age. The mare's milk continues its normal flow and amount, although it dramatically loses its nutritional content concurrent with the reduced foal's antibody blood titre. Consequently, the foal loses in two ways—antibodies and nutrition.

Since the newborn's autoimmune system fails to function until around 12–16 weeks, this age group must be carefully monitored (lower antibody level and lower milk nutrition). I strongly suggest that all foals from 11–12 weeks of age (not before) receive all approved vaccines, thus stimulating and perhaps activating the foal's own immune system.

Chapter Four

CONGENITAL, HEREDITARY, AND DEVELOPMENTAL CONDITIONS

The overall conformation and physical characteristics of a young foal can be fully examined and evaluated as to potential by a skilled eye. The highly visible physical traits and characteristics are of hereditary or congenital origin. More often, though, the value of a horse is more dependent upon the hidden, inherent talents and innate abilities—which, while also of hereditary origin, are unfortunately quite obscure. A method of measuring these elusive faculties may someday come to light.

Gambling on the presence or absence of the out-of-sight capabilities has frustrated breeders and potential buyers of young athletic horses since time began. The wise horse breeder attempts to combine performance bloodlines with desirable physical traits and characteristics, then hopes that the offspring will have superior mental capacity. Perhaps this is why the old saying, "Breed the best to the best and then hope for the best," prevails.

When a foal is born with a birth defect or some glaring undesirable trait of hereditary or congenital origin, the average mare owner automatically elects to change stallions the next breeding season—and rightfully so. This common-sense judgment is certainly not meant to incriminate the stallion, but simply to eliminate the chance of incompatibility and recurrence.

Unlike human medical practitioners, equine practitioners have no practical method to determine during embryonic life birth defects or hereditary malfunction. In human medicine, when a question arises concerning the embryo or fetus during gestation, amniocentesis (the aspiration of amniotic fluid through a long needle precisely placed into the uterus for the purpose of subsequent analysis) sometimes can provide certain valuable information, such as sex determination and recognition of a few well-known birth defects, as well as limited information on chromosomal aberrations.

It is a different situation in equine medicine. The brood mare has the least stable reproductive system of all domestic animals. There are a few courageous veterinarians who perform paracentesis in the equine. I prefer to believe that, in most cases, the dangers of such a procedure far outweigh the knowledge so gleaned.

We sorely need research to determine what effects surgical invasion, dietary intake, drugs, or chemicals exert, either favorable or detrimental, on the potentially vulnerable, rapidly growing fetus. Most thinking horse people who own breeding animals abide by the old rule, "Absolutely no unnecessary drugs, no chemicals including fertilizers, and no foreign materials" near their pregnant brood mares.

The mare's placenta is quite enigmatic, as its functions disallow the passage of beneficial antibodies to reach the fetus, yet it has been documented that almost all drugs given the mare during gestation freely enter the foal's body. This diabolic information should alert all brood mare people to the responsibility and dangers of tending the pregnant mare.

Some also believe that the very young embryo is more sensitive to chemicals during the period of rapid developmental growth and tissue changes. I am convinced that some congenital aberrations occur by the misuse of drugs during pregnancy. In lieu of research, we can only assume that all drugs or chemicals pose a potential threat to the health and well-being of all embryonic tissue or fetal development.

ULTRASOUND PREGNANCY DIAGNOSIS

The use of ultrasound, a noninvasive method of viewing the equine conceptus in utero from 12 days of conception, is a great advancement in veterinary science when used prudently in the brood mare. It is indeed exciting to see the minute embryo or older fetus actually moving and growing right before your eyes, without any known damage being inflicted.

A recent development permits an equine practitioner with an ultrasound machine to determine sex or gender of the fetus. Although I am aware of the advantages this breakthough will allow, I am also concerned as to what abuses may also occur with this early gestational information and the potential spinoffs.

During my brood mare practice, I have religiously shunned the use of drugs and any unnecessary invasive treatment or procedure, unless the need was critical and strongly indicated.

There are two well-recognized exceptions to this rule. A proper program of vaccination is the first. In addition to the rhino-pneumonitis-prescribed vaccinations given during the lengthy gestation, expectant mothers should receive boosters, ideally administered one month before the due date. These boosters should be limited to those prescribed by an equine veterinarian in attendance. Vaccine selection, manufacturer, dosage, route of administration, and even the description of the precise site of injection, should be carefully identified and supervised in all heavy matrons.

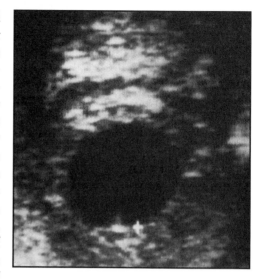

Ultrasound pregnancy print.

The other exception is worm medicines, or anthelmintics, used to control and destroy internal parasites. This delicate area also rates close and careful supervision or surveillance by your veterinarian. Any anthelmintic administered during gestation should be scrutinized and selected first for safety and second for effectiveness without toxicity.

A good rule to follow is that no pregnant mare should receive any worm medicine later than her ninth month of gestation. Stress good, clean, natural food and fresh water with free access to salt at all times.

Your veterinarian is the best judge of worm medicines, their uses and safety margins, especially when intended for use in brood mares.

Although effective against most internal parasites, one particular group of anthelmintics, called organophosphates, are, in my opinion, unsafe for use in pregnant mares and should be avoided. Also, many birds die from ingesting the residue of this anthelmintic found in manure or horse droppings. Ecology-conscious folks frown on all organophosphates.

A foal arrives in the world endowed with an unknown genetic structure. Some individuals are laden with obvious problems detectable at birth, while others possess predetermined hidden defects scheduled to appear later on at variable or unpredictable ages.

Occasionally, inherited defects are so severe that death ensues before delivery. Others are manifested immediately or shortly after birth, accounting for stages of questionable health and a precarious life quality in the newborn. Other genetic traits or characteristics remain hidden until the foal reaches a precise age or moment of a developmental stage, or even maturity, before becoming apparent. At that time it can be determined whether the defect is treatable, amenable to surgery, manageable, or in fact life-limiting.

Depending upon the type and severity of the affliction and the availability and state of the art of veterinary medicine, some foals endure and survive.

INHERITED AND CONGENITAL PROBLEMS

- Monster foals:

    Hydrocephalic (water head).

    Schistosomis reflexus.

    Fetal anasarca (hydrops amnion).

- Cerebellar hypoplasia and degeneration.

- Heart defects:

    Interventricular septal defect.

    Patent ductus arteriosus.

- Defective soft palate (cleft palate).

- Defective colon or rectum:

    Atresia coli.

    Atresia recti.

- Jaw deformities:

    Brachygnathia (parrot mouth).

    Prognathia (sow mouth, monkey mouth).

- Polydactylism (extra appendages).

- Eye lesions:

    Cataracts.

    Undersized globes.

    Iris discoloration.

    Retinal detachment.

Persistent hyaloid vessels.

Corneal dermoids.

Inverted eyelids (entropion).

Everted eyelids (ectropion).

- Leaky navel cord (pervious or patent urachus).
- Urinary bladder defect:

    Ruptured bladder.

    Leaky bladder.

- Limb deformities (weakness and crookedness).
- Locked stifles:

    Upward fixation of the patella.

    Lateral fixation of the patella.

- Contraction:

    In utero—major cause of dystocia.

    Clubfoot.

    Nutrition-related.

- Hernias:

    Umbilical.

    Scrotal.

- Defective guttural pouch (tympany).
- Wobbles:

    Equine ataxia.

    Equine incoordination.

- Retained testicles:

    Cryptorchidism.

    Monorchidism.

- Seizures (various causes).
- Epilepsy.
- Narcolepsis.

- Jaundice:

    Isoerythrolysis.

    Icteric.

- Immunodeficient foals.

- Dentigerous cysts.

- Hemophilia.

- White muscle disease.

MONSTER FOALS

Monster or extensively deformed foals are rare when compared with their bovine counterparts. Deformed and incomplete calves are not uncommon and seem to be accepted as a matter of course on farms where large numbers of calves are born.

Equine fetal monsters are rarely carried to term, and are usually aborted during the latter months of gestation. Any arrest in the progressive development and growth of the fetus will inevitably cause intrauterine death; prompt abortion then occurs in the mare. The deformity per se may not necessarily terminate fetal life. Death with subsequent abortion occurs when one or several essential life-support components fail individually or collectively to maintain fetal growth.

A monster foal cannot function effectively and cannot endure the extrauterine environment. The degree of aberration determines whether the foal is considered to be merely deformed or actually a monster. The few times that I have observed monster foals in my practice, they arrived in the world barely alive, so the inevitable decision to put them to sleep became somewhat easier. Severely afflicted foals, those with incomplete and missing body areas and parts, deserve swift and humane euthanasia.

There are three recognized types of monster foals, all of which usually are born dead or die shortly after birth.

Hydrocephalic foals, suffering from what is commonly called "water on the brain," are most often premature, undersized, and underdeveloped. This easily recognized condition is characterized by an exceptionally enlarged cranium, a staggering unsteady gait, and various central nervous system symptoms. No treatment is known, and euthanasia is indicated.

Schistosomis reflexus is a congenital absence of the ventral abdominal wall and skin covering; thus the entire abdominal viscera is exposed. Some refer to this as the "inside-out stomach." In the rare cases carried to term, these foals are usually born dead.

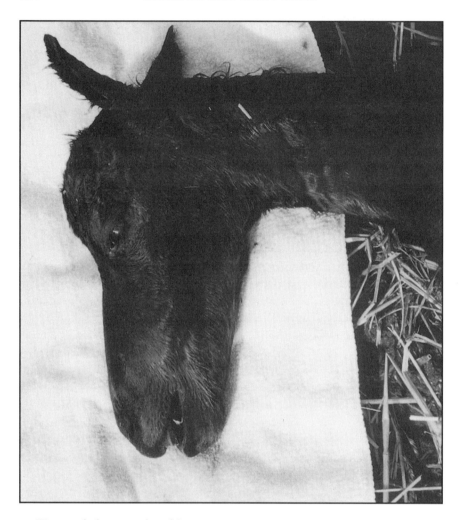

Water on the brain, an aborted fetus.

Fetal anasarca (hydrops amnion) is a condition of hereditary or congenital origin, which affects both the mare and the foal.

During embryonic life, the fetus is enveloped inside of a smooth grayish white sac called the amnion, that part of the placenta which contains and constantly bathes the foal in amniotic fluid. The normal fetus continuously swallows amniotic fluid during the entire gestational period. When a fetus with a faulty digestive tract is unable to adequately swallow amniotic fluid, fetal anasarca develops in the foal, with hydrops amnion suffered by the matron. Also acknowledged as possible contributing causes are faulty placental circulation and perhaps a diseased or infected uterus.

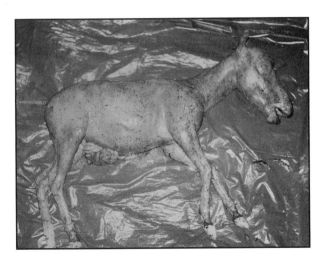

Aborted schistosomis fetus.

In either case, an excessive amount of amniotic fluid accumulates in utero, usually at seven to nine months in gestation, causing edema and ascites (undue water retention) in the tissues of the fetus with profound stretching of the mare's uterus. These mares suddenly take on the appearance of carrying quadruplets, sway from side to side, and, although attitudes and appetites remain good, all involved barn personnel become upset, anxious, and quite nervous.

I have witnessed mares just able to clear a normal-sized barn doorway and on occasion watched some actually increase in size daily. Although they seemed content and obviously comfortable, it was almost frightening to see the degree to which the mare's body can truly stretch. These individuals were in fact suffering with the perplexing entity called fetal anasarca or hydrops amnion.

Excessive stretching of the uterus often results in uterine inertia, or total inability to contract, regardless of whether the fetus is aborted or the foal is presented at term. Once diagnosed, uterine inertia requires a manual delivery. This just adds to the dilemma.

The overabundance of intrauterine fluid creates unusual pressure on the closed cervix and rigid cervical canal, but fortunately, nature allows varying degrees of softening and subsequent dilation, thereby permitting some leaking to occur. With the uncomfortable mare quite unable to foal unassisted, recognition of the dire situation is imperative, and a prompt hurry-up call to the local veterinarian is in order. The veterinarian should aid in the delivery and is sure to be rewarded by a bath of 20 to 30 gallons of stored amniotic fluid that gushes forth to soak clothing, hair, and shoes, as well as flooding the entire stall. This tepid, distasteful bath would be bearable if only the foal were not always dead.

Aborted anasarca fetus.

All of these foals are waterlogged, have a bluish gray tint, and are slightly swollen in appearance. Autopsy usually reveals one or more developmental defects in addition to the primary condition of fetal anasarca.

Did the uterine circulation malfunction, causing an accumulation of amniotic fluid? Or did the fetus, with its inability to swallow, cause the condition to develop?

NOTE: It may be of interest that, to my knowledge, no mare that experienced this horror once ever suffered again from the same condition, nor did any lose the ability to produce normal foals.

CEREBELLAR HYPOPLASIA AND DEGENERATION

Cerebellar hypoplasia and degeneration is thought to be of hereditary or congenital origin. To date, this condition has been reported only in the Arabian breed of horses. Symptoms are seen from birth to six months of age; colts are affected more often than fillies, but all those afflicted possess an undersized cerebellum with multiple histologic tissue changes. Head and body tremors progressively interfere with the foal's ability to walk and, in advanced cases, paddling and compensatory efforts are elicited along with visual aberrations and defective blinking reflex.

In the absence of any known treatment, the degenerative processes continue uninhibited. Euthanasia is the only humane solution.

HEART DEFECTS

Heart defects of hereditary or congenital origin are uncommon in the equine. There are, however, two such conditions infrequently found in foals, called interventricular septal defect and patent ductus arteriosus.

Interventricular septal defect consists of an unnatural hole in the heart wall that allows leaking and reduced efficiency in cardiac function. Patent ductus arteriosus is a faulty duct or one that does not close correctly, thus causing reduced oxygenation and great circulatory inefficiency. This condition is diagnosed with much greater frequency in humans (among whom victims are called "blue babies") and in dogs. Sophisticated surgery is available today to all but the unfortunate equine. Perhaps someday!

The incidence of these conditions is rare and the treatment nonexistent. The combination of weakness, unthriftiness, and intolerance to exercise gives warning that the foal should receive an in-depth cardiovascular examination. Cardiovascular evaluations require specialists to diagnose and predict an accurate prognosis.

Electrocardiogram (EKG) and echocardiogram (U/S) are two available tests for determination of heart conditions aiding greatly in a definitive diagnosis.

DEFECTIVE SOFT PALATE/CLEFT PALATE

Defective soft palate is an inherited or congenital condition that is noticed at birth or shortly thereafter. No one could miss seeing the admixture of milk and nasal fluids oozing from the newborn's nostrils during and immediately after nursing. This startling finding is diagnostic of a defective soft palate. The normal equine soft palate extends fully back into the pharynx and does not allow free passage between the oral and the nasal cavity. With its twofold function, the normal soft palate helps direct the ingested milk to the esophagus (the entrance to the stomach) and prevents any fluid or solid food from entering the respiratory tract. In contrast, a defective palate is incomplete in length, or contains a rent or aperture in the palatal tissue. Any departure from the norm in this membrane separating the two important cavities creates a functional inefficiency. A major portion of the nutritious milk thus misses the esophageal opening, escapes into the pharnyx, and flows out the nasal cavity.

Since the rent is located well back into the throat area and out of sight, the diagnostic symptom of a defective soft palate is milk flowing out of the nasal cavity during the act of nursing or suckling. Because of this loss of milk, these foals seem to be constantly nursing in an attempt to fill a void, and they consistently choke, cough, and gag. Fatigue soon develops. Not only do they suffer a deficit in nutritional intake, but with such inefficient feeding they are also busy nursing when they should be resting.

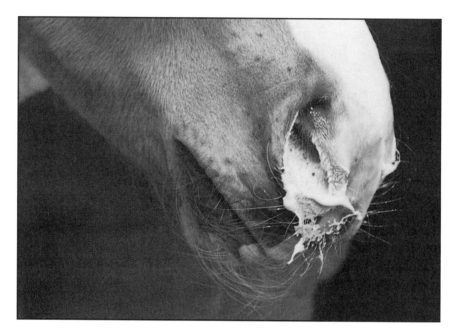

Milk suckled escapes out of the nostrils.

A soft palate defect or cleft palate in a foal is completely hidden, and the characteristic symptoms are the only method of initial diagnosis. Our modern flexible fiber-optic endoscopes enable the practitioner to view the palatal area and location of distress. Diagnosis is easily confirmed.

ALERT: If this condition is ignored or goes untreated, the threat of aspiration pneumonia is great in the large percentage of cases. The greater the frustration and fatigue, the greater the chance for accidental aspiration of milk—with pneumonia rapidly ensuing.

This palate defect should not be confused with a parallel human condition commonly referred to as harelip, or cleft palate. The human affliction is apparent visually and audibly and, fortunately, amenable to corrective surgery. This is not the case in the foal with a cleft palate. Surgery to date has been very disappointing. These foals continue to manifest poor nutrition, fatigue, unthriftiness, and grave weakness. Pneumonia is a constant threat. Prognosis is poor.

DEFECTIVE COLON OR RECTUM

Defective colon and defective rectum, known respectively as *Atresia coli* and *Atresia recti*, are commonly classified as hereditary or congenital in origin and are relatively rare in occurrence. The two conditions are similar by virtue of their proximity to one another and the symptoms produced in each case. In Atresia coli a developmental deformity occurs anatomically in a section of the small colon that ends abruptly in a blind pouch. The opposing section of the colon also ends in a blind pouch. In some cases several feet, or even entire sections, of the colon are missing. In cases of Atresia recti, the rectum also ends in an abrupt blind pouch and is usually found closer to the anus.

In both findings, the foals appear normal at birth, only to develop symptoms of colic shortly thereafter, especially after ingesting colostrum.

Anytime I administer an enema to a newborn foal with no results, I am apprehensive. Because of the substantial lack of tone in the rectum and colon, little if any liquid from the enema is returned; I then have to consider the grim diagnosis of Atresia coli.

In Atresia recti, the enema content usually returns somewhat, but is lacking both fecal material and coloration. Either of these findings should arouse suspicion and signal the necessity for careful observation for signs of future discomfort.

Both incomplete gastrointestinal tract conditions are untreatable, except for surgical intervention. The only hope of survival for such foals is early diagnosis and prompt surgery. Anastomosis, or connection of the blind intestinal ends, has proven successful if performed within hours of the moment of birth. Prompt recognition is essential but unfortunately rare.

FOAL DENTAL CARE

Foals seldom require dental care under one year of age, although most are born with baby teeth already in place.

A dental examination is required, however, when symptoms are presented of head tilting, lowering, or elevating in an unnatural, painful fashion associated with the mouth, jaw, or head posture. Dental and head maladies are commonly of traumatic origin. Symptoms such as excessive salivation, reduced ability to nurse, depression, and no control over the tongue—sometimes hanging freely outside of the foal's mouth—indicate a need for an in-depth dental examination. Many very young foals entered my hospital with just these telltale symptoms. I would always order radiographs and prepare for surgical intervention.

A "danger period" exists early in life during the socialization period with other brood mares and foals. Sometimes possessiveness and jealousy prompt aggressiveness, and unfortunately injury results. The baby foal is often caught in between and becomes the victim.

The classic injury, the type that I encountered in my practice, inevitably occurred at the paddock gate, usually on the initial turnout day. All can be avoided if you read carefully the section on initial turnout day. (See page 247.)

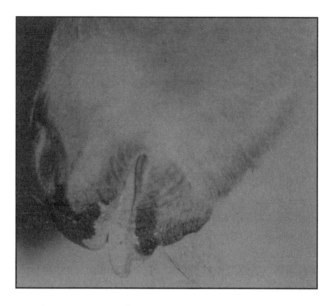

Classic symptoms indicating trauma to the jaws.

To repeat, most foals are born with baby teeth already in place: two incisors in the upper jaw and two matching incisors in the lower jaw, although some arrive with pink gums and hidden incisors ready to erupt within hours. Their specific purpose is grasping or prehension of food. The muscular tongue quickly propels ingesta into the back of the mouth where larger teeth, called molars (grinders), are hidden from sight. Then mastication and initial digestion begin just prior to swallowing.

One additional and quite important function of the incisors (front teeth) is age determination throughout the life of the horse. I am certain that you understand the old adage, "Never look a gift horse in the mouth."

Foals arrive with a total of 16 teeth; four temporary (baby) incisors and 12 temporary (baby) molars. These baby teeth will eventually be replaced by a permanent set of teeth by the age of five years or a "full mouth." At that time, a full mouth totals 36 for the mare and 40 for the stallion or gelding. The four additional teeth, two above and two below,

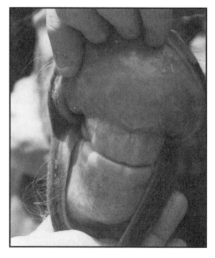

Newborn gums covering incisors.

are called canine, tushers, or bridle teeth and are located in the interdental space. This differentiates the horse from the mare.

Age is determined by the shedding of baby teeth and the eruption of permanent teeth, along with evidence of tooth wear. Also, the jaw angulation changes with age. Horses' teeth continue to grow throughout their entire lifetime. This single fact distinguishes the equine from other species and explains why horses so frequently need dental care.

Since this book is devoted to the equine under 12 months of age, I suggest the interested reader seek out one of the many manuals available with a wealth of information on equine teeth. Most have charts demonstrating how to determine the age of horses.

JAW DEFORMITIES

Parrot mouth and sow mouth are two jaw deformities seen in the young foal. Both are considered to be of hereditary or congenital origin, and both constitute an unsoundness. To date, no satisfactory treatment has evolved.

In parrot mouth (also called "overshot jaw" or brachygnathia), the lower jaw (mandible) is shorter than the upper jaw. This can be an unpleasant sight for the foal owner, who always anticipates perfection. It is unclear whether overgrowth of the upper jaw (maxilla) or a defective lower jaw creates the parrot-mouth appearance.

Sow mouth (also called undershot jaw, or prognathia) is a jaw deformity opposite in appearance to parrot mouth. The maxilla (upper jaw) appears to be shortened and defective in this case.

In either case, the shorter jaw is currently labeled the defective member, although this topic is still controversial among authorities. Concurrent thinking agrees that the mandible (lower jaw) is the defective member in both conditions. If you ever have an occasion to look into the mouth of a pig, you will see how apt the name of this deformity is. Sow mouth is not as common as parrot mouth.

With misalignment of large dental arcades, as happens in cases of jaw-size disparity, improper apposition of the incisors results in abnormal wear and uneven overgrowth of tooth surfaces. The anterior and readily visible incisors are involved, along with the large, numerous, and hard-working molars located well back in the mouth and out of sight. A painful condition can develop when the incisors on the shorter jaw become inflamed and embedded in the soft tissue of the other jaw, rather than meeting and opposing their counterpart teeth as nature intended. Any misalignment of dental arcades interferes with proper mastication and directly affects the health and well-being of the horse.

Fortunately, it does require an extreme defect of the jaws to interfere with the newborn's ability to nurse and feed. Later on, grazing can become almost

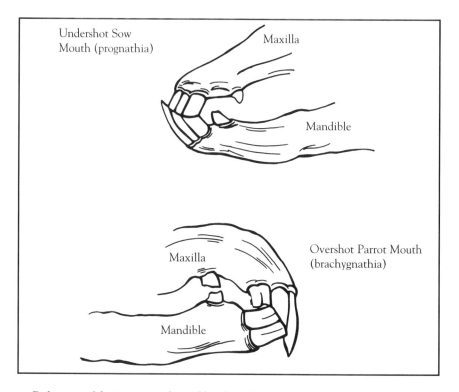

Deformities of the jaw: prognathia and brachygnathia.

impossible with an extreme deformity because seizing of grass by the incisor teeth is dramatically impaired. These foals would not survive if left alone on the short grass of the range, but within a protected environment, with concentrates and lush hay and pastures, they live to become useful animals. The front teeth, or incisors, serve only for prehension; the large molars, out of sight, serve for grinding purposes. Frequent and regular dental attention to remove the offending tooth edges that develop on the molars through the imbalanced apposition will always be needed to enable them to grind their feed properly.

ADULT HORSE TEETH

Continuous eruption of the teeth throughout life is a phenomenon peculiar to the equine. All of the horse's permanent teeth, with the exception of the canine and wolf teeth, are constantly pushed out from the root level by a continuous process of cancellous bone proliferation. Essentially, the growth rate is controlled by the efficiency of the opposing teeth. Normal apposition is vital for even wear and to maintain a smooth dental arcade. In the absence of an

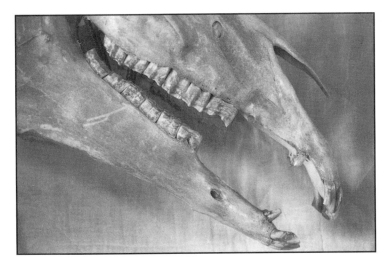

Equine jaws and teeth—molars, canine, and incisors.

opposing tooth, growth will progress uninhibited, causing discomfort and inefficiency in mastication. In extreme cases, growth may even progress to the point where the uninhibited tooth locks into the opposite jaw.

There is an anatomical reason for frequent need of dental attention in the adult horse, involving primarily the hidden and quite out-of-sight molars (grinders). A normal horse's upper jaw (maxilla) is wider than its lower jaw

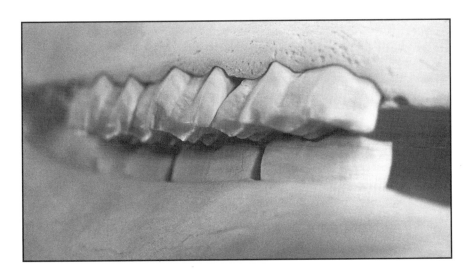

Partially unopposed equine molars.

(mandible)—thus the dental arcade is unevenly apposed. The areas free of apposition constantly form sharp, painful edges on the outside upper jaw and the inside lower jaw. A dental procedure called *floating* (rasping) removes and smooths the sharp, painful edges.

Since the equine jaw requires a peculiar side-sliding motion in order to masticate ingesta, neglected long points on the molars inhibit efficient chewing and may cause the horse to gulp its feed whole.

A semiannual dental inspection for all horses with normal or abnormal mouths is essential for good health.

POLYDACTYLISM

Polydactylism, or extra appendages, is rarely seen in the equine. In all known occurrences, the additional limb has been an extension of the splint bones (metacarpals) affecting the inside of the limb only, and always the forelegs. The few confirmed cases were located on the medial aspect of the forelegs, and all were successfully removed surgically.

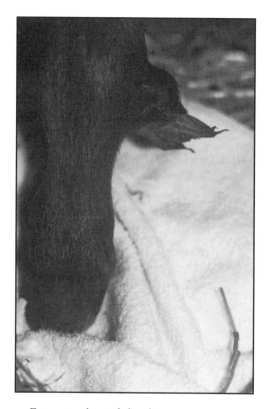

Extra appendage:polydactylism.

One case was documented in a Standardbred foal in Australia, one case affecting an Arabian foal was reported in the United States, and some years ago I had the dubious honor of discovering the only case recorded of an extra limb on a Thoroughbred. I radiographed the filly's leg and found a complete extra leg, including a miniature cannon bone, sesamoids, and phalanxes I, II, and III, all in minute detail, but oh so definitive! I was so excited that I took the time and wrote a scientific report on my findings.

After surgery, the filly grew into a full-sized, perfectly functional race filly, with no evidence of this phenomenal hereditary anomaly. Her dam subsequently produced several foals by the same sire, and none suffered any form of polydactylism.

After a modest race career, this filly produced several foals, none of which had an additional appendage.

I thought I was seeing things one afternoon at the backstretch, when a good horseman asked me to examine a fractured splint bone. The patient in question was a

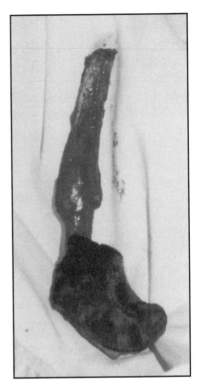

Post-op removal of miniature leg and foot.

four-year-old gelding, a veteran of many races. When I palpated the area, instead of palpating a splint bone, I actually discovered an additional miniature cannon bone, ankle, and foot on the inside of his foreleg. The owner was startled when I told him it was not a fractured splint bone. We scheduled radiographs for the next morning, but when I arrived, the horse had been shipped to another track. I was crushed! This proves that this condition may not be as rare as reported, perhaps just misdiagnosed.

EYE LESIONS

Visual defects of hereditary and congenital origin are considered rare in the equine. However, cataracts, undersized globes, iris discoloration, retinal detachment, persistent hyaloid vessels, and corneal dermoids are found on occasion.

The normally sighted foal requires from 48 to 60 hours after birth to develop efficient vision for coping with the external environment. When there are suspicions about a foal's visual acuity, professional help, with the use of an ophthalmoscope and mydriatrics to dilate the pupil, can determine ocular and visual problems.

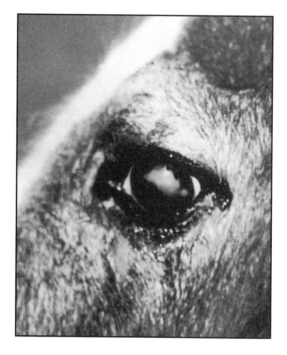

Cataract.

Eye lesions stemming from an irritated cornea frequently occur in little foals. Hay, straw, and dust are familiar offenders, but these are environmental factors.

I have observed many newborn foals with weepy eyes and irritated corneas—the result of a protracted delivery. All responded well to the instillation of ophthalmic ointment containing a small amount of hydrocortisone.

ENTROPION

Inverted eyelids, or entropion, cause a severe corneal irritation (keratitis) of hereditary or congenital origin. Entropion is characterized by a turning in or folding under of the lower eyelid, causing the eyelashes and outer hairy surface of the lid to come into intimate contact with the sensitive cornea, thus causing severe irritation. This is by far the most common eye lesion seen in the newborn foal. It most often involves the lower eyelid and is generally, but not necessarily, associated with premature, weak, and especially dehydrated foals. Discomfort, profuse tearing, frequent blinking, and photophobia (sensitivity to light) draw attention to the condition.

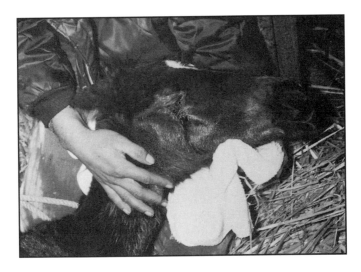

Inverted eyelid with keratitis.

Temporary relief can be achieved in some cases by careful manipulation. Lubricate the eyes and lids well with a bland ophthalmic ointment; avoid the use of corticosteroids. Manually evert (turn out) the affected eyelid by gently rolling the excess skin outward using your thumb. The skin will readily return to its original location, so this procedure should be repeated as often as possible, preferably every hour around the clock. Care should be taken to avoid further irritation and trauma.

WARNING: If this condition is permitted to go untreated for even a few hours, the corneal surface becomes dry, and damaging secondary changes develop. The cornea will develop a generalized bluish haze and minute local spots will appear, indicating the result of continuous irritation and trauma. Keratitis (inflammation of the cornea), corneal ulcers, blepharospasms (uncontrollable blinking), or eventual blindness may follow.

If the degree of inversion is great, and manual efforts toward correction are fruitless, then surgical correction is indicated to prevent further irritation and restore the cornea to health. Correction involves a simple horizontal incision that reduces the excess skin, followed by the placement of a row of well-spaced sutures to complete the tuck-like surgical operation. Surgery is so successful and rewarding in cases of entropion that I would rather operate early than chance the development of corneal irritation and ulcers.

ECTROPION

Everted eyelids, or ectropion, are a hereditary or congenital eversion (turning out) of the eyelid and are very rare in foals. The only cases of ectropion I personally have seen, however, have been the direct result of trauma; they were, therefore, not hereditary. All were corrected quite easily by minor surgery.

LEAKY NAVEL CORD

Leaky navel cord (pervious urachus or patent urachus) is a relatively common condition in the newborn foal. The urachus is a small tubular structure contained within the umbilical cord that carries the fluid waste from the fetal bladder to the placental tissues during prenatal or embryonic life. After birth, when the umbilical cord ruptures, natural closure of the urachus should occur. When the urachus closes as it should, urine is then permitted to pass from the bladder out through the urethra.

Leaky navel begins when the urachus fails to close, allowing continuous dribbling of urine from the area of the navel. Dribbling from that area develops into a flow of urine when the foal attempts to urinate. This condition is not difficult to recognize, for the urine can be seen escaping from the midline of the abdomen rather than through the normal opening. In the case of a colt, a leaky navel may go unnoticed for a few days because of proximity to the sheath. But it is always a dramatic and shocking phenomenon for the owner to observe when a filly suffering a leaky navel urinates.

Since the urachus is embedded in the navel cord stump, a faulty urachus— one still leaking urine—will result in a persistently wet, soiled, warm navel stump, providing an ideal environment for pathogenic bacteria to grow; thus, there is a continual threat of infection, even systemic infection.

Spontaneous correction is rare in untreated cases. The majority of these faulty closures require daily cauterization with silver nitrate or tincture of iodine. Along with daily treatment, daily inspection for evidence of drying and shrinking of the navel stump is important. Medication should be discontinued only when the umbilical stump responds and shows no evidence of moisture or urine stains. When the foal is first recognized as suffering from a patent urachus, a complete physical examination and a complete blood count to screen for septicemia, immunodeficiency, and any other disease condition should be performed.

WARNING: A leaky navel usually can be corrected within a few days, but its presence should represent a warning sign. It has been my experience that a high percentage of pervious urachus cases are associated with various forms of intrauterine infections. The condition should be treated as a simple leaky navel, but you should be alert for hidden signs of systemic infection that may soon become evident and quickly overwhelming. See SEPTICEMIA, page 63; JOINT ILL AND NAVEL ILL, page 67.

BLADDER DEFECTS

Bladder defects are found shortly after birth in foals with symptoms similar to those of ruptured bladder. Although a ruptured bladder is thought to be caused by physical trauma sustained during delivery, small rents and apertures found in the bladder wall are believed to be of hereditary or congenital predisposition.

All bladder leaks or ruptures produce almost identical symptoms, and all are amenable to corrective surgery. Consistent symptoms are periodic straining, abdominal distention, and slight temperature elevation and dullness, with a panting-type respiration. The mucous membranes develop a yellow tint as the condition progresses.

If this condition goes unrecognized and is untreated, vision will fail as convulsions develop. Your veterinarian will confirm the diagnosis by performing an abdominal tap (paracentesis) to retrieve free urine from the abdominal cavity. Emergency surgery is the only lifesaving procedure and usually produces complete recovery.

LIMB DEFORMITIES

Weak or crooked legs have always been a major concern to the brood mare owner. A normal foal arrives with a well-developed musculature and a God-given balance in the tone of the antagonistic flexor and extensor muscle groups. The sought-after straight-legged foal is able to gain proper postural stance without undue effort.

Every year, a certain percentage of foals are born weak or with crooked legs. Because they are not carbon copies of paintings or engravings of the ideal foal, their owners are unnecessarily yet naturally disappointed.

Most limb deformities are of hereditary or congenital origin, and certain changes are strikingly prevalent in some bloodlines, indicating dominant familial tendencies.

In the past few years, however, researchers have pointed to trace minerals as a possible cause.

Found either in excessive or deficient amounts, these minerals—i.e., high zinc, low copper, and iodine, potassium, iron, magnesium, selenium, and calcium/phosphorus imbalances—have become suspect.

The constant desire to grow a super foal results in excessive feeding, especially with a protein push to the brood mare carrying a fetus and to her suckling or weanling foal of that year. Excessive energy or protein intake by the brood mare perhaps causes this trace mineral imbalance—thus limb deformities appear. Quality protein, trace mineral, and vitamin supplements are all very costly. I have never seen this type of limb deformity in a poor man's barn.

Some horse families carry specific talents, such as speed, jumping ability, or traits of disposition, that may be hidden or unanticipated: These traits can be either reinforced or eliminated unknowingly in breeding programs. Crooked limbs or conformational defects are inescapably evident, but they may be avoided by careful study and diligent research into the history of the produce of the dam and the get of the sire.

Many of these problems are the result of uterine size and position, hyper- or hypo-nutrition, and varying amounts of exercise by the dam; the majority are self-correcting within a few days with normal exercise and supervision.

A foal's limbs may deviate in four distinct directions. Anterior-posterior (or front-and-back) deviations are essentially the result of an imbalance between the flexor and extensor muscles and tendons (or soft tissue involvement); medial-lateral (side-to-side) deviations are primarily the result of skeletal deformities. Looking at the foal from the side, the deviations may be anterior (in a forward direction) or posterior (in a backward direction); viewing either from the front or rear, deviations occur medially (toward the midline) or laterally (away from the midline).

In cases of flaccid or atonic flexor tendons, which result in weak pasterns, the deviation of the ankle is in the posterior direction.

Many limb deviations correct themselves as long as the foal is able to get up and nurse. Given a little time, even foals that require assistance do surprisingly well. Some, however, require more drastic assistance in the form of braces, casts, and foot balancing. Some cases require simple taping (no support—only protection covering the soft tissue of the bulbs of the heels).

WEAK PASTERNS

Foals with weak pasterns, who are, as we say, "down in the pasterns," represent the most common, yet least serious, in this category. The extreme is the foal that actually walks with the backs of its ankles literally on the ground. Do not despair: Over the years, it has been proved that good nutrition and carefully regulated exercise bring about miraculous improvement, permitting the deficient muscle group to regain or establish its tone. Some of the most severely affected foals grow into useful adult horses able to compete effectively in performance events.

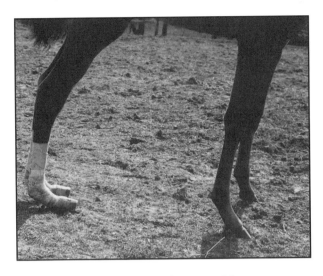

Weak flexor tendons in a foal that as an adult won races.

WARNING: Weak pasterns are caused by a decrease in flexor muscle tone; stretched flexor tendons result in an overextended ankle that is allowed to drop back and down. Flexor tendons become weaker with support, and the weakness can then become self-perpetuating in "ankle-down" foals. In these foals, any type of supportive bandage is strictly contraindicated. In extreme cases, as when the ankle has dropped down and is touching the ground, protective patches covering only the heel area are required to prevent abrasions and soreness, which might stop the foal from engaging in much-needed exercise.

Foals with the slightest involvement correct themselves in a few days; those without severe deviations usually correct within a few weeks.

Although all bandages and support appliances are to be avoided, the application of elongated shoe branches can be helpful in some extreme cases. Older foals so affected do remarkably well and within a few months achieve a stance approaching normal.

Extremely flaccid tendons are seen in weak, premature foals, septicemic foals, or foals from poorly nourished dams; but I have also seen an equal number produced by well-fed, well-managed mares. Obviously, the cause remains unknown.

CALF-KNEED

Posterior deviation of the knee (calf-kneed) is an indication of initial weakness of the flexor tendons and is often a reflection of the anatomical structure of the

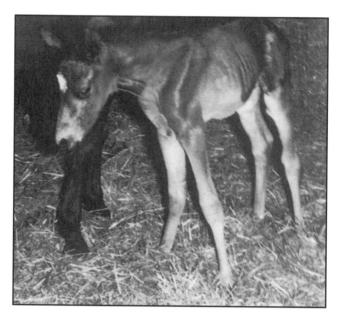

A calf-kneed, weak foal.

knee joint. A condition called calf knee, or being "back at the knees," is frequently seen in conjunction with weak pasterns and on occasion as a separate
entity. Calf knees are a common finding in premature, undersized, or underdeveloped Thoroughbred foals. I have also seen a high incidence of Calf knees
in large, well-built Quarter Horses with exceptional bloodlines. Unfortunately,
the prognosis is the same for all breeds. This inherited condition will always
represent a problem; very little definitive correction can be accomplished if
radiographic studies show that the weight-bearing planes of the joints are genetically imperfect.

In the adult, this entity has been associated with increased tendon tension in
the deep digital flexor tendon (DDFT) and ultimately with degrees of navicular
bursitis and disease. Those individuals suffering with "back at the knees" also
were found to have early degenerative changes in the navicular apparatus.

When foals have sprung knees or are "over at the knees," with an anterior
deviation, it is an indication of an imbalance in tone of the flexors and exten-
sors, with the superficial flexor tendon (SFT) exerting the stronger pull. Unless
the angulation is extreme, there is no cause for concern. With normal nutrition and sufficient exercise, the deviation disappears by the time the foal is
weaned.

RUPTURED COMMON DIGITAL EXTENSOR TENDON

Do not confuse sprung knees, which usually occur in both forelegs in the neonate, with another knee condition, also of congenital origin and seen at birth, called ruptured common digital extensor tendon. Both entities are painless in the neonate. In this condition, a soft fluid pouch is found directly over the knee, with a rupture of the foreleg tendon that simulates sprung knees in appearance only. A definitive diagnosis can be ascertained by careful palpation of the knee area. Sprung knees reveal only bony tissue, whereas rupture of the extensor tendon produces a soft, fluidy pouch. The former afflicts both legs, and the latter appears usually in one leg only. Treatment of choice for this ruptured tendon is stall rest with application of supportive splints, fiberglass casts, or tube casts. Prognosis is good.

ALERT: However, I have observed a close relationship between ruptured extensor tendon and contraction of the deep digital flexor tendon occurring in the same leg. The term contraction is controversial in the neonatal equine world; however, the affected flexor tendon appears shorter than its corresponding skeletal frame. With minute growth an inequity increases the tendon tension, which directly affects the angulation of the skeletal limb, and all joint planes become out of balance. The ruptured common digital extensor tendon is highly visible and easy to palpate in contrast to the deep digital flexor tendon, which is hidden from view. In lieu of a satisfactory method to measure tendon tension in the foal, the practitioner must rely upon clinical symptoms.

An inferior check ligament desmotomy surgically corrects the contraction, prevents the formation of a clubfoot, and enables the foal to support its body weight, achieve ambulation, and cope with nursing. Under these conditions I have found the coexisting ruptured extensor tendon to be self-healing and of no consequence.

Knees that deviate laterally (bowlegged or the reverse of knock knees) represent potential unsoundness. Unlike the previously discussed limb abnormalities, this condition is self-perpetuating. With normal exercise and work, the condition either remains the same or gradually worsens.

Knock-kneed foals, or foals with knees turned toward each other, face a much brighter future.

When the inward deviation is slight, it is self-correcting with time, exercise, and good nutrition. Even moderately severe cases seem to correct themselves if given a chance. Time is the essential factor.

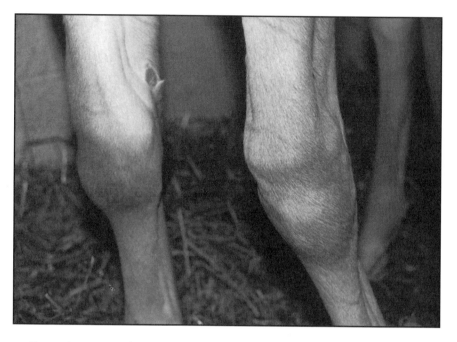

Ruptured extensor tendons.

An old rule of thumb usually proves to be quite accurate: A medial deviation offers a fair-to-good prognosis, whereas a lateral deviation carries with it only a guarded prognosis.

To understand why lateral and medial deviations respond in opposite ways, it is necessary to visualize the distribution of weight as it is placed on the forelimbs of the equine. Stand in front of the foal and imagine a plumb line dropped from the point of the shoulder to the ground. Ideally, this line should bisect the fore-limb into two equal parts, but unfortunately this is rarely seen. The reason for this has continually eluded me. I could suggest poor selective breeding, unbal-anced diets, etc., but perhaps a better reason would be the disparity between the foal's trunk or body size and its inordinately long limbs.

In any case, veterinary science theorizes that 90 percent of the weight and stress is placed to the inside of this perpendicular line, thus creating a laterally directed force onto the joint planes. Outward deviation would therefore have a tendency gradually to intensify the effect of these forces or, at best, to allow the leg to remain unchanged. On the other hand, a medial deviation seems to receive benefit from exercise and growth.

Extreme cases of knock knees will not self-improve. There are two very serious and distinct forms of knock knee that deserve differential diagnosis and specific treatment. Epiphyseal line imbalances and defective ossification

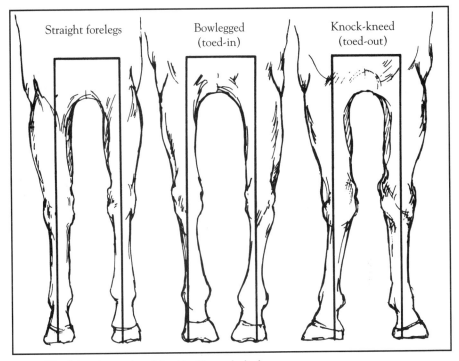

| Straight forelegs | Bowlegged (toed-in) | Knock-kneed (toed-out) |

Plumb line from point of shoulder bisects the limb.

(development of bone) of the carpal (knee) bones are the two congenital entities that not only require special attention, but also have guarded-to-poor prognoses.

An epiphyseal line is a growth zone located on the lower end of the long bones, and, unlike true bony tissue, it remains vulnerable to body weight and stress changes until maturity, when, around 18 to 24 months, the open zone closes.

Through trial and error, veterinarians have concluded that although epiphyseal lines are found on the other long-bone extremities, the radius bone in the foreleg of the horse is highly representative of the animal's stage of maturity or, more importantly, of its degree of immaturity. This fact is the reason why most good yearlings are routinely radiographed before serious training is begun. No young horse should be subjected to hard training under this age.

A normal epiphyseal growth line is difficult to precisely locate clinically when examining the leg, but it can be evaluated and graded as to condition through X-ray studies.

When inflamed or irritated, the epiphyseal growth line can be easily seen clinically.

Enlargement develops on the inside upper area of the knee, clearly visible and quite unmistakable. As the epiphysitis worsens, an enlargement appears on the outside of the leg, opposite the inside swelling. Although knees are erroneously thought to be involved, it is pathology from a variety of body stresses that causes epiphysitis. In fact, it is not the knee, but the lower end of the long radius bone above it, that possesses the growth line.

Unlike true bone, these bands of relatively soft bony tissue are actively engaged in bone growth in young immature animals. When weakened by stress or disease, these areas continue to grow but subsequently become either widened or crushed and compressed by normal body weight and use. These bone zones characteristically react in a lopsided manner that invariably causes a lateral (outside) crushing and a compensatory widening on the medial (inside) aspect so typical of the knock-kneed foal. Limited exercise cannot be overemphasized. A surgical procedure called stapling is effective in retarding further separation, and a second surgical process called periosteal stripping has also received good

Knock-kneed foal (fair prognosis).

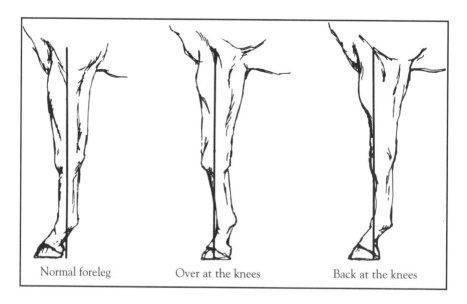

| Normal foreleg | Over at the knees | Back at the knees |

Plumb line from point of shoulder bisects the forelegs.

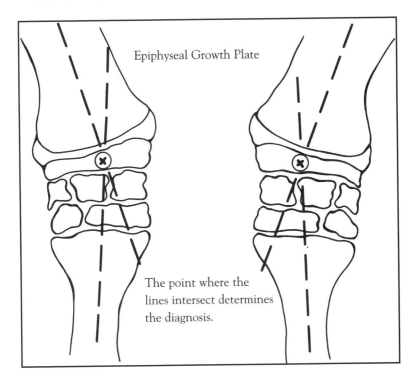

Epiphyseal Growth Plate

The point where the lines intersect determines the diagnosis.

Knock-kneed foal.

grades. But surgical intervention is valid only if performed at an early enough stage to prevent the likelihood of still more damaging secondary changes developing in the ankle and foot. Timely removal of knee staples can, in some instances, prevent compensatory torsion (twisting or turning forces) from affecting the ankles and feet.

The other serious congenital knock-kneed condition found in newborn foals is defective ossification of the small bones that make up the foal's knees. Incomplete or defective ossification of the carpal bones is a true cause of medial deviation of the knees and has been found in concert with epiphyseal line imbalance in the same leg. Since ossification of these bones occurs late in fetal development, during the final stages of gestation, it is quite easy to see that any premature birth or any delay in the ossification process could conceivably result in a foal with weak cartilaginous carpal bones, incompletely ossified. These small cartilaginous bones fail to provide adequate support for body weight and usually are crushed and diminished in size, simulating an uneven epiphyseal line. Radiographic studies aid in a differential diagnosis.

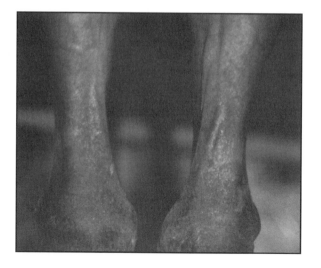

Post-stapling knees.

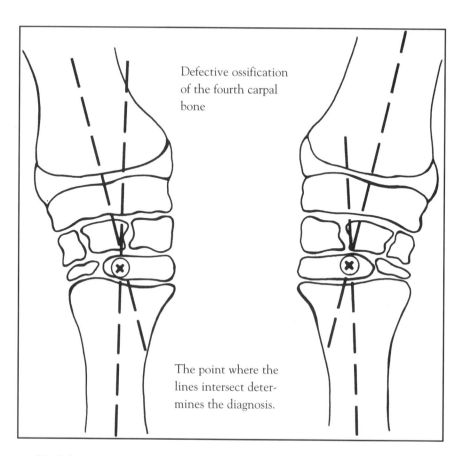

Defective ossification of the fourth carpal bone

The point where the lines intersect determines the diagnosis.

Knock-kneed foal.

ALERT: The concerned new foal owner can determine whether his or her foal has treatable epiphysitis or the dreaded defective ossification of the fourth carpal bone. Request, from your veterinarian, X-rays of both knees, taken front to back. Then draw a straight plumb line through the long bone (radius) above the knee and draw a straight line up through the cannon bone. The point at which the two lines intersect provides a telltale diagnosis. If the lines intersect at the epiphyseal line above the knee, epiphysitis is the definitive diagnosis. If they intersect at the location of the fourth carpal bone level, the diagnosis is then defective ossification of the fourth carpal bone, indicating a poorer prognosis. Any foal owner can do it. Just ask for an anterior-posterior X-ray view of the epiphyseal growth line and carpal area. (See line drawings, pages 131 and 132.)

Treatment consists of rest and application of supportive splints and lightweight casts to prevent further excursions of the foal's limb. The preceding line drawings illustrate the two causes of medial carpal deviation.

TOED-IN (PIGEON-TOED), TOED-OUT (SPLAY- OR DUCK-FOOTED)

Foals have a tendency to either toe in or toe out; it is always a pleasant surprise to see a foal stand straight and true. Whether your foal's feet turn in (pigeon-toed) or toe out (splay- or duck-footed), the ankle, pastern, and foot are all involved.

A toed-out foot usually indicates reduced flexor tendon tone, allowing the ankle to deviate medially, which results in a lateral deflection of the pastern and foot. Quite often these foals have weak pasterns, for this position creates uneven stress on the joint surfaces and joint planes and subsequently stretches the adjacent supportive ligaments. The altered gait causes interference, and trauma is then sustained in the form of bruising, for the one forefoot strikes against the medial aspect of the opposite ankle during movement, called interference.

If untreated, the possibility of future unsoundness is evident. Good nutrition and regular exercise, combined with minimal but regular conscientious foot care, are essential factors in bringing about improvement in this condition.

BLACKSMITH'S, OR FARRIER'S RASP

To correct a toed-out foot, obtain a blacksmith's rasp. Every week or 10 days, carefully rasp or lower the lateral or outside of the bottom of each forefoot with several carefully guided strokes from the heel to the toe. The small foot will then have a tendency to straighten. Any owner can purchase a rasp and maintain the vital on-time regular foot care.

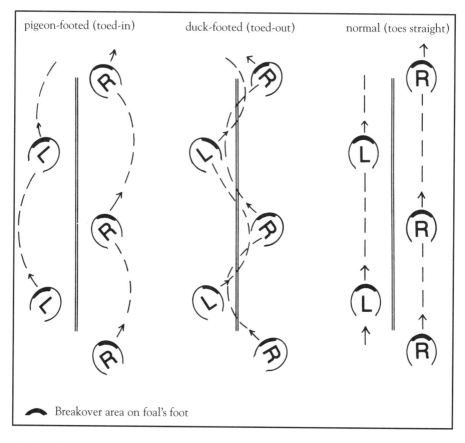

pigeon-footed (toed-in)   duck-footed (toed-out)   normal (toes straight)

Breakover area on foal's foot

Gait analysis.

POINTED TOES

Every neonatal foal develops pointed toes within the first few weeks of life. Pointed toes encourages a foal to walk crookedly and thus develop crooked legs. The blacksmith's rasp once again comes to the rescue. It does not require a weekly call to the farrier. Any owner or caretaker can handle the foal and concurrently teach the foal manners.

NOTE: The rasp should be guided around to the front of the foot to the center of the toe; one or two rounding strokes will effectively remove the point that normally develops. This will round off the toe growth and shape the young foot as it should be. The foal will then be encouraged to break over at the toe of the foot, as is normal in forward motion, and not at the inside toe area so characteristic of toed-out foals.

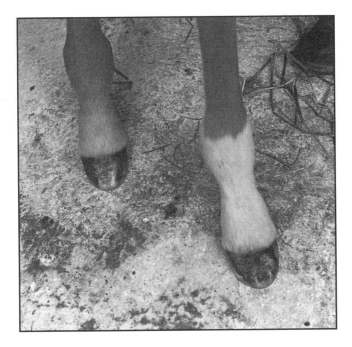

Foal feet (properly shaped).

If this normal foot growth is unchecked and the foal is allowed to continue to break over either side of the foot's center, the foal's unnatural gait will place damaging stress upon its soft, pliant bones and cartilaginous joint surfaces.

A toed-in stance is much less frequently seen than the splay-footed position. In fact, a minor degree of toeing in is considered by old horsemen to be an indication of increased strength, although severe toeing in is comparable to severe toeing out: Both indicate weakening mechanical and conformational defects. Similar joint stresses are inflicted, and the same threat of future unsoundness exists if either problem is allowed to continue unchecked. Interference in its varying degrees can be managed through conscientious shoeing. Toeing in, however, consistently produces the undesirable paddling gait, difficult, if ever, to mask.

With a toed-in deviation, the foal has a tendency to break over on the outside of the toe, producing a paddling gait. Here, too, the blacksmith's rasp is the best defense. Again, the rasp should be used gently to remove the point of the toe, actually rounding the front, thus forcing the foot to break over at the center of the toe as nature intended.

This time, the inner or medial side of the bottom of the foot should be lowered slightly; the same balancing schedule should be maintained as for pigeon-toed foals.

Contrary to some who strongly believe that no amount of foot balancing can provide a sound means of helping crooked-limbed individuals, I contend that with moderate efforts, a favorable response can be achieved. But all corrective measures must begin early in life and end well before bone maturity and epiphyseal line closure. Whatever your efforts, the degree of improvement achieved will depend upon the initial degree of deflection and amount of intrinsic basic limb involvement. But improvement will be seen.

In those cases refractory to consistent, methodical rasping methods, the leg deviation may cause a skeletal change, resulting in joint-plane tilting—either a medial or lateral tilt of the foal's leg joint. At that point, it may be necessary to take additional corrective action.

If the rasping efforts produce no result by two months of age, radiographs can be used to confirm the presence of joint tilting. This finding consistently accompanies serious toe deflections and carries an ominous sign of future unsoundness. It is now imperative to begin definitive corrective measures to reestablish the level of all joint planes before permanent changes occur.

To achieve this, the foot should first be balanced as previously directed for either type of toe deflection. For toe-out cases, apply a small custom-made split shoe to the inside half of the foal's foot. In toe-in cases, apply the partial shoe to the outside surface of the foot. But in either case, carry the split shoe slightly around or beyond the center of the toe. Square the steel in the toe area to force the foal to break over precisely in the center of the toe, thereby directing a straight stride.

Repeat this procedure every three weeks for three to four shoeings. If initiated when the foal is very young, the results should be favorable.

Any conformational deformity of congenital origin carries with it the possibility of consequences that will affect the horse's future ability; no one can predict the degree with accuracy. Many horses have unusual drive, ability, and talent; they compensate for their handicaps and continue to succeed. Obviously, if you were considering the purchase of a foal, you would not wish to acquire one with weak or crooked limbs, but if the foal that God and your brood mare gave you is not perfect, it does not mean that its future is necessarily bleak. The genetic structure of any individual horse can supply that mysterious ability to achieve if its environment provides the opportunity for the foal to get on with growth and work.

ANTERIOR POSTERIOR DEFLECTIONS

Anterior posterior deflections of the ankle and knee are usually tendon- and muscle-related and produce problems that are the reverse of previously described medial and lateral foot deviations. Anterior (forward) deviations of the ankle are more serious for a new foal and carry with them a less favorable prognosis than do posterior (backward) deviations.

Casts and braces should never be applied to an ankle with a posterior deviation. Reduced tendon tone is the principal cause, and immobilization only weakens the involved structures. The opposite side of the coin, "knuckling over" or anterior deviation, often responds well to light braces or casts if applied specifically and only during the foal's first 24 to 48 hours. If knuckling over persists beyond this brief period, surgical intervention may be needed to correct the uneven tendon pull that causes this abnormality.

Occasionally, a condition similar to knuckling over, with the same tendon imbalance cause, is seen to affect the foal's foot. This foal travels on the toe and is unable to force the heel down to the ground. This toe-dancer posture is caused by an uneven tendon pull and gradually, yet relentlessly, develops a clubfoot. (See CONTRACTION, page 141.) Inferior check ligament desmotomy is a very satisfactory solution.

Hind-leg deviations or abnormal angulations are a common finding, especially in large foals. Although they are seen more frequently, the problems of the hind limbs are less serious than those of the forelegs. Perhaps the fact that less body weight is supported by the hind legs is a factor. The position of the fetus in the uterus, the nutrition and exercise of the mare during gestation, and, most importantly, the genetic makeup of the foal are the major causes believed to be responsible for crooked hind limbs.

The most common conditions found in the hind leg include straight stifles, sickle and curby hocks, bandylegged, cow hocks, weak or cocked ankles, and subluxation of phalanxes I and II (long and short pastern bones).

Straight stifles are found in a straight hind leg and represent a potential weakness leading to future unsoundness. This is an anatomical problem and predisposes to various forms of lamenesses. Everybody likes the appearance of a straight hind leg except equine practitioners, who are aware that a straight hind leg involves a straight stifle resulting in a strained hock. I have also found back soreness associated with this condition.

The straighter the leg, the less angulation at the stifle joint and the greater threat to future soundness. With reduced angulation between the large femur bone above and the tibia below, the patella is allowed extra movement, which causes pain and discomfort. Snapping, crackling, and even a locking of one of the three patellar ligaments may occur in straight, loose, or tight stifles. Normal growth, physical condition, and exercise will sometimes bring about increased tone and improvement.

Blistering, injections, or a simple surgical procedure called medial patellar desmotomy may be necessary for permanent improvement.

Sickle hocks and curby hocks are usually very evident immediately after birth. When viewed from the side, the foal is much taller at the withers than at

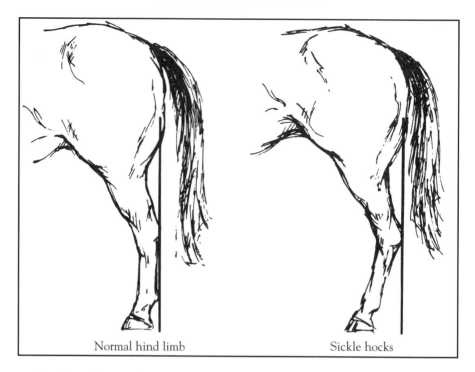

Normal hind limb   Sickle hocks

Lateral, or side view, of hind legs.

the croup, and it seems that the hind end has a difficult time following the front end. From the stifle joint on down, the hind legs are curved forward and under the foal and are shaped like the blade of a sickle—hence the name.

Sickle hocks are almost invariably accompanied by curbs, which are strains or protrusions of the planter ligament at the back and bottom of the rounded hock. Rounded hock is a general lay term describing any combination of sickle hocks, curbs, or any and all weakened standing positions of the hind leg.

It is amazing to see how much improvement the foals born with rounded hocks show by the end of a few weeks of life, and an even greater surprise to see much more improvement by the end of a few months. This is particularly gratifying because there is no specific treatment to offer. It does not take a particularly astute horseman to observe residual evidences of these early physical deviations, but most of these foals mature and become serviceable adults.

When I see a big, good-looking colt come into the world, often my momentary enthusiasm wanes when the colt stands and suddenly his rounded hocks become depressingly evident. Even though it is not a serious deterrent to his performance, this deviation forecasts an almost automatic exclusion from a future on-the-line show career. I am always pleasantly surprised when I see a large colt with clean hind legs and normal hocks. It is thought by some that large overgrown foals may be somewhat crowded in utero during the last two months of gestation, when growth of the fetus is reported to double in rate. Large feti must crowd and cramp their large hind legs up under their body. The hocks are the major joint affected, perhaps because of location on a lengthy limb.

Of course, large fillies can also arrive with crooked hind legs, but they are definitely in the minority. Gender seems to be a factor.

Other hind-leg departures are more easily seen from the rear of the foal, looking forward. This vantage point permits you to imagine a plumb line dropped to the ground from the whirlbone (tuber ischii) of each hind leg, effectively bisecting the leg and foot. A bandylegged or bowlegged foal stands with the hind feet close together and with hocks outside the plumb line. In time, with proper exercise and nutrition, one may see some very slight improvement of this condition.

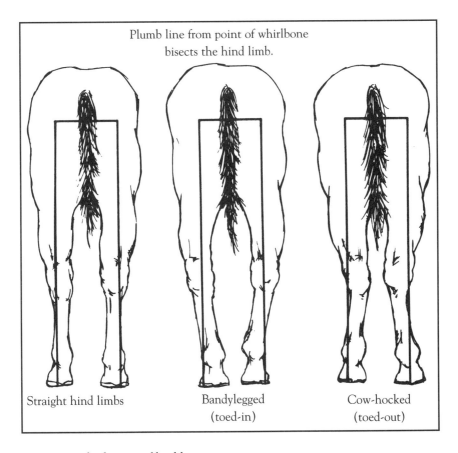

Posterior, or back view, of hind legs.

Occasionally a weak foal is seen with one bandy leg and the other leg following the contour of the curved leg in parallel fashion, as if in imitation of the deformity. These foals have swaying hindquarters that seem to defy the forces of gravity, so they stand as if on the side of a hill.

In spite of the severity of this form of limb deviation, these foals usually straighten surprisingly well. Discouraged by the newborn's appearance, inexperienced owners have suggested euthanasia, but rapid improvement soon eradicates this idea. Always remember: As long as a foal is able to get up and down to nurse, exercise, and rest, the strides he can make in musculoskeletal improvement can be fantastic. Many newborn foals that appear to be cripples do grow into useful, happy adults. It is important to seek advice from experienced horse breeders or an equine practitioner of many years.

Cow-hocked foals stand with the hind feet in a toed-out position, with the points of the hocks and the ankles falling to the inside of our imaginary plumb line. There may be some improvement with exercise, growth, and good nutrition, but this deviation will continue to plague the foal to some degree for the rest of its life.

A cow-hocked horse will brush or strike each rear ankle with the opposite foot as that leg is advanced. This problem is called *interfering* and can be the cause of intermittent lameness in a working horse. Corrective trimming or shoeing will help to alleviate the amount and severity of this self-inflicted wound. Balance the foot and simply square the toe to direct the foot to break over the center of the toe, thus directing its stride forward and straight. It does require constant shoeing care and supervision, as the limbs continue to resist change and tend to remain the same. Corrective shoeing and balancing *can* be helpful in the adult horse. In the adult horse, after balancing the hind feet, I consistently recommend a hind shoe I designed for just this condition. I request the farrier to make a medium-weight steel shoe with a squared toe, a smooth heelless inside branch, and a drawn-out trailer with a 3/8" turned heel on the outside branch. This shoe type has served many performance horses very well.

LOCKED STIFLES

Locked stifles, or upward fixation of the patella, is a quite common congenital condition. A straight hind leg predisposes the stifle to locking of the patella. Its ligaments intermittently catch onto the inside femoral trochlea, causing a locking of the leg in backward extension. Because of the obtuse angle found in straight hind legs, an imbalance exists between the stifle joint ligaments and bony elements, which allows the major patellar ligament to catch onto the bony protuberance of the femur bone and lock into extension.

Fixation of the rear leg in extension can be frightening to both the animal and the handler. Initially the animal is unable to move and then inadvertently moves, allowing the patellar ligament to slip free, relieving the horse. One or both patellas can be involved.

DANGER: In some cases, forcing the animal to back can quickly unlock the stifle. As a last resort, place one hand firmly on the stifle and push inward while the other hand lifts the leg and pulls outward. This does require strength and ability on the part of the operator, so try to arrange to have a helper or two with you.

If locking is persistent and recurrent, local injections of counter-irritants can afford temporary relief, or a clever surgical procedure called medial patellar desmotomy can provide permanent correction. The surgery is so successful and provides such comfort to the often anxious patient that I always feel badly for a horse when the owners decide against the procedure.

CONTRACTION

Contraction refers to the unnatural tendon tension exerted on the skeletal structure of young developing and growing animals. It is a devastating entity of the equine that can threaten life during fetal development or profoundly limit the ability and careers of those foals able to survive and be delivered. Fate of the fetus is greatly influenced by the degree of contraction and the developmental age when afflicted.

When one hears the term *contraction*, a contracted tendon immediately comes to mind. This is erroneous. *Contraction* is not understood and is inaccurately used today to cover a large variety of conditions with many separate and confusing causes. In the next few pages I will clarify to the best of my knowledge the various forms of contraction known to me through 38 years of equine reproductive practice. It is curious to me that this term was nonexistent 30 years ago. It seemed to suddenly appear

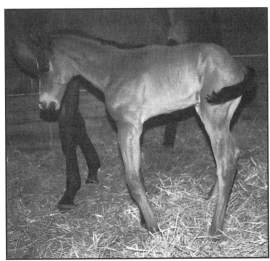

Mild contraction.

in super brood mares and well-bred foals and has since steadily increased in incidence. Someday veterinarians in equine practice will have a better understanding of this dreaded and, in my opinion, quite preventable condition.

Contraction is a generalized condition, affecting primarily the neuromuscular system and secondly the skeletal frame. Because of the relentless and unnatural pull or tension, contraction causes the bones, and especially the distal ends, to bend, twist, and become distorted. The crippling effects vary from single-foot contraction to the case of the unfortunate foal with total skeletal involvement, causing the death of the fetus.

Aborted contracted fetus.

When a fetus in utero is involved, characteristically the spinal cord, skull, and limbs become severely contracted and distorted into a mass almost unrecognizable. One consistent finding is a scoliosed (curved) spinal cord associated with contracted foals aborted or delivered. Although difficult to determine by physical examination, scoliosis of the thoracic (chest) area is believed by some researchers to exist in all foals or horses manifesting a single contracted limb. This is not to be confused with nutritional contraction, where two or more limbs are involved, and appears or develops in an older age (yearling) group.

In a truly contracted fetus, the contorted members ankylose (lock) and are rigidly fixed into position. The immovable joints and joint structures cease to develop, are incomplete, and so are never functional, regardless of remedial measures or heroic surgical attempts at restoration.

DYSTOCIA

In a near-term fetus when intrauterine death occurs and abortion is imminent, the rigid mass cannot be delivered unassisted; the only exception is the undersized fetus that succumbs early in gestation, permitting adequate passage through the mare's birth canal. Unfortunately, most cases of contraction are discovered late in gestation and more often at the time of parturition. Ninety-five percent of all difficult births (dystocias) suffered by brood mares are caused by some variation of contraction. These contracted or ankylosed foals-to-be are frequently found in aborted masses. But extreme trouble begins when an affected fetus continues to live and grow inside the uterus, with no feasible way to get out.

With the exception of a breech presentation, delivery of a normal foal in a natural method can only be achieved by the full extension of both forelegs in advance of the foal's head and long neck. Nature left no room for error here. Because of the rigidly fixed flexion of the forelimbs of a contracted foal, the overall diameter of the shoulders and thorax is greatly increased. Thus, from a purely mechanical standpoint, passage of a contracted foal or large fetus through the pelvic canal cannot be accomplished.

As the attending veterinarian, I know the frustration of finding upon examination an immovable, malpositioned, rigidly locked fetus, especially in a high-strung mare. Sedation given intravenously usually allows for reevaluation; then all hope for a live foal is crushed when neither foreleg will respond and extend into position to allow manipulation and ultimate delivery. This is an emergency!

Such impossible deliveries require a fetotomy, embryotomy, or cesarean section to remove the unyielding mass and save the mare. This is a red-alert situation, requiring total attention, energy, and all possible skills and knowledge to relieve the mare quickly but considerately. The method in which she is handled will not only be lifesaving but will greatly influence her reproductive future. Undue rough handling can injure her delicate cervix and birth canal and render her subfertile or even sterile. Either way, her immediate future hangs in the balance as she must be relieved of the foreign mass posthaste.

A fetotomy performed on the spot with expertise is acceptable, but a cesarean section is much to be preferred if a suitable equine surgery is available. As the foal is already lost, this surgical approach offers the most humane and advanced method to provide for the well-being of the mare and her reproductive future.

Once the twisted mass has been removed from the mare, by whatever method, all areas of the body and limbs will be visible and can be assessed. Varying degrees of thoracic vertebral deformities, asymmetric cranial distortions, and torticollis (wry twisted neck) are some of the common body distortions observed in these unbelievable tissue masses.

By virtue of their small size, some foals amazingly make it into the world even with the handicap of both forelegs locked at knee level. They are unable

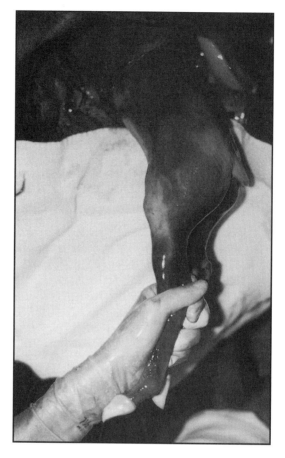

C-section.

to stand to nurse and consequently attempt to walk on their malformed, incompletely developed knees. What a tragic sight to see these otherwise apparently normal foals scrambling around searching for food and demonstrating a grim determination to survive. They invariably possess additional hidden spinal lesions and are therefore hopeless cripples. For humane reasons, euthanasia is indicated.

What causes this godless contraction? The subject is highly controversial; there is no definitive known cause. Conjecture runs rampant. Brood mares fed too well, with diets superhigh in protein and even added supplements, commonly abort or deliver dead or alive contracted foals. *I have yet to see a brood mare owned by a poor man abort a contracted foal or suffer a contraction-related dystocia.*

CLUBFOOTEDNESS

Contraction figures in many other situations as well. For instance, everyone around horses is familiar with the entity called clubfoot, seen equally in foals and adults. Clubfoot is another manifestation of tendon contraction.

This foot handicap is an insidious, hidden time bomb in the newborn foal, not revealing its crippling effects until a certain predictable timetable is fulfilled. Contraction of one foreleg is first seen at birth, or within the first few months of life. During this early postnatal period, one or infrequently both forefeet gradually assume a clubfoot appearance. Excessive heel growth with minimal toe growth occurs as a compensatory action.

Foals are not born with a clubfoot. The malshaped foot is merely the manifestation of unnatural tendon tension exerted on the skeletal structure of the leg and foot. The foot responds to the undue tendon tension and grows misshapen to accommodate the tendon imbalance. The affected tendon is the deep digital flexor, whose attachment is found on the bottom surface of the os pedis or coffin bone of the foot. The constant ten-

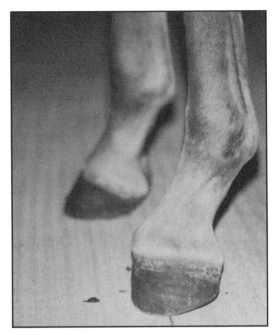

Classic clubfoot.

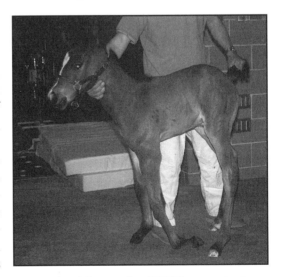

Deep digital flexor tendon (DDFT) contraction in newborn.

don pull causes the foot to be pulled backward into a flexed position, resulting in degrees of altered foot shape, from that of a toe-dancer stance to actual knuckling over.

DEEP DIGITAL FLEXOR TENDON (DDFT) CONTRACTION, OR CLUBFOOT

Most of these foals arrive at the hospital with a fore-limb hanging in a flexed position, incapable of supporting body weight and knuckled over at the ankle. If the problem is ignored, the front of the ankle soon becomes denuded since the foot is almost useless. This newborn (one to seven days old) is assisted when trying to rise and supported while nursing, and must usually be carried into the hospital.

A critical assessment of the foal's limb is now essential to obtain proper treatment. An experienced equine veterinarian is best equipped to make this decision.

If the limb of the newborn responds to manual manipulation and assumes a position of full extension, precisely at phalanx II and phalanx III, then use of casts and splints will suffice. However, when phalanx II and phalanx III resist manual extension, then true contraction of the deep digital flexor tendon is evident in the form of an ankylosis.

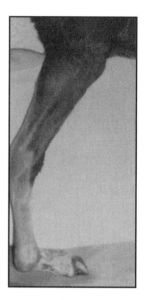

Newborn dragging fore-leg; DDFT contraction (pre-op).

Until just recently, there was no known treatment for cases of contracted tendon with ultimate clubfootedness, and thus no future for the foal. A dramatic corrective surgical procedure called inferior check ligament desmotomy is now available for these cases. Although this surgery is highly successful, it has been accepted by uninformed veterinary groups only very slowly.

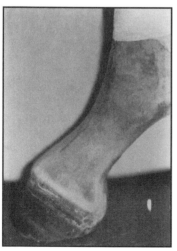

Desmotomy (transection of a ligament) is performed just below the knee and in essence lengthens the affected tendon without touching the tendon tissue. The inferior check ligament encompasses and lightly supports the deep digital tendon. By transecting the ligament, the tendon is released and lengthened by several centimeters; thus the heel can rest comfortably on the ground, and the foal can live a normal life.

Although the farm was much too far out of my usual practice area, I consented to visit because I heard about a newborn foal with a paralyzed foreleg.

Post-op, corrected clubfoot.

When I arrived I saw a 48-hour-old foal in a dusty paddock dragging one foreleg. With a closer look, I saw that the front of the affected leg was bloody and denuded from the midline cannon to the coronary band.

The old mare stood by patiently with much the same expression on her face as I felt I must have registered on mine. I was stunned!

I instructed the groom to bring the two into the barn, out of the dirt and heat. After they were placed in a stall, I cleansed the abraded tissue, applied ointment, and covered the area with a sterile pack from the veterinary unit.

This foal was suffering from deep digital flexor tendon contraction of congenital origin and would ultimately develop a clubfoot. I

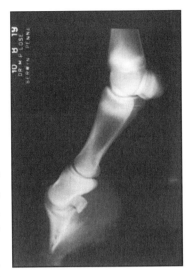

Pre-op X-ray.

arranged for transportation to my hospital and alerted the personnel to admit the mare and foal. A routine inferior check ligament desmotomy corrected the condition. This filly enjoyed a successful racing career and to my knowledge is sound and serviceable today.

This is a very successful surgery offering a total cure for clubfooted individuals or those with the potential of becoming so. It is also effective for those with various lesser degrees of contraction and associated lameness. The affected foot

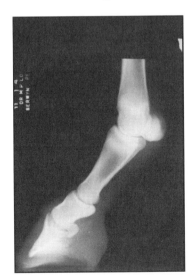

Post-op X-ray.

should be balanced immediately after surgery, with emphasis placed on maintaining a low heel for the first six weeks postoperative. Within eight to 12 weeks of the surgery, the former clubfoot will appear identical to its non-clubbed counterpart—and remain so throughout life. If not offered the surgery, the foal will perhaps hobble around on its toe, grow a high compensatory heel, and form a stubby-shaped dish-like toe. But assuredly, if the foal survives to any age, it will grow a club-shaped foot and have to not only live with this handicap but be expected to compete.

Classified as a coronopedal contraction (phalanxes II and III), this malshaped foot is caused by the relentless and ceaseless pull of the deep digital flexor tendon attached to the

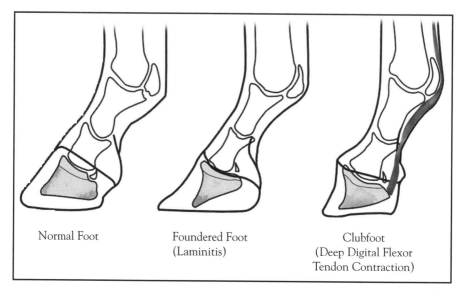

Normal Foot   Foundered Foot   Clubfoot
(Laminitis)   (Deep Digital Flexor
Tendon Contraction)

Differential diagnosis. The foal owner can make his or her own diagnosis by requesting a lateral view of the foot, pastern, and ankle view.

bottom of the os pedis or coffin bone. The backward pull on the tip of the os pedis (bone of the foot) makes the foal travel on its toe, with the heel elevated. A compensatory subluxation occurs in the front of the coronary band, causing sufficient discomfort to create lameness. The tip of the os pedis is forced downward and backward into a position that requires it to support the entire weight of the forelimb, similar to a human walking on very high heels or the tip of the toes.

With this painful, stilted gait and continuous internal pressure, the naturally tough and durable hoof tissue soon thins and gives way at the toe. A separation (or opening) develops, carrying with it the threat of infection and even sometimes fatal osteomyelitis.

NOTE: It is my strong conviction that clubfootedness is of hereditary or congenital origin and will breed true. A mare or stallion showing any degree or tendency toward clubfootedness should never be bred, or the foal will more than likely have a contracted DDFT and develop a clubfoot.

During my youth, with my narrow point of view, I watched from the sidelines many horses with varying degrees of foot contraction compete well at the races and other forms of competition. How much or how far could these courageous individuals have achieved given a normal angled foot?

There are many known Thorough-bred champions who possess the gene for contraction; hence, clubfootedness is destined to continue to plague our better horse families.

In the past, breeders were left with little solution to the contraction deformity. Naturally, horse breeders preferred a runner with any form of mal-shaped foot, rather than a perfect footed non-runner.

In 1975, as an equine veterinarian, with the knowledge of other researchers, I began performing a modified approach of inferior check ligament desmotomy for the correction of increased DDFT tension, which corrected and permanently cured the frustrating, crippling clubfoot.

The skeletal axis and foot angulation realign themselves for the life of the individual. To witness what this surgery can accomplish, and allow these wonderful well-bred foals to grow up and achieve their goals in life, was and still is life-fulfilling for this horse doctor.

Inferior check ligament desmotomy is just a little short of miraculous!

NUTRITION-RELATED CONTRACTION

Another form of contraction rapidly increasing in incidence and creating alarm among horse breeders is nutrition-related contraction. This is a separate entity, in my opinion, and should not be confused with the clubfoot syndrome. This type of contraction is thought to be acquired through external environmental influences, yet can be strongly enhanced by a familial predisposition. For example, certain Thoroughbred families seem to carry a high incidence of nutrition-related contraction and, given the proper circumstances, any large, fast-growing, leggy individual appears to be a prime subject.

Onset of symptoms is consistently associated with certain older age groups and fluctuations in and particularly excesses in nutrition. Nutritional imbalances can easily occur, especially during the supervulnerable fast-growth periods that all colts and fillies encounter and endure. Nutritional imbalances are thought to be created by feeding supplements and overfeeding of protein. Nutritional contraction is commonly found in barns housing very expensive, well-bred thrifty young horses, from 18 to 22 months of age.

Provide an overabundance of rich nutrition with predisposed fast-growing individuals, and nutritional contraction will often be observed with growth spurts in the skeletal structure. This scenario creates an imbalance. The bottom line in nutritional contraction is that the growth rate of the bone outstrips that of the tendon, and a painful imbalance quickly develops.

Unlike the clubfoot syndrome, this is not seen at birth but is observed predictably in older foals during distinct growth time frames. The salient

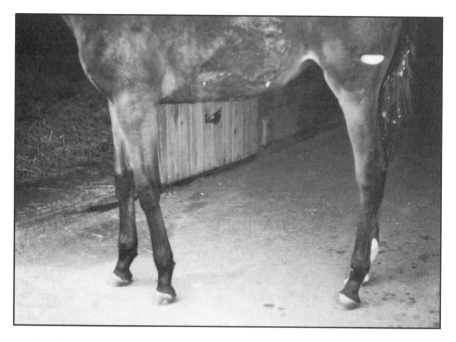

Rapid onset of symptoms.

symptom is a flexor deformity of the metacar-pophalangeal joint (ankle) that produces a stilty, trembling, painful stance with ankles knuckled or cocked forward. Initially both forelegs are affected, and ultimately the hind legs may become involved. Often all four limbs are affected, especially if it goes untreated.

Nutritional contraction differs from other contractions in five distinct areas: Nutritional contraction is caused by growth rate in conjunction with nutrition; the affected tendon is the superficial flexor; the joint involved is the ankle; and all four limbs are affected. And in select cases it can be reversed, with modern veterinary practice and good horse husbandry.

To repeat, it is not seen until 12 to 18 months of age, although I have observed the ankles of several younger, even sucklings,

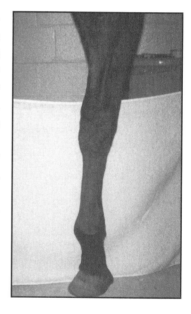

Cocked ankle and knee.

begin to knuckle over at five to six months or close to conventional weaning time. Again, these are periods of nutritional change and notable increased growth rate. Interestingly, all foals experiencing this problem were thrifty and possessed greedy appetites.

In nutritional contraction, one often sees a fine yearling, ready to be sold, marketed, or broken, knuckling or cocking over at the knees or ankles. As the contraction progresses, the animal typically has difficulty supporting its weight in an erect standing position; its reluctance to move is only too evident. These yearlings show a desire to get down and rest; it then becomes difficult for them to regain their feet. Tremors, with painful instability, are frequently seen in their deformed and weakened limbs.

The excessive and unbalanced pull of the superficial digital flexor tendon causes the ankle to flex forward and at the same time causes the pastern to straighten. Concurrent flexion of the knees is thought to be a reciprocal or compensatory action. Neuromuscular involvement originating in the thoracic spine, perhaps as scoliosis or from a hereditary or congenital source, is suspect. The more popularly accepted cause is the rapid spurt of bone growth,

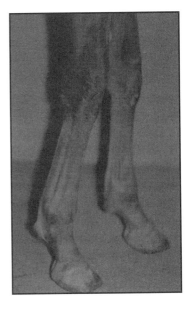

Sprung knees, low heels, and long toes. SFT primarily.

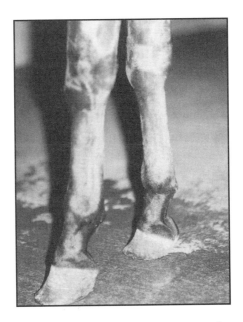

Both DDFT and SFT involvement; upright pasterns, stilty gait, and high heels. Combination of both flexor tendons.

due to excessive dietary protein, that has outstripped the growth rate of the muscles and tendons, especially in length. Increasing incidence of this nutrition-related contraction has been found in cases where excessive protein is fed, along with mineral and vitamin additives, in order to encourage rapid growth and development—perhaps to grow a superfoal!

Occasionally both flexor tendons are involved. (See the photograph above.)

NUTRITION-RELATED EPIPHYSITIS, APPLE ANKLES, AND ENLARGED JOINTS

The epiphyseal line, or growth zone, is located above the knee and is very sensitive to excessive nutrition and exercise. Large well-bred individuals during precise growth periods seem most vulnerable. Although this malady is not fully understood, epiphysitis develops as a painful enlargement above the knees, along with ankles that appear apple-shaped.

I have seen both knees and ankles affected during rapid growth periods in young predisposed horses. Surprisingly, this condition can be arrested with stall rest and the near-starvation diet described below. Under equal conditions, some individuals suffer tendon contraction, while other individuals develop epiphysitis, apple ankles, and enlarged joints.

Often when I am first called to see an affected yearling, the owner's concern is with the hindquarters. Their apparent weakness is in fact an attempt on the part of the suffering young horse to shift some body weight off the painful forelegs by sliding the hind legs forward. This maneuver creates a humpbacked individual. These yearlings experience difficulty in getting up; once the forefeet are extended, they are hesitant to continue to rise. They may remain in a "sitting-dog" position before finally rising to their feet. This gives the erroneous impression that the hind legs are the primary cause of the difficulty.

Since many cases were being euthanized and some insurance companies were actually accepting contraction as just cause for humane destruction, a few frustrated practitioners tried an unconventional and purely unprofessional approach. The common denominators were high nutrition, expensive supplements, and excessive protein intake.

Although they lacked a scientifically documented cause for this devastatingly painful and life-threatening condition, they decided that at the earliest sign or onset of any symptom—attitude, tremors, or any instability of the foreleg—the commonly well-bred, young, usually leggy, and fast-growing individual would be immediately placed on a near-starvation diet. This regime requires total dedication by all involved with the patient. The program must not be violated for any reason.

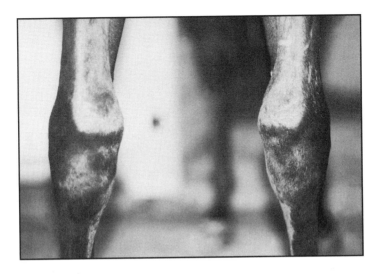

Classic epiphysitis.

Free-choice water, salt, and hay basically constitute the meager diet. The water should be clean and fresh, the salt lick freely available, and the hay straight timothy. Clean, dust-free horse hay is ideal, with or without color. Confinement in a quiet stall is mandatory to allow for needed rest and restricted use of the painful, distorted limbs and tender feet.

Weight loss in young growing horses is dramatic in response to the light diet, especially during the first week or 10 days. And then, almost as insidiously as the beginning signs appeared, the symptoms of discomfort begin to wane. Brighter eyes, expression, and appetite—and less time lying down in the stall—are the first indications of a turnaround in the severity of tendon pull. Then the animal shows willingness to walk more freely, making more frequent turns within the confinement of the stall. Usually, at about the third week on the starvation diet, less knuckling and steadier ankles will produce a reliable stance and an even greater willingness to walk around the stall.

So the owner must keep the faith and maintain the austere feeding schedule; the regime should be continued for an additional two weeks after the initial signs of symptom reversal and relief of discomfort.

Although it borders on the cruel, this method has produced exciting results, with total remission in a large percentage of the cases. I have known survivors of this regimen to quickly regain their weight loss and to remain symptomless, serviceably sound, and relatively healthy throughout their lives.

Of course, not all cases of nutritional contraction respond favorably; those that do not are candidates for corrective surgery. Called a superior check ligament desmotomy, the surgery of choice for nutritional contraction should not be confused with the one described for clubfoot correction. This check ligament, located above the knee and holding the superficial digital flexor tendon in a secure and tense position, is transected. Its release causes an actual lengthening of the involved tendon without touching the tendon per se. This additional length of tendon allows the ankle to relax and return to its normal posterior position; in essence, the pain subsides with the realignment of the normal leg axis. The superior check ligament desmotomy, in essence, lengthens the superficial flexor tendon and parallels the deep digital flexor tendon desmotomy for correction of clubfootedness.

WARNING: If you suspect that your foal is a candidate for contraction, carefully monitor the danger periods, such as immediately after weaning and from 18 to 22 months of age. Do not allow concentrates in the diet to exceed 6 quarts daily after weaning, and 12 quarts daily during the 18- to 22-month period; protein content should not exceed 12 percent. Roughage during these danger periods should consist of timothy hay with some green color, and not alfalfa or any legume hay, as normally suggested at other times.

There are those within the profession who honestly feel that contraction in its various forms initially begins in the brood mare who is overfed and bombarded with every vitamin and mineral supplement during gestation. Until scientific research accurately defines the various causes of and cures for contraction, the subject and its treatment will remain highly controversial. In my opinion, until we discontinue breeding horses with obvious contraction or contraction tendencies and cease the mindless overfeeding of concentrates in order to produce a superhorse, this destructive process will surely continue. Only through education can this scourge be overcome.

I have never seen a nutritionally contracted foal in a poor man's barn, where obviously no expensive feed additives were used. This problem suddenly appeared in the early Sixties when horse people believed that they could grow a "superfoal." All pregnant mares were immediately overfed, and I began to see a form of fetal contraction that caused traumatic dystocias, including contracted limbs and generalized musculoskeletal disorders. These distorted contractions were discovered both before and after birth in various forms.

Rupture of the common digital extensor tendon is frequently found accompanying forelimb contraction. This presents itself as a fluidy pouch found directly over one knee. Do *not* confuse this condition with "over at the knees."

SPINAL DEFORMITIES

When foals are born with contracted forelegs and normally shaped feet, their inability to support body weight is very noticeable; however, the cause of contraction and primary lesion is very obscure. Etiologic lesions are believed by some researchers to be located in the thoracic vertebrae and closely associated with spinal-column deviations, such as scoliosis or lordosis. When extensively involved, these spinal aberrations are easily identified. But beware of the varying minor degrees that are so destructive and yet so insidious. Scoliosis (curvature) and lordosis (swayback) are commonly difficult to diagnose in the young foal; consequently, most cases are found at postmortem.

HERNIAS

Hernias are defined as a protrusion of an organ, or any tissue, through an abdominal opening. They occur either accidentally in nature or from an enlarged natural opening in the abdominal wall. The emerging organ or tissue is usually enveloped within the intact peritoneum and covered with the skin.

Foal hernias are not commonly found at birth, but become obvious within the first 24 to 40 hours of life. Umbilical and scrotal hernias are the two most common in the foal and are considered to be of hereditary or congenital origin. A large percentage of the defects noticed shortly after birth will correct themselves by weaning time without any treatment.

All hernias have a toughened ring of abdominal tissue (an "escape door") through which the intestines prolapse. The ring is located at the neck of the hernial sac and is usually smaller in circumference. The sac is formed by the peritoneum, a durable grayish white glistening membrane lining the inner abdominal wall, and it is pushed out the hernial ring by the escaping intestines. The sac envelops and holds the hernial contents intact.

WARNING: All hernial sacs containing intestinal material represent a potential threat of strangulation. Once diagnosed, strangulation is a life-threatening condition requiring emergency surgical intervention and correction. When the contents of the herniated sac either twist or become crowded or entrapped, the ring constricts on the tissue, and the circulation is promptly compromised. Pain is immediately evidenced, tissue swells, and strangulation becomes a frightening reality.

Prognosis depends upon the length of intestine involved and the amount of damage sustained by the delicate intestinal-tract serosal covering from the trauma and diminished blood supply. The most critical criterion is the length of time from the onset of symptoms to time of surgery.

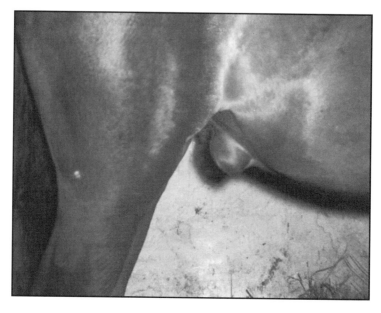

Umbilical hernia.

Strangulation can occur at any time, without any advance warning signs. This is why I heartily respect all hernias and do not rest fully until each is appropriately amended. When a hernia is discovered, it is wise to have your veterinarian assess the offending mass to determine the size, whether a loop of intestine is present or not, and the risk involved. Skillful palpation can determine the ring size and distinguish a reducible from an irreducible hernia.

TWO TYPES OF HERNIAS

A reducible hernia is one that responds to skilled and careful manual reduction. It may still represent a potential problem if it becomes twisted inside and suddenly entraps. An irreducible hernia, caused by either the development of adhesions or a twisted or entrapped loop of intestine, is one that requires emergency surgical intervention. Surgery is the only method of preventing the onset of peritonitis, which is almost always lethal.

THREE HERNIA LOCATIONS

An umbilical hernia is usually, in a colt or filly, recognized as a small protruding sac hanging from the abdominal wall near the navel. It is clearly visible to all.

A scrotal hernia affecting colts, on the other hand, is well hidden, high up between the hind legs, and is not as easily discovered. A loop of intestine slips down through the inguinal ring beside the testicular cord and becomes entrapped in the scrotal sac. A number of these are present at birth. There are, of course, those that, after professional assessment, require prompt surgical correction to avoid strangulation and illness, but generally I have learned to sit quietly by and observe them as they efficiently correct themselves within a few days, needing no human intervention.

Abdominal hernias, hernia-like protrusions occurring in the abdomen and in various places other than in the navel or scrotal areas, are of traumatic origin and should be seen by a veterinarian for an accurate diagnosis and prognosis.

WARNING: Most foal hernias carry a good prognosis if managed properly. Early correction, shortly after recognition and well in advance of complications, will prove the efficient course. However, do not allow anyone other than a qualified surgeon to attempt repair of a hernia. Do not permit any form of haphazard corrective device or material, such as tape, gauze, clamps, string, wire, belly bands, etc., to be used. These contraptions are not only unsuccessful, but they also truly represent a hazard to the foal's life!

DEFECTIVE GUTTURAL POUCH

The guttural pouch is a large sac interposed in the eustachian tube, which connects the middle ear with the pharynx. On either side of the pharyngeal wall is a flap-like valve which opens wide with each respiration, admitting air into the eustachian tube and the guttural pouch. The function of the guttural pouch is not fully understood, but it is thought to have a bearing on equilibrium and even on hearing.

In older horses, the guttural pouch frequently becomes infected and inflamed, and sometimes distended with fluid, pus, or just plain air, in a condition called tympany. Pharyngitis, laryngitis, and all forms of infection can easily gain access to the eustachian tubes through the orifices in the side walls of the pharynx.

Foals seldom suffer from ascending infections in the guttural pouch, but do quite frequently develop tympany. In this special instance, tympany means "air-filled," and foals who suffer from it are found with one or both guttural pouches distended with air. Tympany of the guttural pouch is a condition of congenital or hereditary origin. Air inadvertently gains entrance through a malfunctioning flap of soft tissue that is positioned on the side wall of the pharynx and covers the eustachian tube; this tissue sometimes acts only as a one-way valve. The flap traps air entering the pouch and causes it to distend. Respiratory infection with

Tympanitis   Strangles (*Strep. equi*) (various sites)

Tympanitis vs. strangles, differential diagnosis.

pharyngitis, strenuous coughing, or most likely a foal's panicky screaming for its mother will cause air entrapment, if such a hereditary or congenital predisposition exists.

I have seen young foals under stress or fright suddenly manifest guttural pouches so distended with air that their faces and necks were physically distorted. Although it is a painless condition, some younger foals seem distressed and uncomfortable. The foals whom I have attended were asymptomatic until the circumstance developed that allowed air to enter and become entrapped. The sudden onset of swelling in the parotid area—which extends from the base of the ear to the angle of the lower jaw and under the mandible—closely resembles a case of strangles.

Fear of strangles is allayed quickly when the swelling is touched. The underlying structures are soft, cool to the touch, and have the unmistakable feel of a partially inflated small balloon. The foals are not sick, have no elevation of body temperature, and do not show any sign of discomfort; thus tympany is the diagnosis. Conversely, the three salient symptoms listed above for tympany are always present in strangles.

Treatment

A conservative method to achieve temporary relief is to introduce a tiny catheter through the slit-like orifice under guidance of a fiberoptic scope, thus allowing a great rush of trapped air to escape. Simultaneously external swellings subside. But when an individual foal has recurring tympany, surgical correction of the one-way valve flaps is indicated. This allows air to move freely in and out of the eustachian tube and guttural pouch.

One of my favorite stories involves the first true case of tympanitis I ever saw in practice. I learned as a student that veterinarians were expected to maintain a professional attitude and conduct, and by all means remain calm and reserved, projecting an air of strength to others. Well, this day I lost all composure.

The owners were quite upset to find their foal with huge swelling below the ears and around the throat area. Was it suffocating or strangulating? Could it be strangles? I rushed into the stall, and the foal scampered quickly away, perky as ever. When my hand finally touched the enlarged areas, they were soft, cool, and painless. You can imagine my total relief! Body temperature, respiration, and heart rate were normal.

The small foal had air trapped in both guttural pouches; it was not dreadfully sick with strangles, the feared infection caused by *Streptococcus equi*. It was a simple case of tympanitis, and when given a few days of rest, it resolved itself.

WOBBLES (ATAXIA, OR INCOORDINATION)

Wobbles (equine ataxia, or equine incoordination) is usually seen in young horses from 16 to 28 months of age. Wobbles has also been diagnosed in foals, although only rarely; it is then referred to as foal ataxia. The onset can be either sudden or gradual and is characterized by a wobbly and in some cases uncontrollable hind-leg gait with a clumsy attitude. Once you have seen a classic case, it is not difficult to recognize the loose, free-swinging, swaying gait. Horses so afflicted appear to be relaxed, even uninhibited, and their actions can be compared with those of an inebriated human. Commonly found in young, fast-growing horses, and more often affecting colts than fillies, *wobbles* is a fatal condition in the equine. Recognition is difficult early in the development of this condition and in individuals involved to a lesser degree. However, foal ataxia is progressive, and symptoms soon become intense and extensive. The hind legs are first to be affected; they swing outward in a characteristic staggering fashion, portraying quite well the clinical picture of the word "wobbles." This entity, with all of its abruptness, is actually an insidious condition that develops slowly and then appears without warning. This is the classic wobbler syndrome.

Currently, we understand the cause of wobbles to be the compression of the spinal cord by the bony vertebral column. Lesions develop in the cervical (neck) area of the vertebral column and are commonly found involving the third through the sixth cervical vertebrae. The soft and sensitive spinal cord, full of nerve tracts, is infringed upon by the hard bony vertebrae that under normal conditions surround and protect the cord. For some unknown reason—either trauma, nutrition, or heredity—the vertebrae shift physically, or else the canal through which the cord passes is of insufficient size, perhaps from growth changes; compression of the soft cord results. Nerve fibers and tracts are literally pinched and compressed with subsequent tissue reaction, leading to inflammation with eventual necrosis (cell death). Nerve tracts die, thus nerve impulses cease flowing to precise areas. Nerve impulses to the extremities, especially the hind limbs, are compromised, and this results in degrees of ataxia (leg and body control loss) and paresis (reduced sensitivity)—hence the wobbling gait.

To repeat, classic wobbler syndrome is seen only in young, fast-growing animals, commonly colts, within a specific age group.

Many causes for hind-leg ataxia have been proposed. Popular theories include heredity or congenital origin and traumatic stress to the

Ataxia of the hind legs.

neck during rough or disciplinary handling, especially in long-necked horses, notoriously so predisposed. At present there is no known treatment for classic wobbles.

Although empirical in nature, oral heavy doses of anthelmintics with massive doses of trimethoprim-sulfonamide plus some carefully selected steroids, have been associated with the only known regression of symptoms in some cases.

To predict the course of the disease is easy, but to foresee the rate of progressively irreversible change is difficult. Some animals are rapidly affected, becoming prostrate within days, whereas others may stagger around the paddock for several weeks before advanced symptoms dictate euthanasia. Rate of deterioration depends upon the severity and location of spinal cord compression and/or degeneration.

PARASITE-CAUSED ATAXIA

Internal migrating larvae are another suspected cause of ataxia in the equine. Amazingly, an internal parasite—a gastrointestinal nematode—escapes its conventional tissue in the body and inadvertently burrows into the cerebrospinal tissue and ultimately dies, causing an inflammatory reaction. A "foreign body" reaction results, and degenerative changes follow. I am convinced that parasites are the cause of idiopathic (unexplained) wobbles more often than is ever recognized or suspected. Differential diagnosis is difficult and can only be confirmed at autopsy.

LIVE VACCINE CAUSES OF ATAXIA

It seems only proper to mention here that a new form of ataxia, one associated with the use of certain viral vaccines, has emerged in our young horses. Many affected horses suddenly develop an unsteady gait and a loss in body and leg control; they evidence intermittent dragging and body swaying. They appear to be pain free, much as those who suffer the classic wobbler disease. The symptoms are clear, but the cause is obscure; the only suspect is use of live viral vaccines and perhaps the combination of several vaccines into a one-dose form. Much research is sorely needed in the field of viral vaccines and their use in the equine.

CHRONIC ARTHRITIC CAUSE OF ATAXIA

Older horses suffer degrees of ataxia in quite a different fashion from that of the classic wobbler. The condition is not usually fatal, and the horses develop a low-grade ataxia and adjust and survive over a longer period of time. Deviations in gait, with visible swaying, are commonly observed. Some older horses continue to function in a limited way, while many others are no longer useful. Degenerative changes develop in various sites of the spinal cord, but the area most affected is the lumbar section of the vertebral column. These chronic, irreversible, perhaps osteoarthritic changes and their effects are reflected clinically. This process differs from the classic ataxia seen in young horses because it frequently seems to become arrested, even to become static at times. I have treated some old fox-hunters that evidenced a sloppy, unsteady gait, yet continued to serve for many years, although at a somewhat less efficient level. And then again, I have known some old brood mares that consistently swayed and staggered and yet routinely produced a healthy foal every year.

NOTE: Sometimes, when I am called to examine a horse that is unfamiliar to me, while listening to the heart and lungs I seem to sense an ever-so-slight swaying body movement. This movement, in combination with the seemingly ceaseless replacement of all four feet, is a condition that should never be overlooked. When these horses are asked to move out for a soundness check, they invariably exhibit some degree of ataxia. Unfortunately, this constitutes an unsoundness.

Intensive research with some experimental surgery is currently being conducted to seek a treatment for this fatal entity in young horses. I have learned to expect and have witnessed an increase in the incidence of wobblers in specific equine families, as one would anticipate with any disease for which hereditary influences are suspected as a factor.

OSTEOCHONDRITIS DISSECANS (OCD)

Osteochrondritis dissicans produces joint lesions in foals. Commonly found in the stifle, hock, fetlock, and shoulder joints, slight joint enlargement and lameness is first noticed at seven or eight weeks of age. Definitive diagnosis usually presents a challenge to the equine veterinarian.

OCD is a failure of the joint cartilage to mature and develop properly into normal cartilage. It is characterized by roughed areas and cystic types of painful lesions in the articular cartilages that lead to erosion of the joint surfaces.

Diagnosis requires well-defined radiographs and a skilled person for interpretation. All conservative treatments have been unsatisfactory, and the diagnosis remains guarded to poor. Arthroscopic surgery has given some hope and continues to be explored. Although the cause of this dreaded condition remains unknown, nutritional imbalances and strong familial influences remain suspect.

Treatment

Timely IV injections of hyaluronic acid with IM injections of glycosaminoglycan (Adequan) combined with oral glycosaminoglycan (Synoflex, Flex-Free, and Cosequin) are a current trend among researchers. Clinically, I have confirmed excellent results with early treatment of OCD cases. Unfortunately, it is quite costly.

Favorable results have encouraged authorities; however, early diagnosis combined with strict scheduling is imperative.

In my practice, I have found a higher incidence of OCD in horse farms that emphasized growing a superior young horse. Overnutrition is suspect.

Perhaps, when considering the similarities and overall symptoms, OCD should be classified with contraction, limb deformities, epiphysitis, and apple ankles.

RETAINED TESTICLES

Retained testicles or cryptorchidism is failure, at the alleged proper time, of both testicles to descend into the externally located scrotal sac, the normal position and location for optimal fertility. When both testicles are retained, the animal is sterile, and although it appears as a gelding, it does not consistently behave as one, especially when in the company of other horses.

When only one testicle descends, the condition is referred to as monorchidism. The retained testicle can vary in location from well within the abdomen to just inside the internal inguinal ring, or just lower, inside the inguinal canal proper and down as far as the external ring. Regardless of location and degree, a retained testicle is always defective in development, somewhat smaller, softer, visibly imperfect, and nonviable in comparison with normally descended functional testicles. The individual with one descended testicle is indeed fertile and will, if permitted, consistently produce monorchid foals.

This hereditary or congenital defect is not an uncommon finding and is frequently encountered by veterinarians when castration time arrives.

I see many newborn colts arrive in the world with both testicles normally well descended into their scrotal sacs. The descent occurs during the last third of the gestation period, during fetal development. Within a few days of birth, the testes disappear back into the abdomen to grow, develop, and mature in the warmer temperature in the abdomen. Most colts' testicles have permanently descended by the time they are yearlings, but some individuals may approach their second year before both are permanently located in the scrotum.

In the case of an outstanding colt with show-ring or breeding potential, good nutrition and plenty of exercise are essential. The owner must have an abundance of patience while waiting nervously for the testicle or testicles to appear. Otherwise, prompt and complete castration is the most satisfactory solution. Some of these animals, especially those in training, suffer silently. A colt with a partially retained or low retained testicle is often referred to as a rig, or high flanker. These conditions are at times the hidden cause of many obscure a symmetric hind-leg or gait problems, reluctance to perform, or even outright soreness. After surgical correction, these horses quite often fulfill their roles as useful individuals.

ABDOMINAL RETENTION OF TESTES

Although abdominal retention of the testes is of hereditary origin, the higher temperature sustained by the immature testes while in the abdomen, in contrast to the appreciably cooler temperature in the scrotum, must be considered. Any prolonged time during which the testicles remain in the abdomen, or any delay in reaching the scrotum, their normal habitat, may in fact be responsible for arresting testicular development.

Arrested testicles cannot produce spermatozoa, but are capable of producing the hormone testosterone, responsible for sexual aggressiveness (libido). At times, undescended testes can secrete excessive amounts of the male hormone, which can stimulate nervousness, irritability, and increased libido, resulting in a subtle but hazardous problem of tractability and management. It is not unusual to see erratic behavior and undue aggressiveness, even to the point of viciousness, in cases of abdominal retention of the testicle.

As a rule, treatment has been unsuccessful. Hormone therapy has proved to be of little or no value. The use of a testicular prosthesis, for cosmetic purposes, is unsportsmanlike, unethical, and detrimental to the betterment of any breed. Prompt castration is the only honorable and satisfactory treatment.

ALERT: In my practice I have witnessed not only irresponsible but imprudent procedures in the management of animals with genetic reproductive defects. Many horses that appear to be geldings externally are referred to veterinarians because of their aggressive or bizarre behavior. Upon examination, these "geldings" prove to possess a retained testicle that was irresponsibly ignored when a careless castration singularly removed only the one obvious and readily accessible testicle. This is shameful conduct.

To diagnose a cryptorchid or monorchid colt is relatively easy, based simply on the visible absence of the testicle, or by palpation of the scrotum and inguinal canal. However, the situation changes abruptly when a definitive diagnosis is required in a "questionable gelding." Through their unacceptable behavior, these "geldings" commonly and justifiably attract the attention and suspicions of new owners. These owners are then faced with the expense of abdominal surgery or the nuisance and danger of handling an unsatisfactory gelding.

Of first consideration is the cause of the gelding's strange behavioral antics. Are his problems due to a defective testicle; has he a vice, discipline problems, or is he just an ill-tempered horse?

When I examine the possibly false or incomplete gelding, I first ascertain whether the testes is indeed present; if so, I determine where it is located, its size, shape, and consistency. The four steps to a definitive diagnosis are:

1. Complete physical examination, including examination for evidence of prior skin incisions over the scrotal area.

2. Local palpation of the inguinal region, including the external ring, inguinal canal, and internal inguinal ring.

3. Rectal examination and abdominal exploration. At this time, a skilled operator can determine not only the location, but the size, shape, and consistency of the testes, which helps determine the optimal route and approach of surgery.

4. If a question still remains, either from negative palpation results or the animal's intractability during physical examination, a laboratory test is available. A positive diagnosis of the presence of testicular tissue is based on a dramatic elevation of testosterone in response to an intravenous injection of human chorionic gonadotropin hormone. Your

veterinarian will inject 10,000 IU of HCG hormone IV, wait 15 to 20 minutes, withdraw a blood sample, and submit it to the laboratory for analysis of testosterone content.

Although I must admit that I have consistently relied upon rectal palpation for diagnosis, it is comforting to know that this laboratory procedure is available.

Castration is necessary to transform these horses into safe, dependable, and useful geldings. Safety is important to all concerned, but it is also vital to prevent a stallion with a genital imperfection from breeding, thus perpetuating this defect.

NEONATAL SEIZURES

Seizures in neonatal foals are caused by defects in brain tissue electrical activity. Symptoms range from subtle to full-blown convulsions. Within the first few hours, the neonate is often found down in the straw or out on the ground thrashing, twitching, quite unable to rise.

Seizures may begin with simple eye twitching or abnormal eye movement, incoordinated muscle thrashing, and teeth grinding. This sight can be unnerving for the inexperienced horse owner, and panic is commonplace.

Treatment should never be attempted in a cold, dirty barn. After receiving emergency treatment, all seizure foals should, if at all possible, be admitted to the closest ICU unit in a veterinary medical university for needed around-the-clock care.

Hypoxia and ischemia (reduced oxygen or blood flow to brain tissue) are the most common causes of foal seizures. It is believed that undue pressure on the brain tissue is most often associated with a difficult delivery (dystocia) or any birth process that is prolonged. I have witnessed foal seizures with the entities called neonatal maladjustment syndrome and a variety of septicemias. Although the prognosis is always considered poor, a few cases survive with electrolytic fluid IV and intense antibiotic therapy, plus dedicated personnel. For the foal's comfort, tranquilizers may be helpful, but only on the advice of your veterinarian. Blood pressure must be monitored.

Although treatment must be initiated immediately, a specific and differential diagnosis can be achieved with a little time and study. In order to exclude all other similar conditions, a complete neurologic examination is essential, along with a CBC, differential, complete blood chemistry, radiographs of the foal's brain and skull, and perhaps a cerebral spinal analysis.

Treatment of choice consists of Valium (diazepam), repeated as needed. To help control seizures, the use of phenobarbital is often considered. (*Caution:* Slow IV administration is advised when using phenobarbital.) Dilantin may also be added if seizures persists. Dimethylsulfoxide (DMSO) is a known diuretic that reduces brain tissue edema and has a protective cellular effect on the central nervous system (CNS). Its use remains controversial, while its effects are profoundly satisfactory in many cases. Banamine IV is useful, but please avoid the use of acepromazine and Rompun. Constantly monitor blood pressure parameters.

Neonatal foal seizures can easily be confused with idiopathic epilepsy (see below).

FOAL EPILEPSY

Foal epilepsy is mainly seen in Arabian foals from birth through one year of age. Although it is not understood, it is thought to be of congenital or hereditary origin. The brain tissue in these foals seems supersensitive to any change as such—metabolic, toxin, infection, sepsis, etc.

Some fortunate foals, with time, seem to outgrow the epilepsy, especially when maintained on anticonvulsant medicine. This entity has been correlated with the human juvenile epilepsy syndrome. Unfortunately, many affected foals do not survive.

Drugs, specific for seizure prevention, combined with religious nursing care, can prevent additional injury to the already sensitive brain tissue. It is imperative that a conscientious caretaker prevent additional trauma during an epileptic fit by providing protection in the way of blankets, padding, and manual cradling of the affected foal.

Phenobarbital is the drug of choice. Dosage must be carefully monitored and care must be taken to avoid rapid withdrawal, as resumption of seizures may occur. Listen to your veterinarian.

Prognosis is fair to guarded. Long-term therapy has been reported as successful in some cases.

NEONATAL NARCOLEPSY

Neonatal narcolepsy is a rare condition called sleep or fainting episodes. Foals suddenly become unconscious for a few minutes, fall to the ground, evince rapid eye movement, and are unable to rise. Between attacks, these affected foals appear normal.

There is no recommended treatment and the prognosis is unpredictable. I have never experienced narcolepsy in my practice.

NEONATAL ISOERYTHROLYSIS OR JAUNDICE

Jaundiced (isohemolytic icteric) foals or neonatal isoerythrolysis is a hemolytic anemia of newborn foals that develops as a result of the mare's production of

Proper management procedure for isoerythrolysis.

antibodies during pregnancy that war against the red blood cells of her own fetus. The foal's blood type is actually incompatible with that of its dam, and the fetus can, in some instances, act as a foreign body within its own mother. A strange twist of nature's usual efficiency! If the fetus inherits its dam's blood type, all is well. If it inherits its sire's incompatible blood type, the fetus is auto-matically foreign to its own mother. As a result, the foal's red blood cells trigger the dam to begin production of antibodies in her own blood serum specifically designed to destroy her foal's red blood cells!

This potentially tragic condition is analogous to the Rh factor in human pregnancies. Although similar in some areas, in the horse it differs greatly by its quiescent and insidious development during gestation, only to explode with the foal's first few swallows of the mother's milk, immediately postpartum.

If the foal continues ingesting the poisonous milk produced by its mother, the foal will suddenly weaken and be found down in the bedding, disinterested in or incapable of rising. With a rapid respiration and heart rate, pale or yellow (icteric) oral mucosa (gums), and a subnormal temperature, it will rapidly deteriorate, if untreated, and death will ensue in one to three days. Yellow (jaundiced) membranes indicate the destruction and death of red blood cells (erythrocytes) and the hemoglobin content: thus the name neonatal isoerythrolysis.

Fortunately, nothing happens during gestation, as no transplacental exchange exists in the mare; so, excluding other problems, a normal, healthy foal is delivered by a normal-appearing healthy mare. Her colostrum is loaded with lethal antibodies ready for ingestion by her foal.

Many mares are healthy and vigorous during gestation, showing no sign of this hidden condition. In young mares who have never experienced an incompatible blood type and never produced a jaundiced foal, this condition is especially insidious. Without a history to serve as an alert, the first jaundiced foal a mare produces is often lost. An alert, experienced attendant could possibly recognize the symptoms and summon the veterinarian in time.

Contrary to what we know about the highly selective placental barrier, some affected mares do exhibit vague clinical signs during gestation; they then abort or deliver a dead or very weak foal. Some ambiguous symptoms usually seen later in gestation are depression, progressive slowness of gait, a detectable yellowish tint in the mucous membranes (ocular, oral, and vaginal), and inconsistent edematous areas over the entire body. These signs, considered collectively, reflect the dynamic internal conflict taking place.

NOTE: It is my contention that every foal should be given a "quick screening" test at birth to rule out the possibility of a mother with isoimmunization. Since this disorder definitely carries the implication of loss of the foal, a quick, simple, on-the-spot test has been devised by equine obstetricians. One drop of blood obtained as the umbilical cord ruptures and one drop of colostrum from the mare's udder should be mixed and applied to a clean glass surface. After a moment or two, the mixture should be checked for gross clumping of red blood cells, which is a positive finding. A pink homogeneous solution is a negative finding. This stall-side test is unrefined but very practical. If any question arises in the reading or interpretation of the test, a sample of blood from the foal and milk from the mare should be rapidly submitted to the laboratory for analysis.

The foal's chance of survival is increased if an astute veterinarian can make an early diagnosis and take appropriate measures quickly. If the foal is allowed to ingest the milk—laden with hostile antibodies—within a very short interval, blood tests of the foal will reveal a profound anemia, with the vital volume at a startling 50 percent of normal. This sick foal's count will range from 3 to 5 million per cubic millimeter; normal is 10 to 12 million per cubic millimeter.

Blood transfusions are lifesaving if promptly and properly carried out. Great care and precision in determining compatibility for transfusion is also essential. Although this is time-consuming, it is imperative, because if blood samples are not compatible, the transfusion itself can cause death. Never, ever transfuse from the dam, as she is the cause of the problem and her serum is loaded with antibodies lethal to the foal. Select several possible donors and cross-match each until you or the laboratory can confirm compatibility.

Prevention

There is one way to prevent this disease. Before booking your mare, check blood compatibility between your mare and the potential sire. All that you need do is submit a blood sample from each to a reliable laboratory. When you receive a negative laboratory test, book your mare! Blood typing and testing facilities have greatly improved over the years, and as a direct result of this service, the incidence of neonatal isoerythrolysis has indeed been reduced.

If your veterinarian suspects the existence of this problem during gestation, blood samples should be obtained from the mare and the horse to which she was bred. Blood obtained during the latter part of gestation allows the laboratory to determine the presence or absence of agglutination between the dam's blood serum and the sire's red blood cells. If the tests are positive, additional samples obtained much closer to parturition are essential so that your veterinarian will have a lifesaving time advantage. When the foal arrives, blood counts, blood transfusions, and total supportive therapy will be in readiness and can, with modern medical knowledge, avert a disaster.

If your veterinarian suspects at birth the presence of isoerythrolysis, do not wait for laboratory confirmation—act! The mare and foal should be kept together, but the foal should not be allowed to touch the mare's udder under any circumstance. A partition of suitable height should be erected in the stall, allowing the mare to see, hear, and touch her foal, but preventing the foal from drinking the destructive milk in her udder.

As an alternative, a muzzle can be used on the foal, but I think the hazards of this method outweigh the advantages. Constant supervision and attention to details are required during this difficult period of perhaps three days' duration—long enough for all of the hostile antibodies to clear the mammary gland, leaving only harmless milk to ingest.

The mare should be milked by hand every hour to remove the unwanted colostrum, stimulate continued milk production, and avoid development of mastitis in the mammary gland. Although toxic to her own foal, her colostrum can be frozen and stored for another needy foal: perhaps an orphan, a rejected foal, or one such as her own for whom milk is present but unsuitable.

WARNING: The foal must be bottle-fed every hour around the clock, just as the mare must be milked on the same hourly schedule. Ideally, colostrum frozen and stored from another mare will provide all essential ingredients and protective elements so necessary for the newborn. A simple blood/milk screening test should be performed to reassure the safety of the stored preparation before the foal is permitted to ingest even a minute quantity. Second best is the use of a commercial preparation closely simulating the contents of mare's milk, called Foal-Lac, a Borden product. However, there is no substitute for colostrum.

Years ago, horsemen fed a formula of skimmed cow's milk, lime water, milk of magnesia, and Karo syrup. This mixture reliably produced diarrhea. With its continued use, an underdeveloped, stunted foal developed. Fortunately, today we have suitable substitutes scientifically formulated to simulate mare's milk and fulfill the foal's nutritional needs. A mare's milk is characteristically low in fat, rich in protein, and high in lactose, producing a sweet, sticky substance. Cow's milk is notoriously high in fat content; human milk is low in protein.

A mare may produce colostrum for as long as 72 to 78 hours, so the mare must be milked and the foal bottle-fed for as long as the antibody-ladened colostrum is produced. Before the foal is ever allowed to nurse, laboratory determination confirming the absence of the antibodies is vital.

With the help of quick aid and definitive action, I have seen jaundiced foals survive the initial insult and grow into perfectly normal adults.

IMMUNODEFICIENT FOALS

Although this fatal entity is seemingly increasing in incidence, I am more inclined to believe that it has been with us for a long time. Perhaps aided by new and modern diagnostic blood tests, we are now recognizing this awesome problem with increased efficiency.

Successful transfer of immune bodies depends upon several vulnerable or critical areas. It is my opinion that timing makes the difference between failure and a successful completion of passive antibody transfer, whether a deficiency, incompetency, or total failure is present.

The dam, mother of the foal, may fail to produce antibodies during gestation; this results in colostrum with no immune body content. This mare's colostrum would lack the IgG and IgM globulin content found in the normal mare's colostrum. Or the natural globulin content of colostrum may be appreciably reduced by a leaky mammary gland, most often found in brood mares with unnaturally extended gestation periods or a delayed parturition from any cause. Leaking or loss of colostrum from the teats is easily identified by a thick, sticky substance coating the mare's hind legs and feet. Research has confirmed the high levels of preformed or passive antibody content (IgG and IgM) in early colostrum and also has documented the dramatic drop in globulin levels after 18 hours of lactation; it is distressing to watch a mare relentlessly lose her initial colostrum containing these high concentrations of immunoglobulins. Some commercial farms choose to collect, store, and freeze this otherwise lost colostrum.

There is a test available to determine the presence of or level of antibody formation in the mare's colostrum. Called a Colostrometer, this test provides valid information with accuracy. In lieu of a lab test, we must continue to assume that all is well and that the mare's first milk is loaded with preformed protection for the foal. Your veterinarian has access to commercial preparations of IgG and IgM for use intravenously. Do not hesitate.

Another problem in the transfer of antibodies occurs when an already weak or sick foal fails to ingest adequate amounts of early colostrum. In cases of

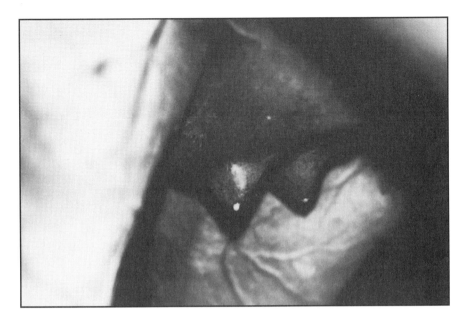

Leaking colostrum.

substandard foals, feeble suckling efforts, supplemental feedings, and drug treat-ment can interfere with adequate ingestion during the critical first 18 hours. Timing is crucial, not only for the colostrum's viability, but also for the foal's capability to absorb the large globulins; so a twofold danger period exists.

By far the most common failure of passive transfer of immune protection occurs inside the foal's small intestine after it has ingested the first milk. Scientists contend that the duodenum is the area where a hereditary or con-genital malfunction can exist in these affected foals.

Normally, the foal's duodenum permits, for a brief period, absorption of large molecular IgG and IgM globulins and their passage through to the foal's circu-lation. The inability of the gut wall to properly absorb, and/or the early shut-down or closure of the gut wall to these large molecular globulins, are two major reasons why the foal may be left totally unprotected from stress, infection, and disease.

To prevent the occurrence of immunodeficiency, some measures are imple-mented to ensure adequate maternal antibody levels before foaling. For the expectant mare, a good diet, abundant daily exercise, and a clean hygienic environment are routine on a good breeding farm. Combine this with an effective parasite-control schedule and vaccination program. Consult your vet-erinarian for a biological program tailored to your specific environmental and geographic needs. Whenever I diagnose a possible immunodeficiency, I suspect a septicemia at work.

NOTE: Even though the mare may have received proper and timely vaccinations throughout her pregnancy, I would suggest revaccination one month before due date. This acts as a booster and thus increases specific colostral antibodies in preparation for lactation and foal ingestion. Tetanus toxoid, rhinopneumonitis, and influenza A-equi I and A-equi II are the three most often administered. If there is a particular problem on a farm, then consider others, such as rabies, salmonella, EEV, strangles, or botulinum.

ALERT: A second preventive measure is logical: Make certain that the foal ingests a minimum of 500cc of safe colostrum during the first 18 hours of life, regardless of circumstances.

INDUCED LABOR

Foals produced by induced labor in brood mares consistently show a low serum content of globulins—and usually these foals perish, even with medical attention. I have always been strongly opposed to the chemical induction of labor in any mare other than for urgent and specific medical reasons. Contrary to other species, the brood mare's inherent physiologic makeup does not lend itself well to any style of induced labor. Brood mares have their own way of forcing people to respect Mother Nature!

Diagnosis of an immune-deficient foal is best carried out four to six hours after the first ingestion of milk. There are two diagnostic serum tests—zinc turbidity and Foalchek. Each utilizes the foal's serum, and both are stall-side procedures. Both are accurate, convenient, and available commercially. It behooves every equine practitioner to keep these tests handy for use at any and all hours. With their use, the foal's immune competence can be quickly assessed and minds set at ease. Or, if indicated, a red alert with appropriate and immediate steps can be arranged for remedial therapy. Whether the result is positive or negative in the case of a weak or questionable foal, I would suggest repeating the test every 12 hours until the foal's overall condition is satisfactory.

ALERT: It is wise at this time (if not before) to draw blood for a complete blood count and laboratory analysis. In immune-deficient foals, blood counts reveal normal red blood cell counts, normal hemoglobin content, but a diagnostic reduction of lymphocytes, called lymphopenia. Normal white cell counts range around 8,000; with this disease the levels have been reported as low as from 2,000 to 4,000. This startling blood picture, in conjunction with blood serum tests, is almost conclusive evidence of faulty immune response. Unlike the latter, an elevated white blood cell count is indicative of a bacterial infection called septicemia.

Treatment

Treatment should be prompt and vigorous. Rarely have I treated a foal suffering only from an immune problem. All cases that I recall were also ill with some form of septicemia, so treatment consistently included antibiotics, fluid and electrolyte replacement, and of course specific treatment for the immune defect.

The treatment of choice consists of a serum transfusion, ideally prepared from a known healthy adult horse. Here, whole blood transfusions are unnecessary and are to be avoided. Commercial plasma specifically prepared and frozen is an easy method but somewhat hazardous, always carrying the threat of a protein reaction. Serum, on the other hand, is totally free of untoward side effects and is literally loaded with the protective antibodies desperately needed by the sick foal. Please heed this advice!

Prepared serum.

NOTE: When confronted with an immune-deficient foal lacking IqG and IgM glob-ulins and no available laboratory, the equine practitioner can simply concoct a per-fectly safe serum transfusion and save the life of the foal. Select as a donor any horse in the barn except the dam of the foal. Never use the mother as a donor!

Usually 700 or 800cc of whole blood is sufficient to obtain the needed 300 to 400cc of serum. The blood should be drawn in an aseptic manner and then prop-erly stoppered and placed under refrigeration until a straw-colored serum is in evidence at the upper portion of the vial. Removal of the serum should be carried out with great care to avoid accidental inclusion of any other blood elements. Allow it to come to room temperature prior to use. The rate of IV injection should be moderate to slow.

I have experienced astounding success in foals treated with serum transfusions. Do not hesitate to repeat the zinc turbidity or Foalchek test every 24 hours for reevaluation purposes. If in doubt, a second serum transfusion is not at all contraindicated. I insist upon preparing and administering my own serum for transfusions and delight in knowing that hardy, viable antibodies produced from naturally occurring antigens from an adult horse are in fact flowing into the suffering foal's circulatory system. What a sense of satisfaction and gratitude!

Immune failure of any degree can be a devastating situation, but when a delayed diagnosis causes the needless death of a foal, it truly is a waste. Every newborn foal should receive the benefit of a CBC and an immune competency test as routine neonatal care.

SUMMARY OF SUSCEPTIBLE AREAS IN IMMUNE TRANSFER

There are four critical areas where immune body transfer possibly can fail:

1. The dam may fail to produce antibodies during gestation, thus the colostrum is void or has a low content of IgG/IgM globulins.

2. Leaking colostrum early before parturition.

3. Sick or weak foals often fail to ingest adequate amounts of early colostrum.

4. For a brief period, a foal's duodenum allows passage of, or absorption of, the large molecular globulins (IgG and IgM) through the GI tract into the system. After a short 18 hours or so this passage closes down and the vitally needed antibodies pass through the GI tract unabsorbed.

COMBINED IMMUNODEFICIENCY (CID) ARABIAN FOALS

Another form of immune deficiency is CID (combined immunodeficiency), a fatal hereditary disease of young foals. Symptoms are weakness, pneumonia of viral origin, and other various secondary infections. It is believed that CID is carried by a recessive lethal gene; a commercial test to identify carriers will soon be available.

Diagnosis

Lymphopenia, the profound reduction of circulating white blood cells, specifically lymphocytes, is a most remarkable diagnostic symptom. Lymphocytes play a major role in the formation of protective antibodies and immune responses of the body. This lethal gene was introduced a few years ago, and without this marvelous research, the Arabian breed, especially the classic bloodlines, would be in danger of becoming extinct.

Microscopic tissue changes are found in the thymus, spleen, and lymph nodes, and are characteristic of this perplexing hereditary disorder. At present, the only diagnosed cases that have been laboratory confirmed have been found in Arabian foals. CID foals who receive maternal passive antibodies at birth via colostrum remain relatively healthy until around two months of age, when the maternal protective bodies reportedly catabolize and wane. With no functioning immune system, these foals die. Arabian breeders have been desperately looking for the answer to this inherited trait.

A commercial laboratory test (Vet-Gem) for the identification of "carrier horses" has just been announced. Undoubtedly, this simple blood test, although costly, will be compulsory soon. All conscientious horsemen will test mares prior to the breeding season. Perhaps this blood test will save the precious Arabian breed. This breakthrough test is exciting but sad news for owners of top horses that test positive; however, the good news is that euthanasia is not necessary—just ovariectomy in the mare and castration in the stallion. Thus these carriers can lead normal lives.

ESOPHAGEAL, GASTRIC, AND DUODENAL ULCERS

I heard of the first diagnosed and confirmed case of stomach ulcers in the young foal about five years ago. Since then erosion and ulceration of the stomach and intestinal mucosa have been reported with increased prevalence. It is most often found in chronically ill or premature foals, especially after a long period of treatment. Cause is essentially unknown; however, stress has long been suspect—thus the name stress ulcers in foals. This entity in the neonate equates with peptic ulcers in the human.

How is stress a factor in the young foal? The ill foal is visited many times a day for treatment of all sorts, some traumatic. Well foals subject to inexperienced personnel or handlers, poor management procedures, irregular schedules, and substandard stalls, fences, and pastures, are also candidates for various forms of ulceration through stress.

Diagnosis

Clinical symptoms of ulcers are relatively specific: Depression, gastrointestinal pain (colic), excessive salivation, and teeth grinding are foremost and usually seen in an underweight and unthrifty-appearing foal. A diagnostic reflux of hot acidic fluid usually occurs with the passage of a nasogastric tube into the foal's stomach. With the release of stomach fluid, signs of relief are usually evident. It is a good practice to administer a therapeutic dose of antacid through the tube while it is in place secondary to the acid release.

To diagnose ulcers, a blood test is first in order. A recent study showed that foals with ulcers consistently had a higher content of pepsinogen in the serum than those ulcer free. Although this test is not totally conclusive, it may be helpful when used with a foal showing classic ulcer symptoms. Although it is not a stall-side test, upper GI studies, with the use of barium, can help identify the condition; however, this sophisticated test requires a veterinary medical facility. Some literature is now available.

A foal suffering from gastric ulcers.

To confirm the presence of ulcers, the fiber-optic endoscope allows visualization and assessment of the gastric and duodenal mucosa. Early diagnosis can result in early treatment and thus improve the prognosis.

Diagnosis in the past has been difficult to pinpoint, and many cases have been confirmed at postmortem. Unfortunately, some foals are found dead from ruptured stomachs or perforated intestinal walls. These losses have been greatly reduced with new information and alert equine veterinarians with their portable fiber-optic endoscopes.

Treatment

When ulceration is even suspected, begin treating with copious amounts of antacids—immediately! Tagamet (cimetidine), at a dose of 600mg four times daily, is strongly recommended. Also indicated are other antacids such as milk of magnesia, Maalox, and Carafate.

Short-course therapy is never successful. Liberal doses of antacids given over a protracted period of time, perhaps six to eight weeks, have proven to relieve some affected foals. But by all means maintain and insist upon quiet and serene surroundings. It can be surely worth the effort. Most all of my patients responded well to treatment for ulcers, after placing them in a good environment.

SHOCKY FOAL

Most foals suffering from shock are found down flat in the straw, with rapid respirations and dilated pupils; they are very weak and unable to rise. A fast and prominent heartbeat (tachycardia) combined with a subnormal temperature usually completes the shocky-foal picture. Capillary refill of mucous membranes is characteristically slow, with varying shades of gum color, from very pale to quite red. Unless accurate and heroic treatment is forthcoming, a lethargic shocky foal can quickly slip into a coma and die quietly.

The reader can easily sense the importance of walk-by checks, on a frequent basis, usually all hours of the day and night during the first few months of a foal's life. Early detection, often called the "third-eye time," greatly improves the chances for survival of the entire foal crop. I know it has helped in my brood mare practice. The successful brood mare farms that I remember all had a designated person who quietly patrolled the nursery on a 24-hour basis.

Shock in the foal is a common sequel to acute septicemias and can overcome the foal quickly and be quite unnoticed until it is almost too late. Septic shock is caused by enteric bacteria, those bacteria that normally inhabit the gastrointestinal tract. Usually gram-negative, these microorganisms produce a lethal endotoxin notoriously capable of causing circulatory compromise with subsequent collapse. Common inhabitants of intestinal contents—*Actinobaccillus equuli*, *Klebsiella*, *Salmonella*, and *Escherichia coli*—are known to cause enterotoxemias that result when these microorganisms leave their normal habitat, the intestinal tract, and invade the bloodstream. This is called septicemia, or blood poisoning. Body tissues and organs suffer reduced oxygen and nutritional content with rapid disruption of the body's homeostasis. Circulatory collapse is imminent.

Shock is not always associated with septicemia. It can rapidly develop when a foal, for any reason, ceases to nurse (injury, exhaustion, extreme environmental temperatures, etc.). Blood sugar drops sharply with dehydration—thus shock ensues.

Vaccinating the pregnant broodmare with Endobactoid the tenth month of gestation could prevent untold numbers of shocky foals.

Emergency Treatment

Emergency treatment must be instituted immediately. Restoration of the circulation and support of body function is of a compelling urgency. There is no time to identify the causative agent, and although blood samples and cultures may be obtained during the "shotgun therapy," the laboratory results will supply useful information only for later treatment, if the patient can survive. An intensive care unit would be a blessing and ideal for the treatment of these foals. In the absence of an ICU, treatment for septic shock in foals, caused by the endotoxins of bacterial invaders, is in the following 11 essential steps:

Treatment

1. Place prostrate foal on an air mattress, in a warm, well-ventilated, but draft-free area.

2. Draw whole blood and run a stall-side test called Toxcheck-LPS. This commercial test can, in two minutes, detect endotoxin in the foal's blood. This test can greatly enhance the prognosis through accurate diagnosis and rapid specific treatment.

3. Rapid, yet cautious, infusion of Ringer's lactate solution IV for support and restoration of body fluids and circulation is first and foremost. For the average 70- to 80-pound foal, 1 liter per hour is a basic rule of thumb. Other species can tolerate double that rate of infusion, but foals *cannot* tolerate rapid infusions of liquid without the risk of pulmonary edema. Lung edema, with its predisposition to pneumonia, can be fatal. So, although hasty treatment is needed, make haste slowly!

4. Incorporate sodium bicarbonate into the Ringer's lactate solution: 168cc of 8 percent sodium bicarbonate for the 70-pound foal will help correct the metabolic acidosis that occurs with any form of disease or toxins.

5. As an added precaution, add Ringer's solution and sodium bicarbonate to the equine plasma or serum to dilute serum protein. If the

commercial plasma product is unavailable, after cross-matching, blood may be obtained from a healthy adult and prepared correctly. Two hundred or three hundred cc of plasma or serum should be ideal for the average foal.

6. In the case of septic shock, a broad-spectrum antibiotic is essential to combat infection. Administer all drugs intravenously. In any case of shock, peripheral circulation is compromised, so any injection other than the IV route may be ineffective, as absorption is inconsistent. The drugs of choice are chloromycetin, oxytetracycline, or neomycin.

7. Provide good ventilation or oxygen administered via a mask or endotracheal tube at a recommended rate of 5 liters per minute. Oxygen supplementation is essential. In shock cases, the tissues rapidly develop an oxygen deficit.

8. Add 100 ml of 50 percent dextrose to each liter of fluid IV described above. Dextrose helps to replenish diminished blood sugar and affords protection for the damaged liver.

9. Corticosteroids are useful if administered early. Hydrocortisone sodium succinate is relatively safe and may be repeated in four hours.

10. Avoid the use of vasodilators and vasoconstrictors. These drugs are dangerous.

11. Closely monitor all external heat used to correct the hypothermia (subnormal body temperature). Avoid over-dry air, and prevent overheating. With warm conditions, the foal's metabolic rate will increase, causing cutaneous (skin) vasodilation and resultant circulatory collapse. Keep temperatures moderate, not warm, while continuing to treat the foal for circulatory compromise and shock.

There is a word of hope. A vaccine called Endobactoid has been announced. It proposes to confer an antibody response that is capable of affording protection when deadly enteric bacteria pass through the intestinal mucosa and gain entrance to the circulation. With routine prophylactic use, perhaps the incidence of *endotoxemia* and septic shock could be greatly reduced or even totally eliminated.

Notwithstanding several years of experimental use and FDA approval, this vitally needed bacterin has not yet been fully accepted by professional horse people.

Perhaps soon, Endobactoid can be included with the other boosters given to all expectant brood mares, one month prior to parturition. This would confer specific antibodies to the foal through the colostrum. What a life-saving practice!

DENTIGEROUS CYSTS

A dentigerous cyst (ear fistula) can appear at the base of the ear in foals from one to eight months of age. Swellings can range from the size of a robin's egg to that of a large orange; all exhibit a persistent and annoying discharge. Interestingly, these tissue swellings frequently contain tooth fragments, hair, and assorted cartilaginous tissue; they are clearly an aberration in embryonic development.

Although these cysts can be quite alarming to the owner, they require only simple surgical excision and removal. Prognosis is good to excellent.

HEMOPHILIA

Hemophilia is an inherited genetic slowness or failure of the blood to clot. It is caused by the sex-linked recessive trait found in colts, although fillies can carry the trait undetected until they reproduce. I have never diagnosed hemophilia in my practice of 35 years; this is a rare condition.

Horses possess the longest known coagulation time in domestic animals. Coagulation requires 12 minutes in a normal horse, one not suffering from hemophilia. Twelve minutes can seem a lifetime if one is watching and counting.

CROOKED LEGS

There are two types of crooked-legged foals: those of congenital or hereditary origin and those of primary congenital origin. The former have been well discussed early in this chapter (under LIMB DEFORMITIES), but the second type of crooked-legged foal may be caused in utero by crowding during the last two months of gestation. Perhaps overgrowth of the fetus and overcrowding causes the long slender limbs to overflex and twist in order to accommodate the size or location of the uterus. These foals are usually well bent, with legs crooked in several directions and having a rubbery appearance; even the foals' heads, necks, backs, and hips look twisted. Devices such as splints or casts will inevitably work well on this category of foal. More often than not, these foals will straighten out within weeks when given proper nutrition, handling, and regularly supervised exercise. Care should be taken to avoid lengthy or overstrenuous periods of exercise.

WARNING: An accurate diagnosis is critical prior to any form of treatment. Crooked legs in the newborn vary greatly. The cause must be distinguished and identified. A very thin margin for error exists between the active and passive corrective approaches. Expert guidance can be reassuring; amateurish attempts should be avoided. They can be costly, and an ill-directed attempt at correction may worsen the condition and make it irreversible.

Please consult an experienced equine practitioner for guidance with your crooked-legged neonate.

SPLINT FORMATION

Splint formation is a hard bony deposit found along both sides of the large cannon bone, involving the smaller splint bones. It is commonly found on the inside splint bone in the foreleg (fourth metacarpus), varying in size from occult or imperceptible to that of a lemon. Usually, splints form when stress is placed upon a young animal. Oral wheat germ oil and rest resolve most fresh splints in young horses. Warm bandages are thought by some to aid in recovery. In older horses, splints become more resistant to treatment.

FRACTURED SPLINT BONES

Fractured splint bones are more commonly found in adult horses. Abusive use or trauma are the usual causes. Early surgical removal of the distal fragments has proven to be a very satisfactory approach.

RUPTURED SUSPENSORY LIGAMENT

Ruptured suspensory ligament is found in older foals. Rest combined with proper shoeing is indicated. Healing consists of fibrosis of the area, and although unsightly, it does not prevent horses with this condition from becoming useful and even competitive.

Prognosis for this uncommon condition is better in the hind leg. Although rest is the best treatment, ask your farrier to extend the branches of the hind shoe for added support. This can be therapeutic and quite helpful; however, elevating the heel is strongly contraindicated in any type of suspensory ligament injury.

As a teenager I trained a steeplechase horse with this condition and, after two years of fibrosing the suspensory hind leg ligament, he won several brush races in good company.

BOWED TENDON/
TENDONITIS

Degrees of tendonitis, or ultimately bowed tendon, are associated with speed and trauma. Two major flexor tendons are found on the back of horses' legs,

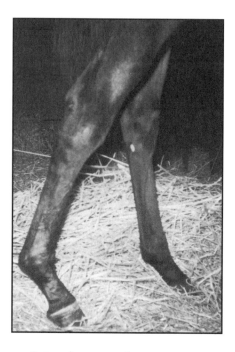

Ruptured suspensory ligament.

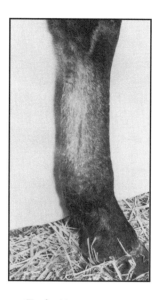

Tendonitis.

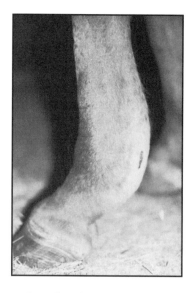

Huge bowed tendon.

namely, deep digital flexor tendon (DDFT) and superficial flexor tendon(SFT). When tendonitis occurs, the superficial flexor tendon is the only tendon affected, and is a precursor to a bowed tendon.

The SFT differs from its partner tendon in that it is much shorter, much wider, and thinner, and is specifically subject to tendonitis. If not rested, protected, and subjected to appropriate treatment for a minimum of two years, inflammation and re-bowing will occur in spite of all efforts. Time seems to be the secret.

Because of tendon tissue's poor blood supply, it is notoriously slow in healing. Time and rest are vital factors.

Ultrasound is used to monitor the healing process of the injured tendon tissue. A veterinarian with an ultrasound machine can guide and advise the owner when to resume slow exercise and supervised training.

I have found that horses with huge bows, with proper time and rest, are able to return to competition, including show jumping, fox hunting, timber racing, and steeplechasing; however, flat racing is contraindicated. Speed is the tendon's worst enemy! A healed bowed tendon can sustain speeds of up to a mile in two minutes. Any speed less than two minutes will inevitably result in re-bow—most likely career-ending.

Chapter Five

ORPHAN, REJECTED, TWIN, AND PREMATURE FOALS

There are those unfortunate foals who come into the world and are immediately deprived of the most cherished thing in the world—a mother! No one is there for protection, guidance, or nourishment, even to snuggle up with. How confusing it must be, and how lost they must feel!

I have seen a tiny orphaned foal lying deep in the straw, literally dwarfed by the huge, otherwise empty stall. I have also seen the distraught and lonely expression of a foal rejected by its hostile, mixed-up mother, and I have watched a twin foal so minute that it could not reach high enough to suckle on the dripping teat high above its outstretched neck and head. Talk about frustration! All of these foals cry out for help.

ORPHAN FOAL

A foal can become orphaned rather quickly by the untimely death of the mare. Brood mares frequently die during delivery or shortly after parturition, leaving the orphan foal to fend for itself. It is a great advantage to the foal's health if the mare survives long enough for the ingestion of a good colostral meal. If this is not available to the newborn, then frozen colostrum from a storage bank is ideal and essential. When the foal misses the ingestion of colostrum for any reason, he then lacks preformed protective antibodies and is vulnerable to all diseases.

All of the better breeding farms have developed the practice of collecting colostrum and immediately freezing this precious commodity for all emergencies—i.e., orphan, rejected, twin, and premature foals.

All alone.

If frozen colostrum is unavailable, your veterinarian will quickly suggest plasma or serum IV for immediate protection from infection. These preparations are loaded with specific protective antibodies, and their presence can determine whether the foal lives or dies. Plasma is permissible but not as safe to administer as a serum preparation. Commercial preparations are available today and appear to be quite safe.

To determine the foal's immune body status, he deserves a CBC and zinc sulfate test. The colostral meal or its substitute, Similac or Foal-Lac, should be followed by the use of Foal-Lac powder mixed with warm water and fed via baby bottles. Although Foal-Lac is a superior milk substitute, it is not a substitute for colostrum, as it supplies only nutrition, not antibodies.

Daily injections of antibiotics for the first week of life are a good practice, along with liver, iron, and B12 injections, plus a careful vigilance on the condition of the navel cord. Ensure that a small amount (1 tablespoonful) of milk of magnesia is added to the diet daily for the first three weeks. Take note of the foal's sleep habits and the amount of exercise that it is taking. All this is routine but oh so wise!

NOTE: At three days of age, a feed tub filled with equal parts of Mother's Oats and Foal-Lac pellets should be placed low enough for easy accessibility to the foal for free-choice feeding around the clock. From three to five days, hand-feed, if necessary, by placing oats and hay particles into your foal's mouth, to avoid notorious foal anemia.

Another pail with Foal-Lac powder mixed into a gruel can be hung as soon as deemed advisable so that the youngster can slowly wean himself from the bottles to the pail. These nutrients should be available at a proper head level and kept fresh at all times. An abundance of clean, green, leafy alfalfa hay and an easily reached mineralized salt lick will complete the ideal dietary picture. Good exercise with kind but firm handling is advised, as orphan foals tend to develop behavioral problems or even psychological disorders in the absence of their mother's influence.

Up until a few years ago, an orphaned foal was automatically sentenced and condemned as a "runt" or a substandard individual with no potential to succeed. A milk formula of cow's milk, Karo syrup, lime water, and milk of magnesia—a combination guaranteed to cause diarrhea—was mixed. This concoction kept them alive, but it must be admitted that the ones who lived suffered nutritionally and were ultimately stunted. In a group of foals, it was quite easy to pick out the orphan by its pathetic weakness and small size.

Today this is no longer the case. I have found that foals raised on our recommended and previously described schedule have been superior to their stablemates raised in the conventional fashion. This should tell us something.

Although it was generally accepted that a formula of cow's milk would barely keep the foal technically alive, its use has persisted over the years. Perhaps the mixtures have endured because no good substitute was available. Goat's milk, with its folklore for curing all ills, has also been tried as a diet for motherless foals. In my opinion, it has no place in a foal's diet. The high incidence of gastrointestinal upsets, often accompanied by gas after ingestion, can be easily explained. The analysis of goat's milk reveals that it contains three times the fat and only two-thirds the sugar content of mare's milk.

A "nurse mare" can be an asset for company, security, and the psychological need of the young, very alone foal. However, the cost of a milk mare that may serve only as a companion is a consideration, as her lactation cycle may not be in synch with the requirements of the moment. Research has revealed that mare's milk reaches its nutritional peak around the fifth or sixth week and dramatically drops from that point. If a frozen colostral meal has been given initially, the immune bodies and laxative principles needed have been provided, and the expensive nurse mare may merely be a baby-sitter and her milk something with which to wash down the food. A nanny goat has been used successfully over the years as a companion and represents a much lesser expenditure.

Benefits accrued by daily critical glances at any newborn during the precarious and sometimes turbulent neonatal period should not be overlooked. To repeat, I define this period of watchfulness as the "third-eye" time.

REJECTED FOALS

Although the circumstances producing orphan and rejected foals are quite dissimilar, they do ultimately end up receiving basically the same regime and treatment.

Rejected foals risk mutilation or even death inflicted by a "nasty" mother, and experience a frightening episode with the final insult of rejection, perhaps creating psychological scarring. A rejected foal is, in essence, an orphan.

I have seen mares attack newborn foals with clashing teeth and striking feet so violently that only the most hardy, devoted, and courageous of grooms managed to rescue the limp and/or injured foal. Had I not witnessed this horrifying incident, I would not have believed it. There is no rhyme nor reason for this total rejection, not any known veterinary medical explanation.

Once a mare has rejected her foal, it has been my experience that no amount of drugs, tranquilizers, handling, or coaxing has ever changed her mind. Don't chance the danger!

Once rejection has been determined, the mare and foal should be separated—an essential safety precaution for both foal and involved personnel. Quickly arrange for bottle feedings of either hand-milked or frozen colostrum, and lose no time in placing the forlorn foal on the orphan feed schedule. Although this tiring schedule requires around-the-clock attention and dedicated people, it is satisfactory, humane, and almost always gratifyingly successful.

ALERT: A word about Foal-Lac, the commercially prepared simulated mare's milk substitute produced by Borden Laboratories. This product has been a delight to use in the case of the orphan, the reject, and the milkless mare (agalactia). In my experience, foals raised on this product have been superior to those foals fed naturally. At the risk of being labeled a traitor to motherhood, I would suggest weaning all foals at 10 weeks, and, in lieu of the mare's inferior-quality milk at this stage of lactation, providing Foal-Lac. I am convinced that larger and better-developed foals would be produced through this dietary implementation.

TWINS

Formerly, the incidence of twin pregnancies was one in every 1,000, but curiously, today the prevalence has appreciably increased, especially in Thoroughbreds. The reason is unknown. Conjecture has suggested indiscriminate use of hormones, increased inbreeding, and possible genetic influences or aberrations. In the horse world, twins are frowned upon and are considered undesirable for two reasons: They are seldom useful, and they are rarely ever competitive.

When a mare produces two or more ova after a suitable cover by a fertile stallion, a twin pregnancy can occur, although with no degree of predictability. No research data is presently available on the controversial subject of super ovulations vs. number of concepti.

There are two types of twins, fraternal and identical.

Fraternal twins develop from two separate fertilized eggs and can result in two embryos of the same sex or opposite sexes. Each embryo is enveloped in its own separate placenta. While both are at-tached intimately, the tissue delineation of each sac is clearly visible upon examination of the afterbirth membranes.

Fraternal twins.

Identical twins.

A 12-day blastocyst.

An 18-day embryo.

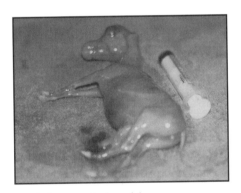

A three-month aborted fetus
(without membrane).

A five-month aborted fetus.

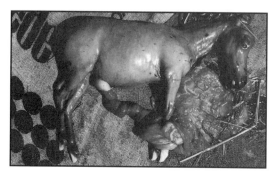

A six-month aborted fetus.

A seven-month aborted fetus.

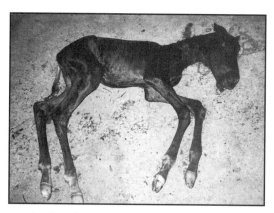

An aborted near-term fetus.

Aborted 10-month identical twins.

Identical twins occur when one fertilized ovum (egg) suddenly divides equally into two complete embryos, thus creating two new foals. This awesome and unexplainable happening is believed to be due to genetic influences. Twinning is thought by some to be familial, especially when all external and environmental causes can be excluded. Delivery of live twins is common in other species, but very uncommon in the equine. Brood mares conceive twin pregnancies rather easily but are subsequently highly unsuccessful in supporting or maintaining the dual pregnancy. Therefore, the birth of live, viable twins is an event!

Abortion in twins occurs in 90 percent of the cases and usually happens around the eighth or ninth month of gestation. This is the time in gestation when the fetal growth spurt is rapid and a major increase in needed room for growth and nutritional requirements has begun. It is only logical that abortions are highest during this period.

It is my opinion that almost all twin abortions, especially those in latter pregnancy, are nutritionally caused. When the equine fetus characteristically doubles its weight, adequate room and nutritional demands in a twin pregnancy are far too great for the average mare. Each fetus competes for space in the uterus, and the weaker of the two usually dies first. A foreign-body reaction is then created inside the mare, who promptly aborts both foals. It seems so unfair to lose a relatively healthy, nearly full-size foal in such a manner! It is an exceptionally "roomy" mare who manages to support two babies beyond the dangerous and critical eighth or ninth month.

Abortion, identical twins (10th month). No evidence of disease but strong evidence of malnutrition.

The mare's uterus is quite inefficient in comparison with that of other species, and its peculiar type of placentation is poorly equipped to provide for two developing feti. Abortion is caused simply from inadequate room and a steady decline to near starvation in the nutritional level. The poignant aspect of twins in the equine is that almost all are perfectly normal, disease-free individuals, growing and developing inside of a normal, healthy uterus, but one of inadequate size and limited capacity. The mare's uterus is poorly designed for more than one pregnancy at a time—yet she has the proven ability to ovulate several ova during one cycle. The equine gynecologist must be consciously aware of this lopsided situation.

While most twins are aborted, some exceptional mares have been known to produce live, viable twins who survive in the outside world and grow into relatively normal adults. To an equine practitioner constantly fighting pathologic diseased conditions, it is indeed a sad sight to see dead twins caused by mere mechanical failure.

Diagnosis of a double pregnancy can be determined manually before but not beyond the 50th postcover day. Beyond this date, the divided egg or double vesicles are not manually identifiable because of the steadily increasing amount of placental fluids, which mask detection. A skilled examination, ideally performed early in the pregnancy (18 to 21 days), can accurately determine pregnancy status.

An abortion technique reported from England has currently raised eyebrows and appalled some veterinarians. When two separate vesicles are discovered in the mare's uterus early in pregnancy, manual removal of one conceptus—or a single abortion—is attempted. One conceptus is literally squeezed and guided out of the cervix, into the vagina, and out into the external environment. These outrageous people claim a high degree of success—that is, the removal of one, while the other remains in utero.

If this method works, it defies all known prinicples of equine fertility. Quite different from all other species, the mare will not tolerate the slightest change in the integrity of the cervical plug or seal during pregnancy, and if it occurs, abortion will assuredly result. Any compromise or interruption of the cervical seal will produce an abortion within 48 hours.

Despite claims to the contrary, I understand through various other sources that both embryos invariably exit and are consistently aborted in toto, in reliable brood mare fashion. I am totally opposed to these blatant abuses.

ULTRASOUND PREGNANCY DIAGNOSIS

Through the use of modern ultrasound machines, a double pregnancy can be positively diagnosed at 12 days postcover. This is a special service, and expensive. If the owner desires, the mare can at this time be promptly relieved of her pregnancy. For commercial purposes, twin pregnancies are usually aborted. The mare can then be rebred and may perhaps produce a single foal; thus, a productive year is not lost. Commercially early determination is essential, however. If the mare is permitted to carry a twin conceptus over 37 days and then it is aborted, her pregnant mare serum gonadotropin (PMSG) hormone serum level, produced by the twin's presence, will inhibit cycling for over 100 days and interfere with the mare's chances for a productive year.

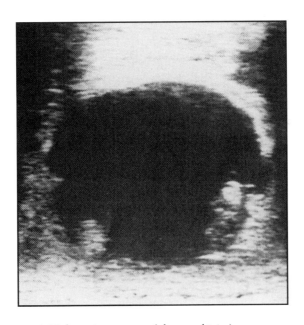

A 12-day twin pregnancy (ultrasound print).

WARNING: Twelve-day postovulation determination of twin concepti, with the use of ultrasound images, is an exciting and convenient commercial breakthrough, especially for large breeding farms. However, I have reservations and unanswered questions. Based on experience as a practitioner, I contend that many normal mares consistently ovulate more than one ovum at each cycle, and often more than one ovum is fertilized, yet at 18 days the majority of these mares are diagnosed as carrying a single pregnancy. What happens to the other fertilized eggs? This paradoxical fact has either gone unrecognized or has been ignored by choice.

MULTIPLE OVULATIONS IN THE BROOD MARE

In over 30 years, I have examined literally thousands of afterbirth membranes and have, in over 60 percent of all single births, found evidence of early twinning, triplets, and even more. Common occupants found in the afterbirth tissue, and proof positive of multiple fertilized eggs, are black cylindrical masses called amorphi globosi. These masses are always attached to the allantois chorion (the membranous sac of the placenta that is most intimately attached to the maternal uterine lining) by a cord resembling a legitimate navel cord. These round bodies are thought to be pregnancies arrested early in the gestation period. Containing various amounts of cartilage and gelatinous material, several of these amorphus

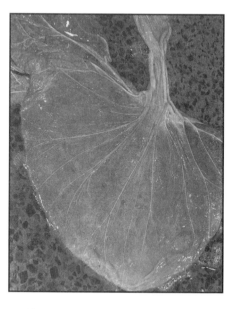

Placenta containing many early arrested pregnancies.

globosus bodies of various sizes may be found in a perfectly normal placenta from a very normal single birth. Also found with less frequency are watery sacs, of all sizes and shapes, each with its own umbilical cord, literally encompassing

Multiple arrested concepti (placenta from a single healthy foal).

the surface of a placenta. Based on this evidence, the untold number of fertilized eggs in the mare could result in a litter! Obviously, some internal force selects the dominant embryo over the lesser members and inhibits the growth and development of all but one, although all are fertilized by spermatozoa.

With the use of ultrasound techniques, are we washing out good, potentially single pregnancies erroneously
diagnosed as twins? Aborting a mare at
12 days based on this method of determination is unjustifiable. I contend that
an unknown percentage of these
"worthless twin pregnancies," if left
alone until the 18th to the 21st postcover day, will suddenly become a single, viable, and valuable conceptus. If
on the routine 20th-day examination
twins are certified, they can then readily be aborted. Ultrasound methods boast
the time savings of eight to 10 days by
offering the breeder the option to divide
or split the mare's normal cycle period,
with the use of prostiglandin drugs. All
this is in the name of economics.
Research and some common sense are
sorely needed here.

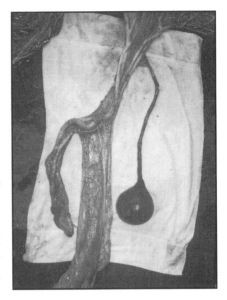

Amorphus globosus.

SYMPTOMS OF A TWIN
PREGNANCY AT TERM

The imminent-term mare carrying live
twins will usually begin to drip milk,
steadily losing colostrum, beginning
several days prior to the due date. She
will continue streaming milk down her
hind legs for up to two to three weeks
beyond due date, then deliver live
twins. The individual mares that I
have known to carry live twins full
term were anatomically large and
roomy. All consistently milked well in
advance of and delivered well past due
date.

During delivery, twins have been
known to become twisted and cause a
difficult birth, if not an outright dystocia. Care should be taken to carefully

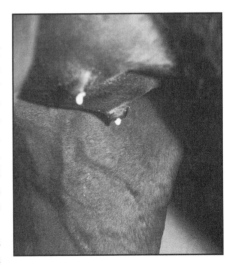

Losing colostrum.

identify any leg before applying traction, as more harm than good can result if there is error. Fortunately, I have never had any problem during parturition of those twins I have delivered. Each was well grown, strong, and presented correctly.

Once twins arrive, the question of adequate milk is always first on the agenda, and without a doubt nearly every mare benefits from a helping hand, a baby bottle, and Foal-Lac to supplement her supply. It is a rare mare who can lactate sufficiently to feed two demanding foals without some outside assistance, and the foals will not receive adequate nutrition

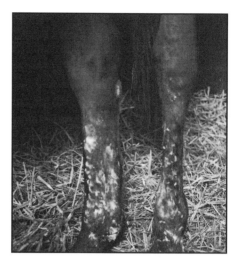

Leaking colostrum on hind egs.

unless given the helping hand they so deserve. Hourly feeding around the clock is in order—usually 6-ounce meals, with dedicated personnel keeping all baby bottles, nipples, and milk containers or pails clean and sterile.

After the first week, milk meals consisting of from 8 to 10 ounces can be given at two-hour intervals, and by the end of the second week at intervals of three hours. Soon, pails hung on the walls can be substituted for bottle feeding. Do not forget that every newborn foal should begin to nibble on hay or grain by the third day of life. Be certain to place hay or grain in the foal's mouth, and, if it is necessary, actually teach it to eat in addition to the instinctive consumption of milk. As a reminder, a mare's milk lacks two vital trace minerals— copper and iron. To prevent foal anemia at three or four days of age, place grain and hay in the foal's mouth if necessary, just to prevent this quickly passing danger period.

NOTE: While on twin foal watch, some shrewd horse people I have known have decided to prepare in advance for two mouths to feed. Instead of watching the colostrum escape down the mare's hind legs, they have prudently collected, but not actively milked, the leaking colostrum in baby bottles, and have then appropriately frozen and stored the precious fluid. Both foals are then assured of a complete colostral meal.

TWIN FOAL BEHAVIOR

I have found twin foals, regardless of whether they are identical or fraternal, of the same or opposite sex, to reliably exhibit various forms of bizarre behavior and to possess erratic personalities. The colts seem overly aggressive, with some individuals appearing slightly retarded in their normal everyday behavior. Most of the fillies seem, in my opinion, mildly mean or ill tempered. Although a few have achieved various degrees of success in competition, none has been outstanding.

Although found consistently, degrees and variations of questionable behavior and even mental awareness exhibited by twins, regardless of type, cannot be truly explained. Lack of discipline must be considered a factor, as most twins are naturally subjected to excessive cuddling and handling and thus become somewhat spoiled, as do most orphans and rejected foals. In fraternal twins of opposite sex, I have invariably observed intensified symptoms of either reduced ability or reluctance to respond to natural and normal everyday challenges. As previously described, the colt usually exhibits unusual aggressiveness, sometimes to the point of stupidity. The filly is usually ill tempered and occasionally aggressive. I have learned to take a special interest in her ability to reproduce. Is a hormonal imbalance experienced during gestation responsible for these peculiar characteristics?

HORMONAL EFFECT ON TWINS

For correlation purposes, I would like to share with you some bovine information. Since twin pregnancies are commonplace in the cow, it is known that, during embryonic growth in a fraternal-twin conception, the male hormonal system develops much in advance of that of the female. The hormones produced early by the male characteristically affect the female partner sharing the uterus. As a result, the reproductive tract of the female twin calf is either incomplete, underdeveloped, or functionally affected at birth. Called a freemartin heifer, this questionable calf has reduced value since she is certain to be productively infertile, if not sterile.

This phenomenon may occur in fraternal twins in the equine. Does the equine species suffer a parallel to this condition of the bovine? Is the filly born twin to the colt infertile, or capable of reproducing? The male twin is unaffected in his ability to reproduce.

I regret that in my practice I have not had the opportunity to examine gynecologically a mare that had been born twin to a colt. Mares from identical-twin pregnancies reproduce regularly, but the lack of scientific records and research on twins of opposite sex leaves many questions unanswered.

I have, however, been able to follow some of the rare male twins through maturity, and I can state unequivocally that their ability to reproduce is unaffected by the female twin's hormones during gestation.

PREMATURE FOALS

Premature foals are those who arrive in the world before the end of the accepted normal period of gestation.

The normal gestation period of the brood mare can extend from 330 to 350 days, with the majority of mares foaling between 332 and 348 days. Any lengthening or undue shortening of this time span is cause for concern and necessitates careful vigilance. However, no fixed, normal gestation period can be calculated because each mare is an individual affected both by the external environment and hereditary influences—her own and those she receives from the stallion to which she was bred. Weather conditions are influential, and certain years can be documented as a particular year in which all mares "carry over," deliver early, or—surprisingly—deliver on time, just as some years have been dubbed as "filly" or "colt" years.

How can one be certain of a shortened period of gestation? With the mare's widely variable time and accepted inconsistency, how does one determine a foal as a "preemie"? There are some who strictly abide by the rule that any foal under 340 days is considered premature. I have seen foals born two weeks early so strong, vigorous, and healthy that without the records and dates, no one could prove that they were truly premature. It has, however, been agreed upon that any foal arriving one month early has little chance for survival. If not dead upon delivery, these foals live only a few hours, even with the finest care.

When a practitioner is presented with a suspected preemie foal, knowledge of the precise breeding date is helpful. A premature foal is usually full or near full size in development, but is profoundly weak, with flaccid muscles and a smooth, soft, glistening coat. Its vision is characteristically poor, and its ears are flopped downward and backward, appearing as "rabbit ears"; they are atonic and appear shapeless and immobile. These foals are unable to cope with the external environment and will surely perish if emergency and sustained treatment are not immediately forthcoming. Animal incubators and intensive care units for large animals are currently available in selected areas, and, in their short-lived existence, they boast saving a respectable percentage of foals.

A premature foal arrives disadvantaged: It departs the intrauterine protection well before it has received full nourishment or fully developed faculties required for survival in the external environment, and is therefore particularly susceptible to infection.

Since equine fetal growth is greatly intensified during the last two months of gestation, any reduction of this growth period lessens the chances for the foal's survival. With prematurity, the intrauterine time, so necessary for the foal's vital systems to reach maturity and capacity to function, is lost. It is, however, important to understand that an early healthy foal has a decidedly better chance for survival than an early septicemic foal.

Prostrate foal.

Recent limited research data has advanced some helpful information in the treatment and nursing care of preemies. Premature foals are primarily noted for poor lung-tissue expansion and reduced oxygenation, nonfunctional gastrointestinal tracts, and distressingly subnormal temperatures. If the foal is free of other problems, overcoming these three major obstacles to survival is the sizable challenge to the ICU team.

First and foremost in the treatment of a preemie foal are provisions for a warm, dry, comfortable, draft-free bed; air mattresses are preferred. An oxygen flow should quickly be established, either through a mask or, better yet, through a small tube to ensure an open airway. To afford an efficient and safe means of frequent nutrition around the clock and the constant support of body fluids and electrolytes, a special catheter is placed intravenously and taped securely into place, with additional tape around the foal's neck for continued stability. This lifesaving support system is constantly maintained until it is determined that the gastrointestinal tract has begun to function on its own. Then and only then can any sustenance—ideally colostrum—be ingested orally.

The importance of elevating and establishing the body temperature to normal cannot be overemphasized. Unbelievably, if the body temperature is 2 or more degrees below normal, all body functions and efficiencies are compromised. Unless prompt and effective steps are taken to correct these hazardous, lower-than-normal temperatures, the foal will fail rapidly. Supply blankets, pillows, and adequate padding in a dry and comfortable area, including heat lamps where necessary. Be careful, however, with heat lamps: They can dangerously dry the air and irritate the foal's respiratory tract. Please keep all electrical appliances out of mare and foal's reach. Heat lamps in stalls should always be infrared. Never use ultraviolet—although bacteriocidal, it can harm the foal's eyes.

Gastrointestinal sounds and fecal movement are absent in the premature foal for a period ranging from hours to days, until independent function occurs. Time is critical now. It is incumbent upon the ICU's clinician in attendance to recognize the foal's initiation of gut movement, as ascertained by use of a stethoscope, and to act promptly to supply colostrum. The duodenum of the newborn is open to absorption of the large molecular colostral antibodies for a short 24 hours or so, after which the absorption is discontinued. Any oral ingestion of antibodies is wasted after this time span. At this point, a nasogastric tube can be slipped into the foal's stomach and sutured into the nostril for stability and comfort. This small tube allows easy access and therefore assures the foal of vital milk meals, administered on schedule. Anyone in attendance can simply administer the prepared meal—at any hour.

All neonatal foals should be carefully observed, but with premature infants, constant monitoring of blood parameters is essential for early detection of infections, septicemias, and immune deficiency.

In my opinion, a barn is an unsatisfactory environment in which to house a premature foal, even when given the most conscientious care. Great strides have been made with the use of incubators and IC units, usually located in veterinary university hospitals. Unfortunately, this does not make them available to the ordinary foal! A specifically designed incubator is the ultimate answer and can save countless lives. With an oxygen supply, humidity controls, and the power to maintain environmental temperatures, the foal incubator provides the vital requirements so needed to sustain life in foals deprived of their superior intrauterine accommodations.

ALERT: Every orphaned, neglected, or premature foal, in the absence of colostrum or first milk, should receive at least 500cc of hyperimmune plasma or serum to assure protection from infection.

I recall staring at premature foals in cold and dirty barns, far away from any town, let alone from a sophisticated veterinary pediatric center, and literally praying for an oven with oxygen or simply a warm place to put the cold, dying baby. Someday!

Chapter Six

THE CONSTANT ENEMY: PARASITES IN THE FOAL

A foal is essentially born free of internal parasites—but this ideal condition is short-lived. From the external environment, parasites, in various forms, promptly invade the neonate's body. Concentrated sources of parasitic eggs and larvae are found in the foal's stall, soil, and feces from the dam and other horses.

Consequently, you should clean your foaling stall wall and floor surface and the initial turnout paddock of all organic debris, especially manure. Following the cleansing and disinfectant efforts of the small turnout paddock, it is wise to apply a thin coating of hydrated lime to all surfaces, and do not use the area until after a rainfall. A light coating of hydrated lime can also sweeten the floor of your foaling stall.

Worming is the treatment used to rid your foal of internal parasites. There is no service that can provide a greater health benefit to your foal than regular worming. This attack against internal parasites should continue on schedule throughout the foal's entire life. Random or erratic worming is futile and foolish. It is not only costly to the owner, but it also represents an insidiously dangerous threat to the health of both young and old patients, involving even their future well-being.

A precisely followed worming schedule can greatly enhance the efficacy of worming by interrupting the life cycle and reproductive proficiency of the parasites. In addition, the veterinarian should alternate the use of anthelmintics (worming medications). The development of resistance to worm medicine can be discouraged, if not totally inhibited, by frequently switching and alternating suitable worm medicines.

Parasites are generally thought of as intestinal inhabitants. However, some worm larvae migrate throughout all internal organs and are assisted by the circulatory system, while others primarily invade tissue. In any case, irreparable damage and destruction to all bodily tissue results, especially live tissue in the neonate. The cause of many adult colics has been traced to bloodworm infestations suffered in early life.

To afford your foal proper health protection early in its life, a methodical and regular effective worming program by your equine practitioner should be specifically designed to the needs of your farm.

On any farm, worming should begin at four to six weeks of age, its frequency determined by the number of horses, square acres of pasture, and the lifestyle of the residents. Even in a squeaky-clean environment, parasites are a fact of life, and deworming should be carried out for the life of the horse.

Parasitism can cause a variety of pathological effects in an adult horse, but the changes and ill effects are quite different and especially severe in foals and growing young adults. In foals, parasitism primarily manifests itself in respiratory problems, sometimes progressing to pneumonia and, often, unthriftiness. In adults, parasitism usually causes death by severe and complicated colic due to blockage of arteries, resulting in poor circulation to the intestines.

Internal parasites represent the greatest threat and continuous danger to your foal's growth-rate efficiency, resistance to disease, and overall health. Foals suffering a parasitic infestation typically show unthriftiness, a potbelly, a ribby appearance, and a starey, rough coat. Noticeably underweight, depressed, teary-eyed, with a runny nose and a cough that resists medical treatment—this is a textbook description of a parasite-ridden foal.

NOTE: Foals do not have colds. When I am called to treat a foal fitting this clinical description, I usually find the foal with a normal temperature and a poor appetite. Much to the owner's surprise, I tube-worm the foal rather than treat for consumptive pneumonia. Tube-worming never produces an instantaneous cure, but the results are rapid enough and always gratifying. Within a few days, the annoying cough disappears, the foal's appetite returns to normal, and it is active, clear-eyed, and playful.

TUBE-WORMING YOUR FOAL

Tube-worming is a simple yet superior method of achieving thorough treatment and is truly imperative to the health—even the life—of the foal. An unchecked internal parasitic infestation can literally destroy the lungs, intestines, and circulatory system of your foal!

The use of a stomach tube may be repugnant to the unindoctrinated owner. However, there is no known method of deworming a horse that is superior to the stomach tube. And actually, in experienced hands, the tube is neither dangerous nor uncomfortable for the foal; also, it offers the great advantage of medicine being delivered and deposited directly into the stomach. The bypassing of the taste buds eliminates the question of drug irritation, and a full, concentrated dose of medicine is delivered in toto. Thus, medicine contacts the entire stomach wall as it passes into the intestine without the presence of an admixture of interfering grain.

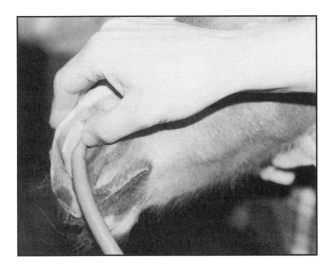

Tubing the neonate.

Although tubing represents an increase in cost, is a chore to the veterinarian, and is time-consuming, its merit is unsurpassed. Tubing with all its advantages diminishes all highly advertised and so-called convenient forms of oral worm-killing medicines (anthelmintics). Powders, drenches, boluses, and even the most current pastes all leave something to be desired. They are either ineffective or so effective that a danger of toxicity exists.

Treatment

From four to six weeks of age, the first deworming is directed primarily toward the destruction of ascarids or roundworms (*Parascaris equorum*), for they are unquestionably the worst enemy of the young foal's pulmonary system and gastrointestinal tract. Ascarids, as found in foals, attack the lung tissue as they pass through during their reproductive cycle, but are not lung inhabitants or lung parasites per se.

Piperazine salts are an old anthelmintic used for many years to combat roundworm infestation in foals. They are not only effective and reliable, but also very safe and still unsurpassed today. Another advantage of piperazine is its capability of enhancing the effectiveness of other anthelmintics. Parasites are seemingly unable to develop resistant forms to this tried-and-true worm preparation. I have routinely combined piperazine salts with one of the benzimidazole drugs while worming older foals for both ascarid and strongyle infestation. Recommended dosage is 350 mg per 10 pounds of body weight.

WARNING: The one exception to the ascarid supremacy rule is the parasitic larvae called *Strongyloides westeri* (stomach worms), infrequently found in the lactating mare's milk. Since this *Strongyloides* larva lives in the mare's milk and is ingested by the newborn suckling foal, it is not unusual to discover the internal parasites in the intestine of a three- to five-day-old foal. After being ingested, the infective larvae settle in and promptly cause diarrhea in the newborn. Diagnosis is confirmed by examination of fecal matter under the microscope, revealing the telltale embryonated egg.

It is curious that only ascarid eggs are present from shortly after birth to six to eight weeks of age, then strongyles appear in concert with the ascarids. Both remain present until around three years of age, then the ascarids leave and the strongyles are present forever afterward. In the adult, pinworms, stomach worms (*Strongyloides*), and tapeworms appear occasionally. Fecal tests are helpful to identify and differentiate all parasites in most cases, but unfortunately, we do not have an accurate test to reveal either lungworms or bot worms in the adult.

In foals over eight weeks of age, treatment consists of thiabendazole at the prescribed dosage of 200 mg per 10 pounds of body weight.

Routine worming should be repeated every month during the first year of life, every two months during the yearling year, and every three months thereafter. The foal's second worming should include treatment for both ascarids and strongyles (bloodworms).

It is important to alternate drugs on a timely basis, as most of our dangerous parasites possess the ability to develop resistance to our better anthelmintics early and effectively.

Your equine veterinarian should help develop a worming schedule specific for your farm's efficiency.

IVERMECTIN WARNING: A very dangerous situation involving a worm preparation exists today. I consider this situation to be highly explosive and want to alert all foal owners. When ivermectin, a worm medicine, was introduced on the market more than a decade ago, full-page colored advertisements in the various horse journals boasted of its killing internal parasites at 100 percent efficacy. However, some meticulous researchers uncovered the startling fact that ivermectin has no or limited effect on ascarids (roundworms), the major parasitic threat to all foals and young horses. Ivermectin is in fact so effective against all other internal parasites that it allows the untouched ascarid population to reproduce in a totally uninhibited fashion, inviting total destruction of the foal.

Consequently, I saw in my clinic some very sick foals with overwhelming roundworm infestations. Fecal examinations were infrequently mysteriously negative. Classic symptoms were weepy eyes, potbellies, starey coat, and very low weight. Nondescript pneumonias and unexplained liver disease and malfunction were consistently part of the clinical picture. Today it is indeed shocking and quite unusual to see a parasite-ridden foal owned by conscientious people with a horse background; however, some of these cases were so advanced that the foals were close to death. All had a history in common. They were religiously wormed on time every month, with ivermectin exclusively. This has all been corrected with a new oral product and education.

Ivermectin, however, in its modified form, is a very effective and perfectly acceptable worm medicine for *adult* horses.

BLOODWORMS

Essentially, there are three bloodworm groups that usually receive immediate attention when their presence is suspect. They are identified as *Strongylus vulgaris*, *Strongylus edentatus*, and *Strongylus equinus*. Bloodworms create a devastating effect upon the foal's intestines, liver, and vital circulatory system; they commonly appear between the second and third month of the young horse's life and must be stopped before they can migrate into and through the blood vessels.

Treatment

Recommended treatment for both ascarids and bloodworms is thiabendazole (200 mg per 10 pounds of body weight) plus 1 gram piperazine citrate; or Ripercol fluid (Levamisole and piperazine; 1 fluid ounce per 100 pounds of body weight).

Although roundworms and bloodworms are the major parasites offending the young foal, lungworms (*Dictyocaulus arnfeldi*), pinworms (*Oxyuris equi*), tapeworms (*Anoplocephala perfoliata*), and the three types of bot worms (*Gastrophilus intestinalis*, the common bot; G.*haemorrhoidalis*, the nose or red-tailed bot; and G. *nasalis*, the throat or chin bot) are also parasites of concern. The suggested drugs and dosage for roundworms and bloodworms will in most cases be effective against any other occasional parasite.

BOT INFESTATION

Bot medicine should be administered in the late fall or winter, as the foal becomes a yearling, ideally after a killing frost in the area. Since bot flies are the source of infestation, it would be foolish to bot-worm before a hard frost eliminates the fly. Wait and tube-worm after the weather changes with a hard frost. The horse will then be free of bots until midsummer, when the bot fly reappears.

The bot parasite is unique in that the bot fly deposits her sticky embryonated egg on the horse's hairs—preferably on the inside of the legs or on the hairs around the mouth. When the legs are licked, the eggs are inadvertently swallowed. The larvae then attach themselves to the stomach lining and remain so attached for months, causing periods of gastritis and colic in certain individuals.

WARNING: Be suspicious of a bot infestation when sudden discomfort develops immediately after a horse begins to eat grain, just as the grain reaches his stomach. This behavior can be diagnostic. In my opinion, bot infestation is responsible for more stomach disorders, acute gastritis, and some forms of colic than other known causes.

Bots were effectively treated for many years with carbon disulfide. This timeless but irritating drug has done a good job for years, although its administration is limited to the stomach tube; however, it must be used carefully and with respect.

I remember hearing horrifying tales about the use of carbon disulfide capsules or "balls"—how they ruptured while the horse was being forced to swallow them, causing severe irritation to the esophageal lining. In unfortunate cases, erosion of the tissue resulted in illness and death.

Nonetheless, we continue to use carbon disulfide as it is still the most effective boticide known to veterinary medical literature. Thankfully, this caustic anthelmintic has been incorporated in a commercial mixture called Parvex Plus (Upjohn). This popular preparation is a superb bot worm medicine and, if instructions are followed, a safe, effective drug. The other boticides, called Dichlorvos and Trichlorfon, are effective but dangerous organophosphates. (Read below.) Ivermectin is a boticide in the adult horse.

In your nonstop battle against parasitism, I suggest that you alternate the use of the benzimidazole drugs, namely cambendazole, fenbendazole, mebendazole, and thiabendazole. All are very effective and very safe for use in all types of horses. Although they are inconsistently effective against ascarids, they are specifically indicated for use against strongyles (bloodworms). When combined with piperazine salts, this mixture is ideal for removing both roundworms and bloodworms in the foal over two months of age.

WARNING: Some of the most destructive parasites are the quickest to build effective resistance to our anthelmintics. To repeat, the key to the prevention of resistant internal parasites is to alter or change the various benzimidazole drugs with each successive worming. In addition, we know that piperazine salts do not cause resistant parasites. Foals can be efficiently wormed in safety with these compounds. Therefore, there is no excuse to use drugs with a narrow margin of safety and toxicity.

PARASITE CONTROL MEASURES

There are many species of worms, but I have touched upon only the most troublesome ones. Your veterinarian can best determine your foal's needs and can better design a specific program. Failure to meet scheduled worming dates can allow massive reproduction of parasites to cause tissue damage that future worming cannot correct.

Land management can aid greatly in controlling these harmful, debilitating parasites. A rule of thumb is one acre of pastureland per horse; this allows for ample grazing and a slower reinfestation rate. Chain harrowing, cleansing pasture areas of droppings, and clipping high grass are helpful; but pasture rotation, which blocks the life cycle of the parasite, is superb in controlling specific parasite reproduction. Some large breeding farms actually vacuum the fields free of manure.

Reinfestation is a constant, never-ending fact of life. Nonetheless, I become upset when I watch a foal, immediately after worming, reach down and fill its mouth with ascarid-contaminated straw. In order to hold the line against the ever-present internal parasites, a well-run horse farm will certainly benefit by having an intelligent farm manager, an interested veterinarian, adequate well-fenced land, and ample housing. I would then be willing to gamble that the worms would lose, at least for a while.

WARNING: Commercial anthelmintic pastes are popular and, as an added bonus, require no veterinary service. Some pastes contain undesirable organophosphate chemicals. Although these cholinesterase-inhibiting drugs do efficiently remove parasites, they also occasionally cause gastrointestinal upsets, especially in sensitive individuals. The organophosphate group of drugs was developed and subsequently advertised with great fanfare in horse journals. They are available under a variety of commercial names. Before using them, do read the fine print and be aware of the

PARASITES AND EFFECTIVE ANTHELMINTICS

WORM MEDICINE	LARGE STRONGYLES	SMALL STRONGYLES	STRONGY- LOIDES	ASCARIDS	PIN WORMS	BOTS
Thiabendazole	x	x	x	x	x	
Cambendazole	x	x	x	x	x	
Fenbendazole	x	x			x	
Febantel		x		x	x	
Mebendazole	x	x		x	x	
Pyrantel pamoate	x	x		x	x	
Piperazine		x		x	x	
Trichlorfon				x	x	x
Dichlorvos	x	x		x	x	x
Carbon disulfide						x
Ivermectin	x	x	x	No	x	x

intimated warnings. Caution—they are also incompatible and react adversely with the commonly used phenothiazine-derived tranquilizers (promazine, acepromazine), especially when administered intravenously. Several deaths have been reported when unknowingly a specific tranquilizer had been injected intravenously within several weeks after organophosphate usage. Chickens and pigeons that search through the droppings of treated horses to retrieve undigested grain are killed by the chemical. Organophosphates are commonly found in insecticides and are responsible for the death of many of our birds.

There is no doubt that these worming compounds remove all parasites and their eggs, but while doing so, they also threaten the health and environment of the host animal. Organophosphates are unsafe for use in horses, ecologically dangerous, and, in my opinion, their manufacture should be abolished.

The equine has survived with intestinal parasites for an eternity, so when designing a worming schedule, please place your emphasis on moderate use of all chemicals, as they are foreign to the foal's body.

Personally, I would rather see a few worms than place my patient in jeopardy.

Chapter Seven

FEEDS, FEEDING, AND NUTRITION

Nutritional requirements vary widely among the different species of domestic animals and continue to challenge the farmer or breeder to provide diets that will achieve maximum growth and genetic fulfillment. The basic difference in species lies in their fundamental classification. Please listen carefully—do not ever borrow or extrapolate known information from one species and apply to another!

HERBIVORE—CARNIVORE—OMNIVORE

The human being and the pig are classified as omnivores (herbivore plus carnivore); the dog and cat are carnivores (meat eaters).

Along with the calf, lamb, and kid, the foal is a herbivore (vegetarian). However, the similarity stops there, as the other three are also ruminants, with digestive systems that consist of four stomachs, while the foal has but one. It is easily understandable, then, why the foal's basic health needs and nutritional requirements are so diverse and specific.

GROWING FOAL REQUIREMENTS

Knowledgeable horse people instinctively place great emphasis on high-quality foods and conscientious feeding schedules. Keep your foal healthy by feeding a highly nutritious and well-balanced diet. A poorly nourished foal will not fulfill its optimum size nor its performance potential, and will suffer for life as a second-grade individual.

It is almost criminal when mediocre care and management inhibit the full development of an individual possessing a superb genetic structure. There may be numerous ill effects as a result of poor nutrition, but certainly the most obvious are those involving anatomical development. A foal suffering from nutritional deprivation is readily recognized as being, to a greater or lesser degree, undersized and unthrifty.

All animals at all ages require protein to survive; the protein content of the diet is most important to a growing animal. The body derives its protein from dietary amino acids, the basic building blocks of tissue construction. Hence the importance of the analysis tag, showing percentage of protein, sewn on the top of each and every bag of grain or feed preparation sold today.

Although there are many amino acids known in nature, 10 essential amino acids are required daily for normal tissue growth in animals. The body can at times generate some of these building blocks, but not always at the rate required to grow, to perform, and to reproduce. Therefore, the animal's daily diet must contain these elements in order to meet and satisfy its dietary requirements— hence the term essential amino acids. The 10 essential amino acids are: arginine, histidine, isoleucine, leucine, lysine, methionine, phenylalanine, threonine, tryptophan, and valine.

Years ago, many farm and draft horses suffered a dietary deficiency as a result of being fed primarily or exclusively corn. Corn at that time was plentiful, fattening, and inexpensive, so naturally it became the sole staple of these animals. However, corn is an incomplete feed. It lacks two essential amino acids—lysine and tryptophan. In horses fed exclusively corn along with the usual timothy or orchard-grass hay, a full-blown deficiency inevitably developed. This deficiency can be easily remedied by the simple inclusion of legume hay, either alfalfa or clover; then the glaring imbalance is corrected. Today it is generally acknowledged that legume hay is almost a complete feed. It possesses high-quality protein, vitamins, and minerals in a readily assimilable form, so it is highly sought after and justly commands a fair price.

The importance of protein in all diets cannot be overemphasized; however, the need is greater in the young, growing, pregnant, or competition animal. A knowledge of food analysis and dietary requirements is important, and much information is available on the subjects. It is equally important that one not misuse this knowledge by assuming that "If some is good, more is better."

WARNING: A dreadful misconception has developed among horse breeders within the past 15 years: Protein, in all forms, has been outlandishly overfed in an all-out effort to grow a "superfoal." This erroneous thinking has proved dangerous and resulted in devastating growth changes in young, fast-growing horses that manifested the clinical form of apple ankles, enlarged joints, epiphysitis, and various forms of tendon contractions. It is my personal opinion that overfeeding of protein, vitamin, and mineral supplements during pregnancy causes 90 percent of all dystocias, by virtue of a contracted fetus while in utero and the various other subtle forms of contraction seen immediately after birth.

I have known breeders to suffer costly and heartbreaking experiences as a result of using commercially prepared "super-additives." Perhaps I can help others by sharing these facts and observations. Please rely on the naturally grown feeds and roughages from enriched soil, as they are in the form most suitable for assimilation by your foal's system.

Although they have been scientifically formulated and developed for the feeding of a foal, I am not convinced of the validity of commercial additives or supplements. Invest your money rather in top-quality legume hay and grain and avoid purchasing costly, highly advertised commercial products. The upper limit of 12 percent protein should not be exceeded in any feed at any age, or you risk nutritional aberrations. See Chapter 4.

DEFICIENCY IN MARE'S MILK

This may be a little-known fact but one of great importance. Let us now return to the very young foal and shed some light on a hidden malady. As early as three days, the average suckling will develop a degree of anemia unless it is vigorous enough to begin to nibble on some bits of grain and hay.

Inherently weak or borderline weak foals may manifest signs of anemia, whereas others, perhaps innately stronger, seem to pass through this threatening period undaunted.

WARNING: Insidiously dangerous, this deficiency is universal, existing in all mare's milk, regardless of breed, diet, or care, and surprisingly involves only the quality of the milk, not the quantity. Abundant lactation or milk flow is deceptive, for the amount of milk is no indication of nutritional level.

Two trace minerals, copper and iron, are totally lacking in mare's milk, and these two minerals are unequivocally responsible for red blood cell formation and hemoglobin levels. Therefore, the foal's dietary intake must compensate for the deficiency in the milk.

CAUTION: Do not attempt to add these trace minerals to the foal's diet—simply determine that the foal is eating hay and grain at three to five days of age, along with drinking milk.

Newborn foals who arrive with normal blood values may be found anemic by day six unless the individual is vigorous enough to begin nibbling on hay and its mother's grain shortly after birth. A constant finding in all mares, this foal anemia mirrors the milk's trace-mineral deficit. The resultant stress created by the anemic condition can lower the foal's resistance to infection and disease.

If the foal fails to consume minute amounts of hay or grain by the third to the fifth day, it will surely suffer some degree of anemia. Most healthy foals begin

NORMAL BLOOD VALUE CHANGES IN THE NEONATE

NEONATE FOAL AGE	RBC (MILLION/ MM³)	WBC (THOUSAND/ MM³)	HEMOGLOBIN (GM.%)	PCV (%)
Day 1 Newborn Hemo- concentration	8–10	8–11	14–16	35–45
Day 5–7 Foal Anemia Period	6–10	7–12	7–14	27–40
Day 21 Normal Recovery	9–12	8–11	12–15	36–41

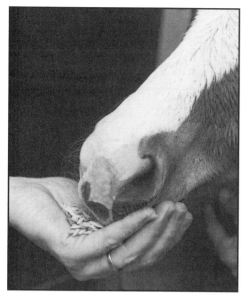

Hand-feed grain.

Hand-feed green leafy legume hay.

eating independently, although sparsely, by the second day. However, be aware that the blood count of foals who appear to be perfectly healthy consistently reveals anemia during this vulnerable period.

If the foal in question seems indifferent to hay and grain, it is then imperative to teach it to eat by repeatedly placing small amounts of grain in its mouth. As soon as good-quality hay and grain is consumed by the foal, the blood analysis improves almost spontaneously.

SIX-WEEK LACTATION PEAK

Around 72 to 76 hours after delivery, the mare stops producing colostrum, and the udder then fills with milk representative of that which will be available until around six weeks, when lactation quality peaks. From this time on, both the quantity and quality of the mare's milk dramatically decrease.

This fact clearly explains why most foals look their best around six weeks of age. They then gradually lose condition and somewhat decline in overall thriftiness. Unless the foal receives additional nourishment, ideally in the form of grain and legume hay (not commercial supplements), it will assuredly diminish not only physically but in actual growth rate.

It has been my experience that those foals given the advantage of a creep feeder starting at three days of age suffer neither the neonatal anemia at day five nor the nutritional letdown experienced around the seventh or eighth week of life by other sucklings.

Longtime breeders who believe in the adage "Nature knows best" are reluctant to adjust old habits and implement changes in feeding practices, especially with suckling foals, but I believe that it is time to change our thinking and see to it that our foals grow to their genetic potential as they should, can, and certainly deserve to do.

In my opinion, the only value of mare's milk, after the six-week peak and its immediate decline, is to aid in washing down the hay, grain, and grass eaten by the foal. This seemingly impertinent, but not disrespectful, attack upon motherhood's efficiency will undoubtedly shock many from traditional complacency and, I trust, convert some to acceptance of newer and better feeding methods.

CREEP FEEDING

From three days of age, all foals should have grain available at all times. It is almost impossible for a foal to compete for even a morsel of grain from his mother's feed tub. Her voracious appetite, size, and capacity to eat faster than her foal make it difficult for even an aggressive, strong foal, let alone a timid or slightly weaker individual, to share. Some mares actually refuse to let their foals eat from the large tub; others tolerantly share their meals. This haphazard method of feeding a foal is inefficient, inexcusable, and, frankly, outmoded.

The average foal will eat a mouthful of grain, then suckle, then go back to the tub for a few more mouthfuls. Therefore, it is essential to provide free-choice grain without competition so that the foal can eat various small amounts in peace and quiet at any hour or time of its choice.

Stall creep feeding method.

Creep feeding is the most satisfactory solution to the problem of adequate nutrition for the newborn foal. This is easy to arrange in the average stall. All that is required is a round, smooth fence rail of sufficient length to fit diagonally across one corner of the stall. Hang the foal's tub at the level of its nose in the corner, then position the rail so that the foal can easily walk under it to reach its tub, but far enough out from the corner that the mare's long neck cannot extend to the foal's tub. A mare's elastic neck has incredible range, so do be careful.

FOAL DIET

Mix 50 percent Mother's Oats with 50 percent Foal-Lac pellets, a Borden product. Provide only small portions at first, keeping the amount fresh and clean. Foals will not eat stale, fly-covered, dirty grain.

Within a couple of weeks, the Mother's Oats can be replaced with large flaked or crimped oats, again fed with an equal portion of Foal-Lac pellets. Some foals will be consuming 6 or more quarts of this concentrate daily at six weeks of age. There are some breeders who prefer to incorporate 25 percent flaked barley with 25 percent crimped oats and 50 percent Foal-Lac pellets around four weeks of age. Creep-fed foals usually surpass in both size and condition those foals who share their mother's tub because their substantial nutritional needs are satisfied.

PASTURE CREEP FEEDING

If your mares and foals are to be kept out on pasture for long periods, a field creep is a definite asset, although it is more expensive and more difficult to build. Mold is a constant threat to any horse owner, so be certain to design an overhang to prevent undue moisture from entering the store of grain. Erect the creep where the mares customarily gather to relax so that the environment is conducive to rest and leisurely snacking. It is a rare foal who eats if its mother has wandered away.

This classic field creep feeder (above) is constructed for the use of sucklings and weanlings. The roof provides protection from dampness and excessive sunlight. Hay (green and leafy, not moist) is stored in the center and grain is provided in the trough, away from dampness. The four-paneled paddock that encloses the creep is precisely 48 inches tall, permitting foals to enter and exit and preventing hungry mares from entering the enclosure.

The creep feeder in the following photograph has some tubs added to the sides, allowing for smaller foals—but farmhands would need an extra eye to watch out for dirt, debris, and mold, which is death to all equines.

Field creep feeder.

A field creep minus the paddock fence. This one is used for older foals, all weaned.

Foal creep feeder.

Notice the fake owl hanging in the creep. Florida has had an unidentified virus carried by all types of birds, so this acts as a deterrent.

NOTE: In summary, foals must have a constant source of high-quality legume hay, good heavy concentrates, and a salt lick (plain or mineralized) at all times in order to achieve their inherent genetic growth potential.

ALERT: In the absence of adequate research, the consensus is that once a foal has reached six or eight months, it should be removed from the free-access grain group and its daily grain intake carefully monitored. Of course, free-access water, salt, and green legume hay should always be available. The reason for the monitored grain allotment is the ambiguous entity called nutritional contraction usually observed in large-bodied six- to eight-month-old rapidly growing foals, or in another age group, those from 16 to 22 months. Please be aware of these dangerous growth-spurt periods.

CEREAL GRAINS

When discussing nutrition, it would be inappropriate to exclude some detail on the various merits, weaknesses, and even hazards of cereal grains and hay types.

Cereal grains, commonly referred to as concentrates, consist of oats, corn, wheat, barley, and rye. Although some barley is fed in limited quantity, horse people are primarily concerned with oats and corn. Rye holds no interest as a food, but its straw is highly prized as superb bedding in some better horse barns.

Cereal grains are characteristically high in net energy and low in fiber, as opposed to roughages, such as hay, fodder, straw, and silage, which are high in fiber and consequently low in net energy. The protein content of grain is notoriously low and also of poor quality. This profound deficiency in cereal grains is caused by their minimal amounts of essential amino acids. A common mistake among horse people in their effort to feed well is an overemphasis on grain intake. This imbalance can seriously affect the nutritional balance in the young, the growing, the pregnant, or the competing animal.

Oats serve as the standard to which other grains are compared. By virtue of their hulls, oats form a bulky and easily digested mass in the horse's gastrointestinal tract.

As a cereal grain, oats are consistently low in protein quality and also low in both phosphorus and calcium. While oats are very palatable and do net the high energy levels so needed by performance horses, oats are very low in vitally needed vitamins A and D. However, oats can be fed properly in a well-balanced diet by combining them with a good, clean, green alfalfa hay. Good-quality legume hay provides the otherwise lacking protein, phosphorus, calcium, and vitamins A and D, so necessary in the diet.

It is my opinion that this previously recommended diet of limited oats with unlimited, free-choice, clean, green, leafy, legume hay with no additives (unless geographically contraindicated) is a tried-and-true safe horse diet. This old and proven method of raising colts has worked very well since the beginning of time; and I can attest, as a young horsewoman and equine veterinarian of 35 years, that this "plain" diet never produced a physis foal (contraction, crooked legs, epiphysitis, apple ankles, OCD, and cervical deformities, to name a few).

Good, clean "plump oats" (Canadian-grown) should weigh around 42 pounds per bushel and are well worth the cost. Locally grown oats (30 to 32 pounds per bushel) should be avoided and not fed to horses. Rolled and crushed oats are to be avoided. Although basically designed to increase digestibility, they have failed badly in the case of the horse. Most of the nourishment escapes during the processing and bagging procedure, leaving primarily dust, debris, and respiratory irritants. Crimped oats are a much more efficient food form, but only second choice to whole oats with all of their nutrition intact.

When molasses is mixed with heavier grains, such as corn, barley, or wheat, the horse's stomach can better accept and digest them. A popular and palatable example is "sweet feed."

COOKED GRAIN

Cooking grain is a superior method of preparing horse grain for the young, growing, or any other horse in the world. It is a highly palatable, highly digestible, and nutritious food. Its greatest asset, though, is the greatly needed intestinal bulk that it provides.

Years ago, it was a common sight in well-run barns to see "cookers" started early in the day and allowed to steep until late afternoon. The large vats, on wood or coal-burning stoves, would be watched by the head groom until it was determined that all grain kernels were soft and split open. When the lid was lifted, eager neighs greeted the escaped aroma. Barns where cooked feed was on the schedule always had fewer colic cases, myositis (inflammation of muscle tissue) problems, or gastrointestinal-related ailments.

To my mind, while more convenient forms of feeding have been substituted, the merit and benefits of cooked grains have never been approached.

HORSE HAY

The word hay is a broad term for any of a group of dried grains or legumes of varying quality. Hay can range in grade from beautiful green leafy legume, glowing with nutritional value, to dried-out brown or colorless sticks and stems of meadow grass possessing negligible food value.

It is unfortunate that among livestock people the complete gamut of roughage, whether edible or not, is considered to be hay. Not so in the world of horse owners or breeders. People involved with high-quality horses demand and usually pay well for "horse hay." And rightfully so. It is not a simple task to select a proper stand of grass in the field, then make, bale, and deliver the nutritious hay to a top barn. Add to this the gamble of weather conditions that weigh so heavily on the successful outcome of making high-quality hay, and one can better appreciate the accomplishment. *The ABCs of horse hay requirements: clean, green, and leafy!*

Conversely, cows, sheep, and goats thrive on all grades of hay—even those rejected for horse consumption. Ruminants actually tolerate surprisingly large amounts of mold, dust, and musty roughages; it is not unusual to see other livestock thriving on hay capable of causing death in a horse.

There are two main types of horse hay:

- *Grass hay*: timothy, bluegrass, and meadow or orchard grass.

- *Legume hay*: alfalfa and clover.

Each type of hay has individual advantages to meet the roughage needs of the horse.

The key to making nutritious hay is the ability to determine the precise time to harvest the crop, based on the age of the plant. A field of immature grass will yield enhanced nutrition and palatability, whereas a mature grass crop will result in reduced nutritional levels and stems with less color and reduced digestibility.

When purchasing hay, remember the four cardinal rules. Hay should be:

1. *Leafy*, with few stems.

2. *Smooth* and soft to the touch.

3. *Green* in color.

4. *Clean*—free of mold, dust, and mustiness.

WARNING: Do not hesitate to break a bale and slip your hand down in between the biscuits or flakes of hay; use your nose to detect odor. Be careful to avoid purchasing mature hay that is being passed off as desirable immature lush hay, usually at a premium price.

When examining timothy hay for use in older horses, be sure to reject any hay with timothy heads longer than $1^1/_2$ inches. The length of the timothy head reveals the age of the hay at the time it was harvested and thus gives some indication of its nutritional content.

Young growing horses, brood mares, and some pleasure horses require vintage legume hay, with all of its nutrients and nutritional superiority. Concentrates are less important and thus play second fiddle to roughage among knowledgeable breeders. A turnabout occurs among performance horses; for them, cereal grains regain their importance.

FESCUE POSITION ALERT: Fescue is a pasture grass found in grazing areas, hay, and even bedding. It grows primarily in midwestern states and has been found recently in Kentucky.

Tall fescue reportedly contains endophytes (fungus) that upon ingestion by pregnant mares causes placental thickening and malfunction resulting in early massive placental separation from the gravid uterus. "Red bag" abortions characteristically occur. This toxic element also causes agalactia (no milk).

Although fescue is difficult to recognize, breeding farm attendants should be alerted to examine all pastures, hay, and bedding.

GRAIN INTAKE VS. HAY CONSUMPTION

We have discussed the hazards of too much protein intake and its adverse effects on muscle, tendon, and bone growth. There has also been in the past a tendency to overfeed young growing horses on cereal grains rather than hay. Historically, hay was erroneously considered bulk, with negligible nutritional value. In my opinion, the emphasis has been wrongly placed. A quality legume hay, or a clean timothy mix of 30 to 40 percent legume, provides vital minerals, vitamins, and high-quality protein needed for both growth and reproduction.

The horse owner should carefully shop and hand-select the precise hay fed to his charges. Although good hay is costly, it is the nutritional backbone and major source of essential dietary needs; concentrates cannot replace it in fulfilling these needs, nor can oats, although it does contribute to the greater energy requirements of performance horses, and of those racing or in active competition.

PHYTIN ALERT: In early yearlings, the practice of force-feeding cereal grains can present yet another significant problem. A compound called phytin, present in all cereal grains, especially oats, can actually inhibit the availability and thus assimilation of essential calcium, phosphorus, and magnesium in the young horse's body, even when these are present in the diet. Phytin is thought to interfere with the normal ratio of calcium and phosphorus, so overfeeding of grain should be avoided.

CEREAL GRAIN WARNING: Also, when overfed on grain rations, these young growing animals are inclined to consume less hay, the true source of minerals, protein, and vitamins. Over a few months, reduced hay intake, plus increased phytin from grain, could conceivably result in a significant mineral imbalance and nutritional deficiency. The physis syndrome (contraction, crooked legs, epiphysitis, apple ankles, OCD, and cervical deformities) quickly manifests its characteristic symptoms in this age group. See Chapter 4.

So after eight months of age, cereal grains should be carefully limited while the foal should be allowed free access to fresh water, a salt lick, and, above all, high-quality hay. Incidentally, top-grade hay with its ready source of calcium, phosphorus, protein, and vitamins not only provides these elements but does so in the proper form and proportion for optimal assimilation by your young growing animal. When hay is grown on well-fertilized soil, it contains nutrients ready for animal digestion, which is not the case in commercially prepared products.

Avoid the use of vitamin and mineral supplements unless specifically indicated by your veterinarian. These commercial products have been incriminated as possible causes for overgrowth spurts, skeletal deformities, and various forms of tendon contraction.

The rule of thumb in feeding "early to late" yearlings is never to exceed 12 quarts of concentrate and never to exceed 12 percent in protein daily. Avoid feed supplements, and supply the best available clean, green legume hay free-choice.

HERBS

There has been a steady, increased interest in herbal medicine in both the human and the equine.

I for one am certain that herbs and their uses will broaden as more is learned about these natural substances. Equine practitioners must use caution when treating with herbs as many of these preparations are, in fact, mixtures and not one simple herb. More research and understanding must take place before anyone can treat with any certainty. In lieu of a predictable and specific action, and without a prescribed recommended dosage, one could hardly treat with confidence.

A few actions are known:

- Kwai has been claimed to lower blood pressure.

- Yucca has been used for arthritic pain.

- White yellow bark is also used for pain but may be toxic in animals.

- Black walnut is toxic to horses.

- Ginseng is claimed to increase energy.

There is no doubt that herbs will, in the future, as more is learned, play a more important role in veterinary medicine if they can be combined with Western medicine.

Acupuncture, also from China, came on the scene several years ago touted as a cure-all, and its use continues with mixed reports.

MINERALS/TRACE MINERALS

The essential minerals needed by the horse to maintain good health are: calcium, phosphorus, chlorine, cobalt, copper, iodine, iron, magnesium, manganese, potassium, selenium, sulfur, and zinc—all of which are found in the normally adequate diet. These are called trace minerals.

One can, through the use of a mineralized salt lick, assure the horse of adequate dietary trace minerals.

The old farmer's saying, "You can't take out what you don't put in," has stood the test of time. In order to produce a nutritious crop from soil that is farmed year after year, after soil testing, expensive fertilizers most likely will be applied to maintain fertile soil.

Legume hay—green, leafy, and well cured, cut from well-fertilized soil—can supply an unparalleled food source, including minerals in the form that can be properly assimilated into the horse's system. Conversely, commercially produced vitamins and minerals, despite great effort on the part of manufacturers to reproduce the "real thing," miss the boat and are neither digested nor assimilated efficiently. Thus, at great expense, the contents are usually passed through the gastrointestinal tract and into the manure pile untouched.

CALCIUM AND PHOSPHORUS

Calcium and phosphorus are vital for a healthy skeletal system, stable metabolic system, and sound dental arcades. A critical balance is maintained, as an interrelationship exists between the minerals in the body; research indicates that if an imbalance occurs, neither mineral is utilized. For a growing or immature foal, a 2-to-1 ratio of calcium to phosphorus is essential. This fragile balance can be easily upset by the inadvertent or ill-advised feeding of phosphorus, not calcium, which is lacking.

Cereal grains are low in phosphorus and equally low in calcium; corn is the worst offender. A good-quality legume hay is rich in calcium and low in phosphorus, but supplies a high-quality protein with a rich source of vitamins A and

D. Here again, however, the phosphorus content is low. A phosphorus deficiency can affect all body functions, especially bone development and fertility. Be aware of this insidious deficiency! Avoid commercial additives or supplements. A deficiency can actually be created by adding one mineral, so overzealous feeding practices are hazardous and should be avoided. Contrary to most thinking, when a deficiency in this ratio does occur, most commonly it is a phosphorus deficiency.

NOTE: All horses at all ages can benefit by the addition of wheat bran to an already adequate diet. Wheat bran is high in protein, high in total digestible nutrients, and, although low in calcium, it is the richest source of phosphorus known.

PREPARATION OF BRAN MASH

Prepare equal parts of wheat bran and any cereal grain; moisten and prepare as a hot or cold bran mash. The mixture provides vital bulk and fiber for the gastrointestinal tract and ensures adequate phosphorus in the diet. It is not only palatable, but also bulky and therefore satisfying. It provides a welcome warm meal in the winter and an equally welcome cool meal in the summer.

As there are many dietary sources of calcium, calcium deficiency occurs much less often than phosphorus deficiency. All legume grasses and hay contain high levels of calcium. I equate bran mash with good old chicken soup.

SALT

Sodium chloride, or salt, is as essential for life and its physiologic processes as water. The use of a plain salt lick is adequate, but the availability of a mineralized salt lick is ideal as it provides all trace minerals—with the exception of selenium. See Chapter 4.

WARNING: A salt lick appears to be perfectly harmless—as well as the logical source for all the trace minerals. Not so. Beware of abrupt changes. When a salt block is suddenly available free-choice after horses have been deprived of salt for a given period, digestive disturbances, colic symptoms, and even mild toxicity can occur.

A salt block is safer than loose salt for use with young horses, especially foals, as loose salt can be consumed much more quickly, inadvertently causing a toxicity and possibly resulting in a very sick foal.

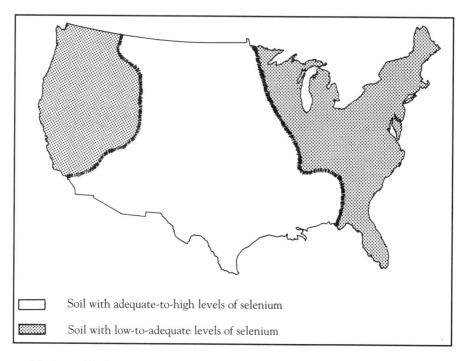

Selenium soil levels.

SELENIUM DEFICIENCY—THE CAUSE OF WHITE MUSCLE DISEASE (WMD) IN THE NEWBORN

Although selenium (Se) excesses and deficiencies are seen in all ages, foals suffer a distinct entity in utero.

In newborn foals, Selenium deficiency is called white muscle disease and is usually lethal. Symptoms are profound muscle weakness, with inability to stand and no capacity to swallow. Death occurs within a short time.

Postmortem findings are extensive degeneration of muscles, which are very pale and swollen throughout, with areas of mineral deposits interspersed in the muscle tissue. Foals affected are all short-lived and commonly diagnosed or confirmed at postmortem. This tragedy can be traced to a selenium deficiency in the dam during the ill-fated foal's gestational period and embryonic life.

The at-risk brood mare should receive a monthly 10 ml injection of vitamin E/Se IM (preferable site—gluteal muscles) combined with a daily feed supplement of selenium to prevent white muscle disease (WMD).

Since there is no satisfactory treatment, prevention is the only answer.

YOUNG GROWING AND ADULT HORSES

The incidence of selenium deficiency seems to be on the increase, unless we are becoming better diagnosticians. Adult individuals, especially racehorses, suffer bouts of myositis, metabolic imbalances and lameness in the form of tying-up syndrome when subjected to any degree of selenium deficit. They respond well to vitamin E/Se, recommended as a monthly injection, preferably administered into the gluteal muscles. Oral preparations are given in the feed on a daily basis.

Low-grade or chronic selenium deficiency can be recognized by malshaped feet, lameness, and irregular patterns or growth ridges on the hoof wall.

Selenium deficiency foot symptoms are pathonomonic—and abnormal foot growth pattern develops with disturbed growth ridges in the malshaped foot wall. Frog tissue assumes a yellow discoloration quite characteristic of selenium deprivation. Balancing and shaping the foot and properly placing nails in the compromised foot wall becomes a farrier's nightmare. Frequent shoeing is required. In these cases, monthly selenium and vitamin E injections are indicated and quite helpful.

Linseed meal is an ideal, safe, and natural source of selenium, in addition to being rich in protein. Please consult your veterinarian, however, before introducing this rich supplement, as a careful dosage must be met to avoid toxicity. This is a vital trace mineral, but also a dangerous one, and must be used with respect. The margin for safety is narrow.

The established selenium requirement for an adult horse is 4 mg per 100 pounds of horse feed; the hazardous toxic level is less than 200 mg per 100 pounds of horse feed. Excess selenium intake produces a toxicosis or poisoning.

CHRONIC SYMPTOMS

Symptoms are hair loss in mane and tail areas, poor appetite, staggering, and the development of excessively moist or wet hoof texture.

Obviously, the chronic deficiency or toxicity symptoms are seen only in the adult and usually in a soil-deficient area, whereas the newborn foal suffers white muscle disease and promptly succumbs. Since it is not included in the mineralized salt lick, selenium must be added to the diet, if indicated. Geographically soil-deficient areas have been identified as low, normal, and high in selenium levels, each creating its own individual symptoms and conditions. Deficiencies are especially found in the Northeast and the Northwest.

In the United States there are precisely identified geographic areas known to be soil-deficient in iodine. All people in these areas, and all livestock, must augment their daily diets with iodized salt. Before the importance of iodine in our diets was fully understood, both humans and animals suffered with goiter development simply from living in iodine-deficient areas.

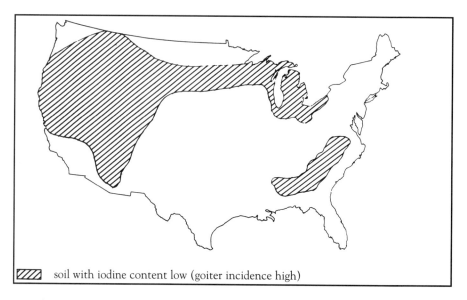

soil with iodine content low (goiter incidence high)

Iodine soil content.

It seems diabolic, but when their diets contain excessive iodine or when an iodine deficiency exists during gestation, brood mares will produce foals with goiters. There appears to be no margin for error. The thyroid gland is enlarged in these foals at birth, and this condition can alert the astute horseman to a possible deficiency.

Foals severely affected during embryonic development are frequently aborted. They may be born alive but weak, or slowly succumb, but in any case, the telltale enlarged thyroid gland (goiter) is clearly visible.

Again, as with some other trace minerals, the margins between adequate, inadequate, and excessive or toxic iodine levels are very narrow. An iodized salt lick can fully provide the necessary iodine required in any diet. Goiter formation, once developed, remains visible the life of the affected foal and can helpfully reveal a geographic area in question.

ALERT: There is one hazard with any salt lick—rapid consumption of or overindulgence in salt can create problems in the form of gastrointestinal upsets that may reach a toxic level, especially with mineralized salt blocks. Salt poisoning most commonly occurs in salt-deprived or neglected animals. Constant or available use of a salt block may help prevent such upsets, since loose salt invites rapid consumption, whereas a salt block requires long, tedious licking to consume an equal portion of trace minerals. A time-tested rule for any foal-keeper is to maintain that watchful vigilance we again call the "third eye."

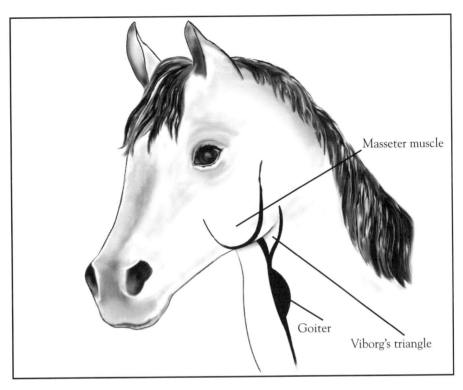

Masseter muscle

Goiter

Viborg's triangle

Goiter (enlarged thyroid gland).

COPPER AND IRON DEFICIENCY

The brood mare's milk is notoriously deficient in the trace minerals copper and iron. It is easy to understand that the neonate foal will suffer from anemia during the first three to five days of life.

To prevent this inevitable anemia, it is essential for the caretaker to observe whether the baby foal is in fact ingesting small amounts of hay and grain. If not, please hand-feed the foal by placing bits of hay and grain into its mouth. You then will soon see the foal begin to eat small mouthfuls on its own and quickly wash it down with its mother's milk. See Chapter 5.

It is rare to see a primary or systemic copper deficiency in any age horse. Just recently, however, some brood mare farms in specific geographic areas have reported foals manifesting varying degrees of knuckling over of all four limbs. A recent report correlated copper, zinc, and magnesium deficiencies with limb deviations. Again, these cases seemed concentrated in precise geographic areas (Ohio, Kentucky) suspected of soil mineral deficiencies. Prognosis is guarded to poor.

All other mentioned trace minerals are abundant in the everyday diet and are thus not problematic, even in horses receiving a mere marginal diet with only average thought, care, and attention.

VITAMINS

Vitamins are dietary organic substances required in minute amounts for normal body function.

These are found naturally in feeds. Any indiscriminate dietary change can easily upset the delicate balance of vitamins and cause a deficiency disease. Vitamin deficiencies cause malnutrition, retarded growth, sex disorders, abortions, and assorted diseases and maladies.

While vitamins are stored quite well inside the body, in the normal environment, their potency is vulnerable and easily destroyed by sunlight, air, moisture, and temperature change. In grains and roughages, a vitamin's strength, maintenance, and stability can be dissipated quickly and its potency needlessly destroyed depending upon the time of year when the hay or grain is harvested, the stage of growth at harvest, and the method and duration of storage.

Vitamins prepared for human consumption are stored in protective capsules and airtight containers, which maintain their stability. Unfortunately, feeds and forage foodstuffs for animals cannot be enclosed and protected in the same efficient fashion to prevent loss of vitamin quantity and quality.

Vitamins are divided into two groups: fat-soluble and water-soluble. Fat-soluble vitamins include A, D, and E, and hold the greatest potential for deficiencies in the horse.

FAT-SOLUBLE VITAMINS

Vitamin A ranks first in importance among animals and people. Since it is plentiful in natural foods, one would think that a vitamin A deficiency should never exist. Unfortunately, lack of vitamin A in daily diets is commonly found in livestock, especially during the winter months.

Vitamin A is essential for good health; since the body produces it from carotene contained in plants, animals must ingest an adequate amount of carotene daily. Intake of 3,000 to 5,000 IU per 100 pounds of body weight has been determined to be the daily minimum requirement of vitamin A for the equine. Fresh green hay or good pasture can more than meet this figure.

Green color represents carotene content. Hay that is stored for longer than one year is known to dramatically decrease in vitamin content. Exposure to light and oxygen destroys vitamin levels in forage, but when it is stored properly inside of barns, the nutritional loss is neither as rapid nor as great.

As cereal grains are low in vitamins A and D, a leafy green hay and good pasture constitute the main sources in a horse's diet.

Poor fertility, anorexia, poor hair coat and hoof texture, night blindness, excessive tearing, and reduced resistance to respiratory infections are typical symptoms of a vitamin A deficiency. Dietary supplements can be used, but it is better to feed an improved quality of green, leafy legume hay than to give supplements that might be ineffective.

Vitamin A is stored in the liver for periods of six or seven weeks, so a horse can tolerate a substandard diet for short periods.

A toxicity can actually result from overfeeding vitamin A, and, to add to the confusion, the symptoms of hypervitaminosis simulate those of a deficiency. When in doubt, call your veterinarian.

Vitamin D does not represent a concern in the diet of horses. For the horse, a herbivore, sunlight and sun-cured forages provide all the vitamin D needed. Plants aplenty contain ergosterol, which is converted into vitamin D2, a precursor of Vitamin D, by the action of ultraviolet rays from the sun. All forms of hay eaten by horses contain a rich source of vitamin D2. The horse's body converts D2 into usable D. Production of the vitamin is activated by exposure of the horse to ultraviolet rays from either an artificial source or from natural sunlight.

ALERT: Do not use ultraviolet bulbs in the foal's stall. See Chapter 8.

Ergosterol is abundant in yeast, so by simply irradiating yeast with ultraviolet light, a ready-made vitamin D2 is available. Irradiated brewer's yeast is a very popular method of supplementing the vitamin D intake in horses during the long cold season with short sunlight hours.

WARNING: Vitamin D is intimately associated with the balance, absorption, and deposition of both calcium and phosphorus. Vitamin D is the anti-rickets vitamin; symptoms of a vitamin D deficiency are calcium and phosphorus imbalance, resulting in calcification or decalcification of tissues, skeletal weakening, impaired joints, poor teeth, and malformation with enlarged ends on long bones, resulting in deformities. Generally no supplement is given, as sun-cured hay, preferably a green, leafy legume, and exposure to sunlight provide natural and abundant sources of vitamin D.

Vitamin E (alpha-tocopherol) is called the anti-sterility vitamin. However, the effectiveness of vitamin E alone to reverse sterility or enhance fertility has not yet been scientifically substantiated. Research does indicate that vitamins E and A work in combination synergistically to produce a favorable response in infertile brood mares. Vitamin E is also thought to be essential to animals for development of muscular, skeletal, and nervous systems.

VITAMIN A (CAROTENE) CONTENT	
FEEDSTUFF	CAROTENE (MG/KG)
(Roughages)	
Alfalfa hay	33
Bermuda grass hay	36
Bluegrass pasture	386
Red clover	34
Timothy hay	11
(Concentrates)	
Oats	0
Corn	2
Barley	0
Beet pulp	0

Vitamin E combines naturally with selenium, a trace mineral found in the soil and in plants. Supplementation of this vitamin-mineral combination, either orally or by injection, has been helpful in the treatment of some muscle diseases in foals, and in myositis cases suffered by older competition horses.

Treatment

Wheat germ oil is a commercial preparation high in vitamin E especially processed from the germ of wheat. While the primary use of wheat germ oil is for the stallions and mares on the breeding farm, I also like to use it to improve the coat on a young horse. If the animal is fed well, wormed, and vaccinated properly and still has a dull, rough coat, then 1 ounce of wheat germ oil twice daily should, over a period of one month, improve the animal's overall condition.

In addition, I have found it to be very useful when a yearling develops a splint formation on its leg from unknown etiology. Double the dosage to 2 ounces twice daily, and bandage the splint, keeping it warm and protected. With rest, within six weeks you may be pleasantly surprised.

The odor of wheat germ oil compound smells like fish oil, and most horses, especially the young, turn away. To overcome this, simply smear some wheat germ oil all over and around the young horse's mouth and feed tub. This will adequately confuse the animal. Then watch it eat!

WATER-SOLUBLE VITAMINS

Water-soluble vitamin B complex and vitamin C (ascorbic acid) do not present as serious a concern as the fat-soluble group. Because vitamin B complex is reportedly synthesized in the liver, no deficiency can easily develop. However, this can only be assumed in the presence of a well-rounded, balanced diet, and in a healthy individual.

Racetrack veterinarians contend that, contrary to this information, the diet of racehorses and other competition or endurance horses should be regularly augmented with B complex and vitamin C (ascorbic acid) preparations before and after competition. Clinical response has convinced those closely associated with performance horses that additional vitamins are valid for high-exertion time spans.

EARLY WEANING

In Chapter 5, while discussing orphaned or motherless foals, the fact was clear and emphasized that these motherless foals physically outstripped the foals raised in conventional ways—with a lactating dam. Has a better method of raising, feeding, and growing foals evolved from the observation of motherless foals?

I have found that early weaning, at approximately three months of age, with good natural foods plus specifically designed dietary supplements, has produced exceptional individuals.

I am convinced that early weaning is beneficial for the foal as well as the mare, especially if the mare is bred back and pregnant. Of course, veterinary supervision and advice should be sought.

A word of caution: When the foal reaches six to eight months old, the supplements (Foal-Lac) should be halted and the foal fed only straight concentrates and high-quality legume hay. This is particularly important if the foal is naturally large and growthy or has a genetic predisposition to be so. *Avoid overfeeding grain concentrates!* See Cereal Grain Warning on page 223.

Chapter Eight

MANAGEMENT AND HUSBANDRY

The solid foundation for good health and successful raising of horses, whether in a large breeding operation or a small stable, is primarily the daily practice of good management and husbandry principles. Although veterinary service must be a viable and vital component of this venture, it is just that, and cannot function alone with any degree of proficiency. Modern veterinary medical service can only complement an already proficient horse operation by essentially decreasing the incidence of disease and increasing overall health.

It is incumbent upon every practicing veterinarian, when summoned to treat an animal, to observe and suggest remedies, either medical or managerial, to enhance the efficiency of the barn or operation. The veterinarian should take the necessary time out of the daily call schedule for pertinent discussion and helpful input. A practicing veterinarian should have a true desire to aid, enhance, and disseminate useful knowledge for the treatment of disease and betterment of raising livestock.

A lifetime could be spent learning principles of equine husbandry, and another lifetime studying soil preservation and crop management. Veterinary medicine, limited to equine practice, requires another lifetime of study and dedication. Each of these disciplines plays a vital role in any successful equine enterprise. As licensed veterinarians, it is our duty to guide and suggest prudent procedures and thus improve and maintain health in the livestock.

Primarily, we should prevent any animal possessing a hereditary or congenital defect from reproducing or competing as a sound animal. It is considered malpractice to medically or surgically mask these defects or encourage anyone to do so. My equine practice was made somewhat easier, as many of my clients were prudent, honorable, dyed-in-the-wool, third- or fourth-generation horse breeders. They culled, or deleted, on a regular basis, any individual manifesting any form of unwanted hereditary trait, in an effort to improve the breed.

Contented imminent brood mare.

Agricultural schools and animal husbandry courses cover the generalized field of domestic animals, including their nature and their needs. Horse husbandry, on the other hand, is a narrow, specialized area that emphasizes the peculiar and unique needs of the equine.

WARNING: Extrapolation of knowledge from one species to another can be hazardous and should definitely be avoided. There is absolutely no relationship to be made between the carnivore and the herbivore; and there is a great distinction to be made between a herbivorous ruminant, such as a cow, and a herbivore, the horse.

The study of horse husbandry encompasses, among other things, basic handling of horses with their characteristic likes and dislikes. Housing, fencing, feeding, and the all-important land and pasture management must be included.

Common abuses are overcrowding, overgrazing, and overfeeding of concentrates (grain mixtures). Overcrowding invites disease, parasitism, and contamination. Overfeeding of concentrates is discussed in Chapter 7. Overgrazing is a fact of life that is becoming more common with the increased number of plea-sure horses and the increased costs of suitable land and sturdy fencing.

Good pastureland touted for raising horses commands a stout figure. The old rule of thumb—one horse per acre of land—has stood the test of time, but I regret to report that I continue to see overcrowding more often than not.

Bluegrass land, noted for its nutritional level for horses, has been at a pre-mium for years. However, bluegrass land may be losing its lofty perch, as some reports have stated that the high carotene and estrogen content of lush bluegrass found during the spring is responsible for early abortion in some brood mares. Rich and lush is not always best! Here again, we seem to assume that if a little is good, a lot must be better.

Amount of rainfall and the growth of grass go hand in hand. An excess of lush grass has been for many years associated with various pathologic states such as founder, abortion, obesity, and colic.

NOTE: Moderation is the key word in raising horses, and excesses in any area should be avoided.

The management of a horse farm or of a single foal is best achieved by a con-scientious, educated, or well-read person who has shown the interest and desire to do the job well. I have never diagnosed a foal with gastric ulcers (see Chapter 4) on a well-run farm. Good husbandry practices are impossible without a knowledge of all the subjects covered in previous chapters—feeds, nutrition, prophylactic measures of a medical or sanitary nature, etc.—as they all interrelate.

RECOMMENDED VACCINATION SCHEDULES OF DAM AND FOAL

Prophylactic vaccines are specific antigens that, when injected into a young ani-mal at the proper age, confer protection to the foal. Actively stimulated protec-tive antibodies are thus produced by the foal's own reticuloendothelial system after three to four months of age. These antibodies are truly specific and protective.

MATERNAL ANTIBODIES

Let me repeat and stress that the immune system in all young foals begins to function around the third to fourth month of life. At birth, the newborn receives passive antibodies from the colostrum that protect the foal from vari-ous diseases.

ALERT: These maternal antibodies wane rapidly around eight to 10 weeks of age. This vulnerable period of susceptibility in the newborn should be recognized and acknowledged as a dangerous time, warranting special attention and added precautions. The precise time or age when the foal begins to produce its own antibodies remains highly debated among veterinary authorities.

The foal's vaccination schedule should begin with the mother, long before the foal is born. It is essential for the brood mare to receive proper vaccines during her gestational period so that her newborn foal will have an adequate level of preformed protective antibodies available in the colostrum. With only a single source for the suckling foal, the mare's vaccination schedule is of paramount importance.

All brood mares should receive routine tetanus toxoid (lockjaw), influenza, and rhinopneumonitis vaccinations *before* being sent to the breeding farm.

After pregnancy has been determined, all unnecessary injections of any form of drug or vaccine should be avoided unless, of course, circumstances dictate otherwise. In the event of an epidemic or direct exposure to an infectious or contagious disease, brood mares should receive only specifically prescribed vaccines. Consult your veterinarian.

Excluding extraordinary conditions, the pregnant mare needs to receive a rhinopneumonitis vaccination, namely Pneumabort-K (Fort Dodge Laboratories) killed vaccine, in her fifth month from the date of her last cover. This killed vaccine is safe for use in pregnant mares and should be religiously repeated in the seventh month of pregnancy and again in the ninth. In the 10th month, specifically one month prior to her due date, the brood mare should receive a booster of tetanus toxoid and influenza. At that time, any other indicated vaccine for the specific geographic area should also be given. These "11th-hour" boosters practically ensure, but not totally, the presence of a respectable level of protective antibodies ready for ingestion by the newborn foal.

SUGGESTED ADDITIONAL BROOD MARE VACCINATIONS

Some other brood mare vaccines to be considered depending upon the geographic location and the advice of the attending equine veterinarian:

- Eastern and Western encephalomyelitis vaccine (EEV/WEV)
- Venezuelan encephalomyelitis vaccine (VEE)
- Botulism bacterin—associated with shaker foal syndrome
- Rabies vaccine

- *Strep. equi* bacterin (strangles), F.D.A.-approved intranasal spray vaccine (Fort Dodge Laboratories)

- Potomac fever vaccine (EPM)

- Lyme disease vaccine

- Enterotoxemia bacterin

PARTURITION TIME

A tetanus toxoid can be administered to the dam if she failed to receive her 10th-month booster.

The newborn needs 1,500 IU of tetanus antitoxin included with the other routine injections, just to be certain of adequate protection.

ALERT: It is my contention that every foal should receive a tetanus antitoxin injection regardless of whether the dam has received a booster. This subject has been discussed and debated at length and continues to remain unsettled among some members of the profession. Many practitioners, however, believe a tetanus antitoxin injection for the foal is an unnecessary precaution. I feel that it is better to be safe than sorry; it has been my finding that some mares, even those boostered, fail to produce protective antibodies, and/or that some foals are unable to ingest, assimilate, or even receive or benefit from antibodies that are available. (Also, I have never associated any harmful effects or any form of liver malfunction with the precautionary use of tetanus antitoxin in the newborn.)

CAUTION: In the newborn, several paths are open to failure of immune transfer, and there is no human way—other than through tragedy—to recognize where the inefficiency lies; I therefore justify my routine 1,500 IU tetanus antitoxin injection to all newborn foals in my care.

Although it has been well documented that foals respond poorly to antigens (vaccines) before three or four months of age, there are practitioners who insist on assaulting the foal's body with constant biologic injections during this early period. This is disconcerting if not actually damaging to the foal.

At age of 14 to 16 weeks, vaccines against influenza (FluVac), rhinopneumonitis (Pneumabort-K), and tetanus (tetanus toxoid) should be administered to the foal. Two weeks following, *Strep. equi* (strangles) bacterin or F.D.A.-approved intranasal vaccine should be given.

WARNING: Strangles bacterin should be used only under the strict supervision of a veterinarian. It should be injected *only in the gluteal muscles* (large muscles of the buttocks). Be certain of an astute dosage determination. This preparation, while affording essential protection, can create a systemic reaction, causing severe irritation of muscle tissue at the injection site. Biological protection is a blessing against the dreaded disease strangles, but its use requires judicial administration.

At the end of the month, the original vaccines—influenza, rhinopneumonitis, and tetanus toxoid—should be repeated as boosters, to ensure immunity.

Advisability as to the use of equine encephalomyelitis vaccine in sucklings and weanlings is subject to the disease incidence, geographic location, and the discretion of your veterinarian. Always check your "booster schedule" first, if movement to a different area or a van ride is necessary.

Influenza and rhinopneumonitis boosters should be given to your foal every two to three months during its first and second years, then every three or four months during its third year. After the first two original injections, tetanus toxoid can be given annually, unless of course the foal sustains a severe laceration or, more specifically, any puncture wound in or

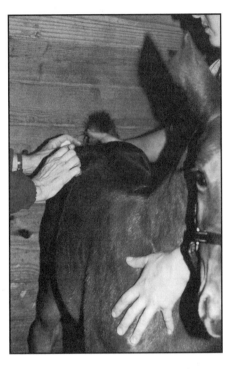

Correct injection site and proper foal restraint.

around the feet. Manure is literally teeming with tetanus spores, so the need for "lockjaw" protection cannot be overemphasized. This need for protection also applies to humans associated with horses.

Around the time period that maternal antibodies begin to wane in the foal—about 10 weeks or so—the youngster becomes particularly vulnerable to infection. A disease called *Cornyebacterium equi*, or recently renamed *Rhodococcus equi*, for which there is no vaccine, causes the notorious and refractory foal pneumonia and can cause foal septicemia. This infection is responsible for a high mortality rate in foals. Fortunately, some broad-spectrum antibiotics are effective, if early intensive treatment is instituted, and some hardy foals survive this scourge.

Some brood mare farms contend on a yearly basis with *Rhodococcus* infection in their foal crop. This soil contaminant sets up housekeeping on populated farms and subsequently infects each foal crop annually. Farm veterinarians, responsible for the health of the foals, have become, in the past, frustrated treating this resistant infection. Recently, they have developed an *autogenous bacterium* by obtaining nasal swabs from the infected foals on individual farms. The samples were submitted to the laboratory for the development of a bacterin, specific for that farm's infection. This approach has been quite successful.

Need for specific vaccinations and frequency of boosters depends greatly upon disease incidence, prevalence, environmental conditions, and weather changes, but most importantly upon the degree of exposure to outside horses and the amount of overcrowding of horse residents on the premises. Management and husbandry can prevent unnecessary exposure to disease and help maintain good health.

Prophylactic measures, such as vaccination schedules and well-timed worm medication, can prevent or contain many would-be diseases and epidemic tragedies. Combined efforts and cooperation on the part of an educated conscientious farm manager and a dedicated equine practitioner can run a horse farm at a high standard of efficiency.

FOAL VACCINATION SCHEDULE

Newborn through first and second year of life:

- At birth: 1,500 IU tetanus antitoxin. (Do not hesitate to repeat dosage of tetanus antitoxin at the slightest indication of delayed healing *or* infection of the navel cord *or* if any puncture wound is sustained before the third month of age, especially any foot wound.)

- At 4 months of age (16 weeks): Influenza vaccine (FluVac; Fort Dodge Lab); tetanus vaccine (tetanus toxoid; Fort Dodge Lab).

- At $4^{1}/_{2}$ months of age (18 weeks): rhinopneumonitis vaccine (Pneumabort-K; Fort Dodge Lab).

- At 5 months of age (20 weeks): Repeat the two original vaccines (influenza and toxoid) now as a booster.

- At $5^{1}/_{2}$ months of age (22 weeks): Repeat the rhinopneumonitis vaccine now as a booster.

- At 6 months of age (24 weeks): Rabies vaccine; repeat every two years. Please consult your veterinarian.

- *Strep. equi* bacterin and encephalitis vaccines can be administered to the foal any time after four months as the prevalence of, or exposure to disease, dictates; repeat annually. Please consult your veterinarian regarding rabies vaccine. Use only if suggested by your veterinarian.

- Influenza and rhinopneumonitis vaccines should be repeated every second or third month during the first year, depending on environment.

- After the first year, an annual tetanus toxoid booster suffices. When injury or infection develops, a booster is indicated.

THE NURSERY STALL

Let us return to the expectant mare carrying the center of the spotlight—a foal. Assume at this date that the matron has received proper prenatal care during her gestation period, and is complacently awaiting the blessed event.

Well in advance of the due date, prepare a suitable stall to serve as the mare's delivery room and as a nursery for the newborn. And, of course, keep watch on the mare!

At dawn on a warm spring morning, 30-odd brood mares rushed through the gate from the south forty into the barn area for breakfast. The foreman noticed a mare due to deliver two weeks hence with large amniotic membranes hanging from her vulva. Panic ensued. After the mare was placed in a clean, well-bedded stall, the foreman sent two men on the double to the south pasture to look for a foal. Then he reached for the phone.

I arrived shortly afterward and confirmed without too much ado that the mare had indeed delivered or aborted. Although my veterinary unit is equipped for rough terrain, the pasture tested its durability. With the barn personnel hanging onto and standing on top of the truck, all searching, we finally found a flat plateau area where the grass seemed somewhat flattened.

The men jumped from the truck and felt the grass for moisture. Yes, the ground was damp, and there were bloody areas—enough evidence to convince me that we had found the delivery site. But where was the foal? I noticed that the bottom rail of a nearby fence looked disturbed and slightly dislodged.

Excitement overtook me. I jumped the fence into a dense thicket. Stumbling forward and peering through vines and brambles, I caught sight of two perky pricked ears. It was the foal, lying in the weeds and thicket with its head stretched high. Just as I saw its alert head, it whinnied!

The men shouted with joy, and I watched the elated group carry the newborn, weak but courageous, up through the almost impossible footing. After a cursory physical examination, the foal promptly walked to its indifferent mother and began nursing.

As I drove the road to my next call, a sobering thought passed through my mind. If the mare had passed her afterbirth membranes up in the desolate field, then no one would have searched for a lost foal. This baby surely would have perished. There is nothing wrong with taking steps to protect your mare and foal from the ravages of nature. I have found naturalists' methods both cruel and wasteful. Go ahead and prepare for the safety and well-being of your brood mare and foal-to-be.

FOALING STALL

It is imperative that the foaling stall be roomy and "goof-proof" so as to avert any possible injury to the long-awaited foal. The size of the stall is an essential consideration. The optimum size is 20 by 20 feet, with the interior surfaces smooth and free of all projections. Large breeding farms usually have foaling stalls with specific dimensions equipped with all facilities needed for parturition. The solution for the one-mare owner is to remove the partition between two existing stalls and so double the space.

Construction

The walls of the stall should be solid to a level of at least three feet, with no holes or openings in which a foal could wedge a tiny foot.

All stall doors should be solid from the ground or floor surface up. Stall screens create a potential disaster unless they are carefully secured with a board at the bottom to cover the open space, and thus prevent a foal's foot, leg, or head from being caught underneath. Remove hay racks, metal or wooden, from the stall, and cover all glass windows with a protective durable screen well before parturition. Wide-spaced bars covering windows and open spaces should be avoided. Little feet can easily become wedged between bars.

Safe stall.

An ounce of prevention is well worth a pound of cure. Logical prevention far outstrips treatment, so use your "third eye" and search the stall well in advance for hidden danger before tragedy can occur.

Feed tubs and water pails should have a rubbery texture and be removable or hung high enough to prevent injury.

I had a call one early morning from an obviously upset owner whose foal of several weeks of age had almost severed its ear and was bleeding profusely. I grabbed a cup of hot, black coffee on my way through the kitchen and managed a few sips along the way. (Sometimes I think my veterinary truck drives itself over rough roads so I can fortify myself with my favorite brew before I reach the scene of an emergency.)

When I got to the barn the waiting owner led me to the stall. It was a bloody scene that greeted me. The foal was standing dejectedly in the middle of the stall, literally covered with blood. One ear hung limply at a crazy, lopsided angle; it appeared to be hanging by only a shred of tissue.

After the foal had been sedated, local anesthesia was injected and the area cleansed. I examined the laceration carefully. Fortunately, it wasn't as bad as it had originally appeared. The ear was almost completely severed, but above the cartilage and muscle that control the movement. As soon as I finished suturing the ear back in place, the foal started moving the injured member. In lack of gratitude, or ill temper, he flattened both ears in disapproval of the whole situation. As I left the stall, he pricked both ears forward and walked over to his dam to nurse.

The owner started an immediate search to find any sharp object or projection that could have caused the ear injury. It wasn't until late afternoon, when the mare and foal were turned out in a paddock so that the stall could be thoroughly cleaned, that a nail was found buried beneath straw, just an inch or two above the floor of the stall. It had been inadvertently driven through a board from an adjacent stall. It had taken the owner several hours to find the nail; the foal had managed to find it without difficulty.

The neonate's stall should be as safe and foolproof as humanly possible, yet not so solid as to interfere with proper ventilation. Adequate ventilation is essential, but care must be taken that the foal is never in a draft or direct air current, either while it is up and playing or sleeping in the straw bedding.

On a cold rainy morning I received a call to come quickly: A mare had foaled and her foal was in trouble. Without waiting to hear details, I dressed and, with a cup of coffee in my hand, ran out the door and shot down the road toward the farm.

It must have rained all night, since my veterinary truck tires sank deep into the muddy lane and slid to a stop just by the familiar barn door entrance. Running into the barn, I almost collided with the distraught owner who, with tears streaming, pointed into the stall. Peering and squinting, I could see a hairy, wet mass wedged between two large 2- by 6-foot stall planks—very dead indeed. The steaming wet mare frantically paced the stall as the owner cringed outside, quite afraid to enter. I waited, caught the mare by her halter as she made one of her circles, then slipped a sedative into her muscle. She hardly noticed the needle prick. Within minutes she quieted down so that the foal could be extracted from the ill-constructed stall wall. Here was a case of a total waste of life, caused by failure to prepare a suitable foaling area for the mare.

During delivery, the highly explosive nature of the equine birth process separates horses from all other species. When the time arrives for foaling, nothing short of the Almighty can impede this dynamic physiologic process.

Motto: Be ready well in advance. You won't want to miss the opportunity to observe and be awed by the magic of parturition.

Disinfection

Cleanliness is godliness, so scrub the stall floor, walls, and ceiling with hot soapy water and a wire brush. If the stall floor is clay, simply scrape a layer away, dampen, and tamp well. Remove all organic material, soak free, and rinse. Follow this initial scrubbing with a strong Lysol or pine-oil solution and wait two hours before rinsing away. Wait three days, then disinfect for a second time using a garden pressure tank with a spray nozzle. The spray can penetrate all cracks and crevices that are missed otherwise. Any disinfectant with a satisfactory phenol coefficient will do, or try a newer povidone-iodine compound. Be sure to include all water pails, tubs, and screens. Large breeding farms have access to steam sterilizers to cleanse the stalls (especially the foaling stall).

If paint is used on the inner surface of the stall, avoid those that are lead-based.

Bedding should be clean, dust-free, and absorbent. Wheat or rye straw is noted for being bright, clean, long-stemmed, and dust- and mold-free. Although expensive and quite difficult to purchase, it is the best bedding for a newborn foal.

Bedding other than the preferred straw, such as shavings, Staz-Dri, peat moss, sawdust, or any processed wood by-product—even the new newspaper product—is unsuitable for neonatal foals. In addition to being irritating to the ocular, nasal, genital, and navel membranes of the foal, these products lack both cushioning and the essential warmth needed by the newborn.

ALERT: After the stall is thoroughly disinfected, it should be left open to air and dry. It will benefit from ventilation and whatever sunlight reaches the stall. The harmful bacteria, specifically *Clostridium botulinum* microorganisms, found in stalls are usually anaerobic in nature and thrive in warm, moist, dark, and dirty areas where there is little or no oxygen. See SHAKER FOAL SYNDROME, page 89.

Safety Night Light

All nursery stalls should be equipped with a small night light, well out of the dam's reach, and kept burning around the clock so that the foal can readily be seen by the matron at all times. Some high-strung mares will panic if they lose sight of the foal.

Temperatures

Hot and cold temperatures are stressful to the newborn. In cold weather, heat lamps can be of tremendous help in dispelling chill and dampness from the foal's stall. When comfortably warm, a foal will be more relaxed, function more normally, and be more contented. Be aware, though, that heat lamps can unnecessarily dry out the air and can also present a fire hazard if hung incorrectly.

CAUTION: Heat lamps hung too high produce inadequate warmth. When hung too low, they may ignite the combustible material in the stall or prove hazardous to the mare's head. Some people prefer to cover lights with metal screens for protection.

ALERT: Be certain to use infrared rather than ultraviolet bulbs in heat lamps. The former produce warmth and are reasonably safe; while the latter are bacteriocidal, they do not produce warmth and can do irreparable damage to the foal's eyes. A heat lamp may serve double duty as a night light.

The entire stall need not be heated; in fact, it is unhealthy to heat it. Foals will seek out a warm spot in the stall when they are chilly. It is actually better for the stall to be on the cool side rather than too warm.

THE FOAL'S PADDOCK

A foal's vision is not acute enough for the first three days for it to be trusted beyond the confines of the stall. After this brief period of confinement, the mare and foal should be introduced to a small paddock in which mother and her newborn can stretch their legs in protected privacy. For a period of seven to 10 days the pair should exercise alone before they are turned out with other brood mares and foals. Mother and baby should be protected from other curious horses for this prescribed adjustment period and allowed privacy in a separate paddock; the new mother will not be especially sociable, as she is extremely possessive and jealous of her new baby.

Unless you want only exercise for the mare and foal, the paddock should have fresh, clean pasture grass and soil and be well fenced, preferably double-fenced, and well protected for the newborn. A well-fenced paddock adjacent to the barn

Both mare and foal need privacy.

is ideal, if it has not been overused and overgrazed, and is not parasite-infested. These unsuitable conditions promote inadequate nutrition and present a very real danger of parasitic invasion of your foal.

On a hot summer day I was at a large stud farm, finishing a long afternoon that was winding up an unusually long day, when the Motorola telephone crackled an emergency. A filly had been cut just above her hoof and was bleeding copiously. My sister had recommended, on the telephone, pressure bandages, tourniquets, and ice—all to no avail. The call was from an owner with only one mare, and this was the very first foal the owner had ever raised. Everything had been done "by the book" to assure the foal's safety and health. With uncharacteristic haste I threw equipment into the unit. I wondered how such an accident could have happened.

It normally would have taken half an hour to drive from point to point, but I pushed to the limit and made the distance in half the time. Within a quarter of a mile from my destination, the dash lit up like a Christmas tree. Every warning light flashed ominously. I prayed the truck would keep going. I arrived with steam pouring from under the hood and hurried to my patient.

Someone was at the filly's head, and the owner was holding up a foreleg with the ankle flexed. The leg was covered with bandages soaked with blood, and the filly was obviously in borderline shock. I started IV fluids immediately, then removed the bandages to examine the injury. It became apparent why the ankle was being held in a flexed position. When the filly bore weight, a gaping wound opened over the heel just above the hoof. Blood poured out. I clamped off the bleeders, continued fluids, and decided it would be judicious to repair the damage on the spot rather than transport the patient to my hospital. Under general anesthesia the wound was cleansed, repaired, sutured and a plaster cast applied to prevent and relieve tension on the suture line.

While the filly recovered from the anesthesia, the paddock was carefully examined. It was a safe post and rail fence. Only one area was suspect. One portion of the fence was covered with honeysuckle vines. Insidiously hidden in the vines was a single strand of smooth wire. The filly had been curiously pawing the vines, caught her leg at the pastern over the wire, and in her panicky efforts to free herself had almost amputated her foot. Fortunately, she had an uneventful recovery; no nerves were severed. The only residual problem was a minor hoof deformity in an area where the growth line of the hoof had been damaged.

During the filly's surgery in the barn yard, some kind unknown soul treated my abused veterinary truck, so I was able to make the short drive home.

WARNING: Initial Turnout Day   Now comes the turnout day. This exciting occasion requires careful planning. Wait until noon of the third day, and hope that the sun will be out and the temperature ideal, with no falling barometer or precipitation, and the footing safe.

Cradle the foal in your arms, with one arm around the chest and the other arm firmly encompassing the hindquarters. Someone should lead the mare ahead of the foal at a pace that allows the pair to remain close, so that they do not panic. The foal's tail, if held up close to the dock, is the handiest and safest means of securing the hindquarters for any purpose, including simply walking, or for any purpose for which restraint is needed.

Turnout day.

Cradling a valuable foal in one's arms is the only method I had ever learned to safely transport a baby foal from its stall to the paddock and back. It is amazing how quickly the foal learns, by repeated trips, to lead quickly alongside the mother.

As a reminder to always keep an open mind, one day I was taken back by a rancher who insisted that he had a better method, especially on a one-man operational ranch. I watched him slide a large soft rope around the hindquarters of a robust foal, and the pair walked quietly together to the pasture. Although I respected this knowledgeable and obviously experienced horseman, I still contend that my method is safest and best.

Insist that your foal be cradled as described and never, ever allow anyone to breach this old method of foal handling. Do not allow anyone to attempt to lead your foal as you would an older horse; any force applied to the foal's head or neck can cause serious, perhaps permanent damage, as the foal's inordinately long, slender neck is especially vulnerable to any stress.

DANGER PERIOD/PADDOCK GATE

When the mare and foal reach the paddock, the mare first should be led through the gate and then turned to face it. This moment is critical and can save the life of the foal or spare it injury if you pay attention. Hold the baby securely at the open gate while the mare is released and permitted to wheel, kick, and run a

Freedom at last.

short distance. Continue to cradle the foal. She will assuredly return to the gate within seconds to check on the location of her baby. Now is the time to release the foal to run with its mother with some degree of safety.

By following this procedure, you may have averted a very common tragedy: You may have prevented the mare from thoughtlessly kicking her baby in a split second of exuberance. If both mare and foal are launched simultaneously, the mare can lose sight of the little one at her side as she gives way to pent-up energy after her confinement.

Regulate and limit the time allowed for the first few outdoor exercise periods; do not permit the foal to become so fatigued that it must actually lie down on the ground. And during the first few weeks of life carefully time the periods outside and avoid extremes of temperature. Under no circumstances should you allow any form of falling weather (rain or snow) on your foal.

Through the first few months (suckling stage) the neonatal foal should not be permitted to become overly tired, wet, chilled, or overheated. A safe, quiet, and clean bed or rest area should always be available. Foals are babies and should be treated as such!

HALTER INTRODUCTION

After a few days of privacy and tender care, your filly or colt is ready to experience its first exposure to discipline: the application and wearing of a small, light foal halter. This age is the ideal time to fit a halter properly on the new foal; this sometimes vigorous feat can best be accomplished by a two-person team.

One person should cradle the foal front and rear while the second person quietly places the halter on the head. The halter should just be snug, not tight! The fit is correct if, after the halter is adjusted, one finger can be placed comfortably under the straps at

A properly fitted halter.

every point. *Warning:* A correctly fitted halter will require weekly minute adjustments to meet the foal's rapid growth and prevent facial soreness.

A halter that is too loose can be a dangerous invitation for the foal to accidentally place its foot through the gap while lying down; or the halter might become caught up in stall equipment or on any object attached to the wall.

Leather halters are preferred. Leather's ability to stretch and even break is advantageous if a small foal becomes caught on some immovable object.

Even though the foal is wearing a halter, it must not be forced or pulled to lead. Until it becomes too large to cradle, the foal should be held and led as it was on its first day in the private paddock. Then it must be gently and considerately taught to lead. A foal should never ever be pulled forcefully by its head or allowed to pull against the halter.

NEONATAL FEET

Some veterinarians advocate the application of iodine tincture to all four feet in the neonate immediately after submerging the navel stump. I have never used iodine in this manner, but the antiseptic is said to have a drying and cauterizing effect on the newborn's soft, leafy-layered feet, and its use may prevent the entrance of unwanted and undesirable bacteria. Within hours the feet are normally dry and firm.

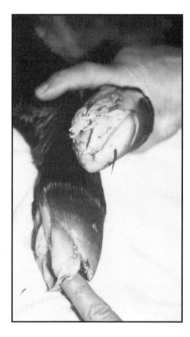

A foal's feet require little care during the first month or two, but around the third month, persistent "points" characteristically develop on the front and center of the foot. When the foal walks or trots, the front foot should break over at the front and center of the toe, as the foot is brought forward. (See BREAKOVER POINT in the Glossary.) A pointed toe makes correct placement of the foot difficult if not impossible, as the foal will then break over on the inside of the foot, causing a toed-out gait, or on the outside of the foot, causing a toed-in gait. These growth points

A newborn's wet, leafy-layered feet.

cause undue stress on the entire limb, as well as stressing the planes of every joint in the affected limb. Frequent inspection of the foal's feet can identify the toe formation.

I have found leg and foot deviations to be self-perpetuating; unless corrective measures are taken immediately, the condition usually worsens. Early efforts to establish and maintain a straight gait have had a direct bearing on many young horses' ability to show and on their future soundness and serviceability. When any interruption is noted in the rounded contour of the toe, a few strokes of a blacksmith's rasp is all that is needed to restore the proper rounded shape and a normal, natural gait.

Any conscientious person can, with the use of the rasp, round the tiny toes every 10 days or so. The sole of the foal's foot, however, should not be touched or dressed.

The only reliable trait about any brood mare is her unreliability. One morning I was summoned to a large breeding farm, where a mare had foaled the night before out in a large pasture—during a rainstorm.

The owners were terribly upset that they had not recognized her imminent condition and had not put her into the regular foaling stall.

The owners' son took me down to the area where he suspected that foaling had taken place. The worn-down grass and debris were very close to a rapidly running stream, and it was fairly obvious that the newborn foal

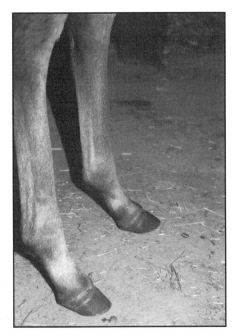

Pointed toes.

had helplessly slipped and eventually slid into the fast current of water. We walked together along the bank and down the stream a few hundred feet and found the small, twisted body of the foal caught up in the vines and brush.

These people were devastated with sorrow and guilt. Brood mares, unlike other domestic animals, do not often show reliable impending signs of parturition, and for this reason many accidents happen, even when people with great experience are present. It is for this reason that the imminent brood mare must be treated with extreme caution and absolutely no second-guessing.

After a lifetime of witnessing every possible tragedy that can befall a brood mare, and particularly the vulnerable foal, I contend that when a person has a mare bred and conception ensues, there exists a moral responsibility to that animal, not only to provide a proper gestational period, but also to arrange and provide for proper housing and attention during and after parturition. The casual attitude taken by the ignorant is that "nature will prevail." Yes, she will—but nature can be cruel and indiscriminating. I have found that the best rule is to provide for them as we would for ourselves.

I would like to emphasize that the study of foal pediatrics is a separate discipline, one with its own diseases and entities, each requiring an accurate diagnosis with known safe and effective drugs, specific dosages, and individual treatments.

Take heed: *Never* borrow information from adult medicine when treating a foal, and never extrapolate prescribed treatments used on babies of another species. This practice can be hazardous or at best counterproductive. Foals are infant horses—not little horses!

I would like to share a true story with you. After 35 years of practice, I thought I had seen almost everything at least once, but just last spring I became involved with a most unusual and exciting case.

My dear friend and neighbor had an aged pregnant mare due around the middle of April. No news is good news, and all was quiet. Then one day I had a telephone message: "Please come; my mare is uncomfortable and several weeks over her due date!" Now, I never become too upset when a mare is seven to 10 days overdue given the possibilities for human error and inaccurate record-keeping. However, I knew this person quite well, and several weeks truly overdue indeed is something to be concerned about. My friends owned but one brood mare and had strained their pocketbook somewhat to support that one during her 11-month gestation period. So as I drove into their long lane and approached the small, well-kept red barn, I held my breath, hoping that all was well.

I found the large pendulous mare standing with her head in the corner, obviously depressed, obviously annoyed, and very tired. Her backbone was prominent and accentuated by the degree of muscle flaccidity and relaxation so necessary in the preparation for delivery. I touched her large tail and found it heavy and weak, and then looked under at her full udder. Although her udder was large, tense, and warm, there was no evidence of wax, let alone milk.

When my friend arrived a few minutes later, she began relating a horror story that told why she had called for help. At this instant, we witnessed what the distraught owner was describing—the mare almost fell down as the foal began kicking violently! A foot punched outward, pushing the abdominal wall so far that I was startled by the sight. I became greatly concerned for the safety of the mare and her uterus, and the foal's life. Either the mare's uterus would rupture, or the active foal's umbilical cord could twist in utero. I promptly sedated the mare lightly and began my careful examination. Without a doubt, I have never palpated a larger or more active foal in utero.

I found the cervix totally closed, so I quickly injected the mare both intravenously and intramuscularly with a drug to allay her anxiety and—most significantly—to cause her cervix to soften and open, thus allowing delivery. After two hours and several violent kicking episodes, her cervix was still tightly sealed. At this moment I knew that both lives, the mare's and her foal's, were in jeopardy and that they must be sent to the hospital. Fortunately, the veterinary medical facility was nearby. A trailer was ordered, and the fatigued mare was taken to the hospital in haste, but ever so carefully.

Within the hour, the exhausted mare was on the operating table, and a cesarean section was under way. Just as I made the incision through the uterine wall and placental tissue, a large wet foot suddenly appeared, kicking upward through the aperture and almost hitting my surgical mask; then it disappeared back into the uterus as quickly as it had appeared. It was so fast and such a shock that I actually did not see it but felt only the amniotic fluid splattering over my glasses and gown. My surgical staff gasped with disbelief. I had heard of super-active foals, but none such as this! Following this kicking episode, I grew even more concerned for the safety of the aged mare's uterus. Time was of the essence.

The oversized foal filled the uterus to capacity, leaving little or no room for manipulation during delivery. My fingers felt the thinned, totally stretched uterine wall with its very large vessels also extended to capacity; they were quite friable and unable to tolerate any additional trauma. I then knew that I must deftly deliver this foal quickly and between fits of temper. As I grasped for both hind legs together, the foal began kicking violently. My assistant reached forward, and we were able to elevate and free it from all tender tissue. After clamping the umbilical cord, we handed the oxygen crew a 90-pound, 36-inch brown colt. While they cared for him, I routinely sutured the uterus and closed the abdomen. By this time we had a dry, vigorous foal looking to nurse, while the old mare was still recovering from the anesthetic. She recovered from the operation and was given a well-earned year's rest.

At three months of age, the huge brown colt won a national championship for sucklings and weanlings!

It has been a joy to spend the better part of my career treating all sorts of foals.

I have always considered myself a lucky person, one who has worked hard but has also received any and all of the fortunate breaks and opportunities available in this lifetime. I guess this lucky aura has carried over to my small friends and patients—the foals. Oh yes, I have lost my share, but let me assure you that they were not given up short of a fierce battle. When a very ill foal survives, all rejoice. When one dies, solace is taken only in the knowledge that no medical stone was left unturned and every human effort was made on behalf of the young life.

Chapter Nine

DO YOU KNOW?

What makes a horse so different? As a child, I read all the horse books I could get my hands on, but only experience and time have given me the answers as to why our equine friend is so unique.

There are a multitude of reasons, but I have chosen 17 of the most predominant mysteries of the horse to share with you:

1. Horses are herbivores; they subsist on a diet of grasses, herbs, and other forms of vegetation. Sheep, cows, and goats are other forms of herbivores. These animals are also ruminants and possess four stomachs. The horse is radically different. It is not a ruminant, and the equine species possesses only one small stomach. This basic difference may account for frequent colic attacks in the equine and may explain the fundamental species-specific husbandry practices.

2. The horse's stomach is unusually small, being one-fifth the size and weight of other similar species. Hence the need for small and frequent meals, along with grazing, which help to prevent gastric discomfort.

3. Gastric discomfort in the horse can be a common and serious problem—the horse has no gall bladder. The liver secretes a yellowish brown or green substance called bile. The bile then empties into the duodenum (small intestine close to the stomach). Bile is essential for digestion and peristalsis. In order to maintain intestinal function and health, in the absence of a bladder in which to store the bile, a constant slow flow of bile exists. All horses appear to eat slowly but on a constant basis; perhaps small meals are consistent with the slow, steady flow of bile into the GI tract.

4. The horse is totally unable under any circumstance to regurgitate. Tragedy can strike when the equine ingests a foreign substance that becomes hostile to its digestive system. Anything swallowed must

continue through the GI tract, unlike all other domestic animals. In remote cases, a stomach tube can be used to release stomach gases from the distended stomach, relieve pain, and prevent ultimate rupture with certain death. The stomach tube also provides a direct route to the stomach, bypassing the taste buds and allowing treatment with the drug of choice.

5. Hay, straw, and feeds containing dust or mold threaten the general health of every horse. Keen observation of the horse's daily diet and changing environment must be maintained to prevent any contact or exposure to dust or mold. Horses are not cows or sheep—no mold!

6. A foal is born—hurry and clear the sac from the nostrils so the precious air of life can be inhaled. The nose is the only way oxygen can enter the lungs; nothing via the mouth. Another disadvantage given to the equine. Nature has been unkind to the equine species, giving the horse only one passage with which to inhale atmospheric air: only through its narrow nasal passages.

7. Guttural pouches: What are they and who has them?

    Every horse, foal, pony, in all equine species, possesses two guttural pouches, one on each side of the head and well hidden by the jaw muscle. The eustachian tube, running from the base of the ear to the inside wall of the pharynx, contains a balloon-like pouch (guttural pouch) in which air or infectious matter may lodge or be entrapped. The function of the guttural pouches is not completely understood—one of the many wonders of the unique horse!

8. "Long in the tooth," an expression that could ruffle your feathers if you have a senior citizen card, comes from the fact that horses' teeth continue to grow throughout their entire lives. In the older horse, the longer the incisor teeth, the greater the tooth angulation. Age is determined by these two factors. Equine dental care consists of regular floating (rasping) performed by a professional, with particular attention given to different stages of growth throughout the equine life. Refer to the basic dental formula (#17 below) prepared to guide you as your horse matures.

    By the way, do you know how to tell what sex a horse is by its teeth? Well, listen closely. Approach the horse, preferably from the left side, and carefully open the horse's lips, exposing the interdental space. This space divides the incisors of the mouth in the front from the large molars hidden in the back of the mouth. This is where the bit normally rests. In the stallion or adult gelding you will find a large, long, pointed tooth centrally located in the interdental space. These are called tusher, canine, or bridle teeth. They are found both above in the upper jaw and below in the lower jaw. The mare or filly, on the other hand, has a smooth, empty interdental space. (See #17.)

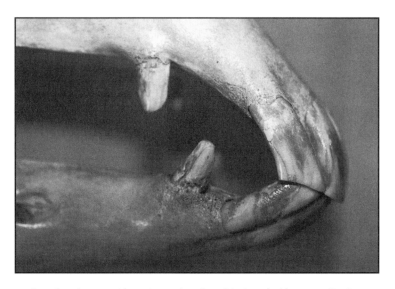

Interdental space with canine teeth and aged incisors (gelding or stallion).

9. All horses have a prehensile muzzle, a bundle of fibro-elastic tissue, capable of stretching eagerly to grasp tiny blades of grass and sorting delicately choice tidbits. The abundance of nerve endings concentrated in that small area of muzzle provides a type of "third eye," perhaps for protection from accidental ingestion. Over a lifetime I seldom found a foreign body in any horse's mouth. (See #4). Truly, the horse cannot see the muzzle area, yet by means of the tactile hairs, he is able to sense with great discrimination anything that approaches that region of his face—even a soft kiss.

10. The horse is a highly selective eater. Just try to disguise medication in its feed and then watch as it suddenly stops chewing, opens its jaw wide and expels the entire contents onto the ground. An array of facial expressions is often displayed during this procedure. After totally annoying the owner, the equine quietly resumes eating exactly and precisely what it prefers.

11. "The look of eagles"—A horse possessing that quality has the depth of yesterday combined with the understanding of today and, most likely, the courage for tomorrow!

A horse's vision is such that a wide range of head and neck movement must take place in order to see efficiently. Horses are noted for their excellent long-range vision; myopia (nearsightedness) is much less common.

Foal's vision, on the other hand, is diabolic. Neonates have poor vision for the first three days and then gradually improve. So please do not allow the newborn to be in an unprotected area during this brief period.

12. Chestnuts, or night eyes, belong only to the equine. Night eyes are small crusty tissue deposits located on the inside of the horse's legs. They are found above the knees on the forelegs and below the hocks on the hind legs. Please memorize the former sentence, because their locations may be a great asset and even life-saving.

    During your lifetime as a horse person, you could suddenly find yourself in the position of helping a brood mare to deliver. A knowledge of the precise location of night eyes could serve you well. This information could help identify which leg is being presented and, by proper manipulation, prepare the foal for delivery through the birth canal.

    Oddly enough, night eyes are unique to each individual horse. They are comparable to a human's fingerprint. Night eyes may, in the future, replace lip tattoos for identification purposes in all breeds of horses.

13. Care of the foal's feet should begin around eight to 10 weeks. The foal's foot problem is not growth, but rather, foot shape. The old adage, "No foot, no horse," continues to maintain great significance. (See Chapter 8.)

14. Unlike all other species, the baby foal enters the world with absolutely no immunity against disease, but then promptly receives an abundance of life-saving antibodies in the first milk it swallows from its mother's teats.

15. The reproductive system of the mare can only be defined as unstable. She possesses an antiquated uterus, a weak cervical seal, and an inefficient placental attachment to the inner lining of the uterus. Over the years I learned one certain rule: "The only reliable thing about the brood mare is her unreliability." I guess this fact keeps all equine veterinarians humble.

16. The equine spinal column is composed of five groups of vertebrae: the cervical (neck), thoracic (chest), lumbar (lower back), and

sacrum (pelvis), plus coccygeal (tail). The vertebra are always consistent in number with the exception of the coccygeal vertebrae, which vary by five or six in number. The normal vertebral formula is C-7, T-18, L-6, S-5, Cy-15-21.

Have you ever wondered why an Arabian horse's back appears somewhat shorter than other breeds'? The only exception to the above formula is the Arabian horse, who is noted for having one fewer vertebra than other breeds of horses.

17.   The dental formula for an adult horse (full mouth):

Twelve permanent incisors plus 24 permanent molars = 36 teeth total in the filly or mare. The adult stallion or gelding has four additional teeth = 40 teeth total. These four additional teeth, two above and two below, are called canine, tushers, or bridle teeth and are located in the interdental space—that wide space between the incisors in the front and the molars in the back of the mouth. This space is where the average bit rests during exercise.

Both genders usually possess tiny wolf teeth, an evolutionary vestige of a premolar, located in the upper jaw just in front of the first molar. They serve no function and have been known to cause pain from bit pressure during exercise, so most equine dentists extract these small fragmental teeth. Wolf teeth increase the total dental formula by two.

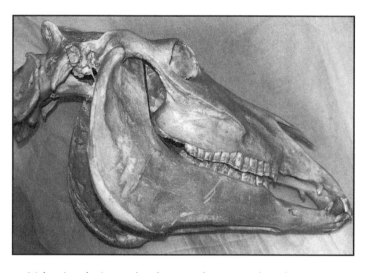

Molars (grinders), interdental space with canine teeth, and incisors.

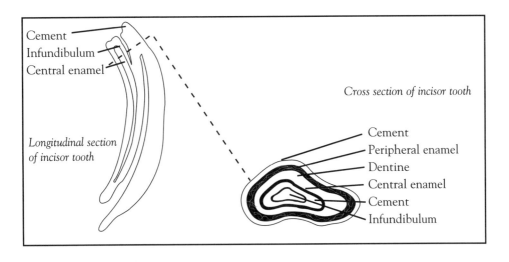

Cement
Infundibulum
Central enamel

*Longitudinal section
of incisor tooth*

Cross section of incisor tooth

Cement
Peripheral enamel
Dentine
Central enamel
Cement
Infundibulum

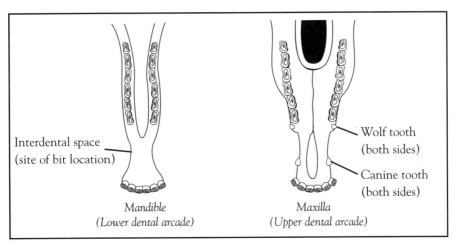

Interdental space
(site of bit location)

Wolf tooth
(both sides)

Canine tooth
(both sides)

*Mandible
(Lower dental arcade)*

*Maxilla
(Upper dental arcade)*

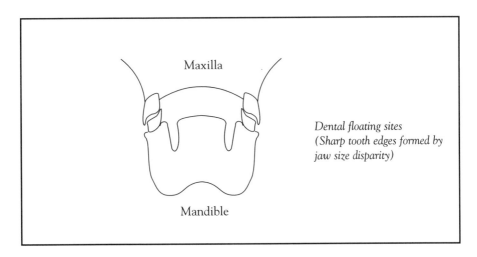

Maxilla

*Dental floating sites
(Sharp tooth edges formed by
jaw size disparity)*

Mandible

Equine teeth.

Most foals are born with four baby incisors and six baby molars; however, some are born toothless with swollen pink gums ready for the incisors to erupt, usually within hours of birth to perhaps a day or two.

Information and charts devoted exclusively to equine teeth, their growth and age determination, could easily fill a book.

HOW I WON MANY A WAGER WHILE IN SCHOOL

The majority of my classmates, while attending The University of Pennsylvania School of Veterinary Medicine, were interested in small-animal medicine, mainly dogs and cats. Every time I would see a row of stalls with the horses' heads hanging out, I would casually state to my fellow students that I could determine the gender or sex of each and every individual horse down the aisle by merely looking into their mouths. They would always laugh, then predictably one would assuredly offer a wager. I never told them my secret, but the empty interdental spaces revealed mares or fillies and those with canine teeth were stallions or geldings. Can you imagine the fun I had?

A MEMORABLE FOALING

Foaling time is always hectic, but the season of 1987 seemed unending. I was trying to endure icy cold days, irritable farm staff, and too many uncooperative mares while watching the breeding-time schedule run out. As I reviewed some of my past experiences, one farm and this story came to mind.

The date was March 15th and ever true rang the ominous "Ides of March" expression!

I received a call from the successful, hard-working manager of a rural Pennsylvania brood mare farm. "Please come, Dr. Lose, Medley is foaling!" I became immediately concerned, knowing that this manager had foaled many mares and was a good horseman. Although I was tired, the thought of a mare in trouble brought new energy into my soul, so my legs started moving toward the door. With thermos in hand, filled with good hot coffee, I slid into the fully equipped veterinary unit and off I went. Icy spots on the road made the trip a little tricky, and what usually took 30 minutes now seemed an eternity, as I careened into the long lane and up to the barn.

As I approached, the manager waved a signal that the foal had arrived and was in the world. My initial reaction was one of relief until I was able to see the manager's face. It was riddled with concern. "Medley's not right, Doc," he said, and my steps hurried towards the stall. Fortunately, the large bay filly had managed to nurse and consume quite a bit of precious colostrum from the uncomfortable mare. Her pain was obviously increasing, so I quickly injected a relaxant IV, just enough to allow her some relief while the fresh and strong foal quickly suckled a few more gulps. My examination concluded that the aged mare had suffered a uterine hemorrhage brought about by many prior pregnancies. She was obviously beyond treatment. Although I was able to administer Naloxone combined with coagulants, her eyes shortly glazed over and the hot perspiration turned to cold black sweat. The foal was now in danger as the mare began to stagger, so I swiftly ordered the men to remove the neonate foal from the stall. The mare collapsed into the bedding and died quietly.

Everyone, including the owner and helpers, was in tears. Exhausted and emotionally worn to the bone, we began the tedious task of gathering equipment and cleaning up. The only one who seemed not to understand the severity of the situation was the vigorous bay filly foal—she was now an orphan. No one spoke a word, but the farm's personnel all knew what bottle-feeding around the clock meant, especially when all felt somewhat overworked at the moment.

I began to think of my schedule for tomorrow, and after giving feeding instructions concerning the newborn, I was mentally homeward bound.

I reached for my stainless steel pails, and as I looked up, I was eyeball to eyeball with a curious "looker" from the adjacent stall. She was peering through the boards longingly, staring at the new foal and softly nickering. She even became more vocal as the foal would shuffle through the bedding. I was so startled and touched by the mare's sincerity and true concern, that I wanted to reach out and touch her in a reassuring way. . .perhaps things would be okay.

I opened her stall door, then noticed her coat was slightly damp, most unusual for such a cold evening. Just then the manager approached, saying she was also due any day or any minute. As I checked her udder, I could see large milk droplets turning to streams of milk as she anxiously circled the stall.

Silently excited, an idea exploded in my brain. I took the concerned mare's pulse and found it to be elevated along with other imminent signs of the first stage of labor. Sure enough, she was going to have a foal in short order. I wasn't going anywhere!

I sat on a bale of straw, with all of my necessary equipment, in front of her stall and tried to relax somewhat. Within an hour's time, she became more restless, started to perspire, and then abruptly broke her water. I pressed the buzzer and alerted the staff. While she was down and very busy delivering her own foal, we hustled the orphan from the neighboring stall and deftly slid her into and underneath the large after-birth membranes, right in beside the legitimate baby.

We all watched and held our concerted breath, as the weary matron rose to her feet. Her eyes enlarged as she greeted both foals and urged them quickly to suckle. Everyone sighed in relief, and we couldn't help but smile. This wise and kind old mare solved an otherwise sad and difficult situation.

A "MIRACLE"

We have all heard, I am sure, of the warning about buying a "pig in a poke." This story is just what occurred to one of my affluent clients—one who was too busy to care about details, yet wanted to enjoy his hobby, cutting horses. Two months prior, he had arranged for delivery of six small steers to his modest horse farm, presumably for practice sessions with his cutting horses.

The dilemma, however, began one morning very early, when the groom discovered one of the "steers" down starting to deliver a calf! Since I was the farm's horse doctor, he placed an emergency call to come quickly. The man was obviously confused and terribly distraught.

Unfortunately, my schedule was so heavy that I had begun the day extra early. It was early autumn, and no brood mares were due to foal for months, so I decided to start my day almost 50 miles away from this loyal client's barn. The telephone rang in my veterinary unit, and the distance made reception faint and quite unclear. I tried to discern which mare was aborting and what the problem was? "The cow is calving!" I could hardly believe my ears. Equine medicine and bovine medicine are as different as day and night! Equipment, drugs, and techniques vary drastically. They needed a cow doctor, not a horse doctor.

I instructed my office to call the anxious man back and carefully explain that he needed a nearby doctor, one who specializes in bovine practice. The cattle dealer had apparently slipped a pregnant heifer in with the steers, who knows? Perhaps a joke on a friend!

Hours went by. Even though I made a number of my scheduled calls, I was still far from home and was confident that a cow doctor had been reached. A serious conversation with a new client was interrupted by another call from the office. The message was, "No bovine doctor is available, and the heifer is still in labor." The groom was terribly upset and asked again if I could please come. I reiterated the fact that I was not a cow doctor and I was still too far away to be of any assistance. I knew of a cow doctor 10 miles from my office and could not understand his unavailability. Never wanting any animal to suffer unnecessarily, especially when it should be handled in a professional way, I continued to feel guilty and uneasy but quite helpless about this situation.

The day wore on, and the last of my patients took more time than I had expected. A gelding had a nasty laceration, and it became tricky and time-consuming to close the gaping area, especially with poor lighting and unskilled assistance. I knew that it could be repaired, but because he was a valuable show horse, scar prevention was also a major consideration and foremost in my mind. All finally went well with the use of some super-suture material and heavy dressings that I found in the corner of my unit.

As I drove away from the barn, I called in to see whether there were any imperative messages that would turn me around at the last moment and further delay a hot bath and a hot meal. Sure enough, after all day, the same heifer had not been able to give birth. I was aghast to think that no cow doctor had been reached and surely the poor mother and calf would not be alive after all this time! As a horse doctor, none of this made sense. I looked at the clock on the dashboard of the veterinary unit and it was almost 10:30 p.m. She must have been trying to deliver for almost 16 hours—if it had been a brood mare, both would have been dead short of an hour or two of onset of labor.

I could not stand it anymore. Frustrated, I swung the heavy unit around and stepped on the gas toward the not-so-far-away farm. The exhausted groom and the confused owner met me at the barn door and pointed toward a large well-bedded stall. I saw a little black sweat-soaked heifer down in the bedding with one small cloven hoof presented. I called for a pail of hot water, a towel, and some antiseptic soap.

When I grasped the foot, it was ice cold. Heaven only knows how long it had been exposed to the chilled air. I could not tell my friend, the owner, but I felt positive that the calf was dead. Quietly I was dwelling on the fact that, unlike that of the brood mare, the cow's placenta is unbelievably efficient. In the cow, the placenta delivers a constant and continued blood supply with nutrition through the umbilicus for long, undetermined time limits, sometimes for many hours. How long can they survive?

My hasty examination revealed that one foreleg of the calf was flexed and folded back under its body. With some sterile lubricant, I was able to re-position the leg. For a second, I thought I felt some movement, but the lack of muscle tone in the leg seemed to belie that possibility.

Once the calf was aligned in proper position, it was easily delivered with some applied traction. The wet coal-black bundle lay in a limp heap. Its eyes were shut with no visible respiration and it seemed quite lifeless indeed. All of a sudden I saw a little twitch and its rib cage began moving. One eye blinked open and the calf took a few ragged breaths. The little durable bull calf was alive, and with each breath became brighter. Soon he was standing and nursing—I was amazed!

As I leaned against the stall boards, I could not help thinking, "What a contrast to the delicate equine matron and her foal!"

Every interested and involved horse person should be aware of the differences between cows (ruminants) and horses (herbivores), each with its different types of placentas. The placenta of the cow has many "button" attachments that allow nutritional and oxygen support for protracted time periods. The mare's placenta, however, is no match. Unlike the ruminant, the brood mare's feeble placental attachment lacks security and quickly peels away, leaving the foal with no support system whether delivered or not. This release, under hormonal control, can occur before, during, or immediately after delivery—sometimes leaving the foal in a precarious state.

Any foal would have been lost if subjected to the ordeal experienced by that newborn calf.

NOTE: The secret to survival in the newborn lies with the type of placentation. So, in conclusion, please be careful to never borrow information about one species and apply it to another! It can make the difference between life and death.

There are times when all treatment seems to fail; in recourse, I turn to my favorite prayer:

> God grant me the serenity to accept the things I cannot change,
>   The courage to change the things I can,
>   And the wisdom to know the difference.

I have enjoyed writing this book and sincerely hope that it might provide information or help in some small way to some small foal.

GLOSSARY

ABERRATION   Deviation from the normal or typical.

ABORTION   Expulsion of an embryo or fetus before it is capable of maintaining extrauterine life.

ABRUPTIA PLACENTA   See PLACENTA PREVIA.

ACIDEMIA   A condition of increased alkalinity of the blood and tissues caused by excessive loss of acid.

ACIDOSIS   A condition of decreased alkalinity of the blood and tissues caused by excessive acid production.

ACTINOBACILLUS EQUULI (*SHIGELLA EQUI, SHIGELLA EQUULI*)   A gram-negative microorganism causing infectious disease in newborn foals (known as "dummy," "sleeper," and "wanderer"), primarily noted for its generalized systemic disease in the neonate.

A-EQUI-I, A-EQUI-II   Abbreviations of two strains of the influenza virus causing flu in the horse.

AGALACTIA   Absence of milk in the mammary glands after parturition or birth of the foal.

AGGLUTINATION   The clumping together of red blood cells or microorganisms.

ALFALFA   Legume hay.

AMINO ACIDS   The building blocks of protein.

AMINO GLYCOSIDES   Important effective antibiotic for treatment of gram negative disease in neonatal foals.

AMNIOPARACENTESIS   Aspiration of amniotic fluid (via a long needle placed through the abdomen into the amniotic sac) for the purpose of analysis.

AMNIOTIC FLUIDS   The fluids in which the embryo is bathed and which are ingested during gestation.

AMNIOTIC SAC   The sac that encloses the embryo; the first membrane visible during birth; the inner of two sacs.

ANAEROBIC   Growing only in the absence of free oxygen.

ANAPHYLACTIC REACTION   An unusual or exaggerated reaction (hypersensitivity) to a foreign substance; may be induced by a small sensitizing injection of that substance; or a severe reaction to a substance inhaled or ingested.

ANASARCA   The accumulation of fluid in the connective tissue of the body.

ANASTOMOSIS   A surgical or pathological connection of a passage between any two normally distinct spaces or organs in order to form a continuous channel.

ANESTHESIOLOGIST   A specialist in the administration of anesthetics in order to induce the desired level of insensibility.

ANESTHETIC   Any drug that produces local, regional, or general insensibility.

ANKYLOSED   Abnormal immobility, stiffening, or fixation of a joint.

ANTHELMINTIC   Worm medicine that is destructive to and causes expulsion of intestinal worms.

ANTIBODY   A disease-fighting serum globulin substance produced by the body in response to an antigenic or foreign stimulus.

ANTIGEN   A substance or complex, usually in protein form, that stimulates the body's immune system to react to it by producing an immune response.

ANTIPYRETIC   Any agent that reduces fever.

APPOSITION   When the opposing surfaces of upper and lower teeth meet in proper position to inhibit improper overgrowth and permit proper mastication.

ARTICULAR   Of or pertaining to joints.

ASCARIDS (ROUND WORMS) Intestinal parasites responsible for a variety of symptoms and diseases. See NEMATODE.

ASCITES   Abnormal accumulation of fluid in the abdominal cavity.

ASPIRATION   The act of breathing or drawing in; also, removal of extraneous fluids or gases from a cavity.

ASYMPTOMATIC   Symptomless.

ATAXIA   Locomotor imbalance; failure of muscular coordination.

ATONICITY   Insufficient muscle tone.

AUTOCLAVE   To sterilize by means of steam under pressure.

BACTERICIDAL   That which destroys bacteria.

BACTEREMIA   Blood poisoning or septicemia.

BACTERIN   A preparation made from dead bacteria to stimulate the formation of antibodies.

BAG   The mare's udder or mammary gland.

BANDY LEGS   Legs bowed or bent in an outward curve; bowedlegs.

BARKER FOAL   A foal suffering from a systemic infection from an unknown cause; characteristically, the foal makes "barking" noises and suffers convulsions.

BASTARD STRANGLES   Occur when *Strep equi* escapes from the lymph glands forming abcesses throughout the body in a chronic nature.

BICEPS FEMORIS   Biceps muscle of the thigh or powerful, double-branched muscle on the back of the leg. Its general action is to extend and/or elevate the limb.

BILATERAL or SYMMETRIC   Having two symmetrical sides.

BIVALENT, TRIVALENT   Capable of immunizing a horse against two or three known variations of neurotropic viruses that attack the nervous system.

BLEPHAROSPASM   Uncontrollable winking caused by involuntary contraction of the eyelid muscle, producing more or less complete closure of the eyelids.

BLOOD COUNT   The calculation of the total number of red or white blood cells in a cubic millimeter of blood.

BLOOD CULTURE   Blood drawn aseptically, then submitted to the lab for identification, growth, and analysis.

BLOOD POISONING   Septicemia, pyemia or Bacteremia.

BLOODWORMS or STRONGYLES   See NEMATODE.

BOT   The larva of botflies (gastrophilus); they are parasitic when attached to the stomach lining.

BOTULISM   Poisoning caused by an exotoxin from the bacillus clostridium botulinum that affects the nervous system. Death occurs upon ingestion of exotoxin. See SHAKER FOAL.

BRACHYGNATHIA (PARROT MOUTH)   Shortened lower jaw in relation to the upper jaw.

BRAN MASH   A meal that is wet and preferably somewhat fluffy. Consists of equal parts of wheat bran and concentrates (grain) mixed with either hot or cold water, as the weather dictates. High in phosphorus and fiber.

BREAKOVER POINT   Flexion of and location on the foot as it is lifted from the ground.

BREECH PRESENTATION   Presentation of the hind legs and buttocks of the fetus during labor; posterior portion of the foal's body with the hind legs appearing first.

CARDIOVASCULAR   Pertaining to the heart and blood vessels.

CARTILAGINOUS   Pertaining to cartilage.

CASTRATION   Removal of the testicles, thereby neutering or gelding a male horse.

CATARACTS   A loss of transparency of the crystalline lens of the eye or of its capsule.

CATHETER   A hollow rubber or plastic cylinder used for passage through blood vessels and body canals.

CEREBELLUM   The posterior brain mass; that part of the brain mass concerned with coordination of movement.

CEREBROSPINAL   Pertaining to the brain and spinal cord.

CEREBRUM   The front and largest portion of the brain, consisting of two hemispheres.

CESAREAN SECTION (C-SECTION)   A surgical procedure in which an incision is made through the abdominal wall into the upper segment of the uterus in order to extract a fetus.

CHESTNUTS (NIGHT EYES)   Small, crusty tissue deposits located on the inside of the foreleg above the knee and the inside of the hindleg below the hocks.

CHOLINESTERASE   An enzyme directly involved with nervous impulses.

CHROMOSOMES   Intracellular rod-shaped bodies that carry genes or hereditary factors within the nucleus of a cell at the time of cell division.

CLEAN LEGS   Normal, undamaged, and sound legs.

CLOVER HAY   Legume hay.

CLUBFOOT   A stumpy-shaped foot caused by increased tension in the deep digital flexor tendon.

CLUMPING   See AGGLUTINATION.

COCKED ANKLES   A broad, nonspecific term that describes an anterior subluxation or any degree of anterior (forward) deviation from the normal articular surfaces of the ankle joint (from variable causes). See NUTRITIONAL CONTRACTION.

COLIC   Acute gastrointestinal pain.

COLOSTRUM   A thin, milky fluid secreted by the mammary gland a few days before parturition; a mare's first milk, essential to the foal's health because it transmits vital passive antibodies, although for a limited time (48–72 hours).

COLOSTRUM BANK   Colostrum that is gathered from mares and prepared, frozen, and stored for future use with needy foals.

COMBINED IMMUNODEFICIENCY (CID)   A fatal genetic immune deficiency found only in the Arabian breed. A laboratory test can now identify carriers.

COMPATIBILITY TEST   A test administered immediately after birth to detect an incompatibility between the mare's milk and the foal's red blood cells. See ISOERYTHROLYSIS.

CONCENTRATE   Cereal grains.

CONCEPTUS   The early product of conception from the time of fertilization of the ovum.

CONFORMATION   The anatomical structure and external appearance of a horse.

CONGENITAL   Existing at birth, but not hereditary.

CONSTIPATION   A condition suffered when bowel movements are infrequent or incomplete.

CONTAGIOUS   Transmitted by direct or indirect contact.

CONTAMINANT   Any impurity; dirt or pathogens with the potential to cause infection.

CONTRACTED FOAL   Generalized description of many kinds of contractions.

CONTUSION   A bruise that does not break the skin.

COPROPHAGY   The act of eating manure (considered a vice).

CORNEA   A transparent membrane forming the outer coating of the front of the eyeball and containing the aqueous humor or fluid in which the iris is bathed.

CORONARY BAND   A band of tissue containing blood vessels and nerves that encircles the top of the hoof.

CORONOPEDAL CONTRACTION   Unnatural elevation of the heel due to excessive and continuous pull of the deep digital flexor tendon, resulting in a clubfoot.

CORYNEBACTERIUM EQUUS (RHODOCOCCUS EQUUS)   A gram-positive bacillus that is a soil inhabitant and the causative agent of foal pneumonia and abscesses found in the gastrointestinal tract and usually throughout the body at three months of age.

COW HOCKS   Hocks that are bowed or bent in an inward curve.

CREEP FEEDER   An area constructed to provide a constant source of available feed for young horses in a peaceful environment.

CRIMPED OATS   Whole oats with cracked hulls; crimped oats are easier to chew and digest and provide better nutrition than rolled and crushed oats.

CRYPTORCHIDISM   Hidden or recessed testicles that do not descend into the scrotal sac.

CURB   Protrusion of the planter ligament at the back and bottom of the hock; such swelling usually causes lameness.

DAM   The female parent.

DEEP DIGITAL FLEXOR TENDON (DDFT)   Main flexor tendon in horse's leg.

DEFECATION   Discharge of feces from the rectum.

DEFECTIVE SOFT PALATE   Inefficient palate of congenital origin.

DEGENERATION   Usually irreversible deterioration of specific cells or organs.

DEHYDRATION   Excessive loss of water from a body or from an organ.

DESMOTOMY   Surgical transection of a ligament.

DIARRHEA   An abnormally frequent discharge of fluid fecal matter from the bowel.

DIFFUSE   Widely distributed; not definitely localized.

DISINFECTION   The process of eliminating disease-producing microorganisms and their toxins.

DISTAL END   The reverse of proximal; located far from the point of attachment.

DIURETIC   An agent that increases the flow of urine.

DOCK   The base of the tail.

DORSOSACRAL   Dorsal surface of foal's spine when aligned with the sacral vertebrae of the mare's spinal column; the normal position for any foal in preparation for delivery (on its stomach with extended head, neck and forelegs).

DRESSING FEET   Trimming and balancing of the horny hoof.

DUMMY FOAL   Septicemia caused by *Actinobacillus equuli* (*Shigella equuli*).

DYSTOCIA   A difficult birth.

EDEMA   Excessive and abnormal accumulation of fluid in the tissue spaces, originating from the capillaries.

EEV   Abbreviation of Eastern equine encephalomyelitis vaccine.

ELECTROLYTES   The ions of the various salts of sodium, potassium, calcium, magnesium, iron, etc., found in the body fluids in precise amounts. During stress or illness replenishment by IV and oral administration is relied upon.

EMBRYO   The early or developing stage of the product of fertilization from the moment of conception until appendages, head, and neck are defined; thereafter it is called a fetus.

EMBRYOTOMY or FETOTOMY   Dismemberment of a fetus to facilitate delivery.

ENDOCRINE SYSTEM   Ductless glands whose internal secretions influence appropriate target glands that, in response, further react upon *their* target glands.

ENDOMETRIUM   Inner lining of the uterus.

ENDOPARASITISM   Invasion of a horse's body by parasites that live within the internal organs.

ENDOTOXIN   Poison in the circulating blood from entrance of gram-negative bacteria from the GI tract.

ENTEROTOXEMIA   Septicemia caused by entrance into the circulation by deadly bacteria from the gut.

ENTITY   A particular and separate thing (pertaining to disease).

EPIPHYSEAL   In the young animal the end (extremity) of the bone is called the epiphysis and is separated from the shaft (diaphysis) by the zone of growth (epiphyseal plate or line), which closes at maturity.

EPIZOOTIC   A rapidly spreading disease attacking a large number of animals simultaneously over a wide geographic area; the animal equivalent to a human epidemic.

ERYTHROCYTE   A mature red blood cell responsible for oxygen transport to and from the lungs to tissues and organs.

ESCHERICHIA COLI   A species of microorganisms constituting the greater part of the intestinal flora of animals (and man).

ESOPHAGEAL OPENING   Orifice leading to the esophagus; located above the tracheal opening and between the guttural pouches.

ESOPHAGUS   That portion of the digestive canal that leads from the pharynx to the stomach.

ESTROUS or HEAT   The recurrent, restricted period of sexual receptivity in female horses.

ETIOLOGY   The study or theory of the cause of any disease.

EUSTACHIAN TUBE   A cartilaginous tube through which the tympanic cavity of the middle ear communicates with the pharynx. The guttural pouch, peculiar to the equine, is a distention in the eustachian tube.

EVERT   To turn inside out.

EXCURSION   Movement of the rib cage in order to breathe out (exhale) or breathe in (inhale).

EXOTOXINS   Produced by *Clostridium tetani* and *botulinum*. Both fatal.

EXUDATES   Material such as fluid, cells, or cellular debris that has escaped from blood vessels and been deposited in tissues or on tissue surfaces, usually as a result of inflammation.

FALLING WEATHER   Anything that falls from the sky, such as rain, snow, sleet, etc.

FAT-SOLUBLE VITAMINS   Those vitamins that can be dissolved in fats or fat solvents, Vitamins A, D, E, K found in the equine.

FEMUR   The bone between the pelvis and the stifle.

FESCUE (TALL)   Contain fungi (endophytes) causing toxicity, abortions and agalactia (no milk).

FETAL ANASARCA (HYDROPS AMNION)   General accumulation of fluid in various tissues and body cavities from failure of the fetus to swallow during gestation.

FETOTOMY   See EMBRYOTOMY.

FINDING   An observation; discovery of a condition.

FIRST MILK   See COLOSTRUM.

FLACCIDITY   Reduced tissue tone.

FLAXSEED   See LINSEED MEAL.

FLOAT   To remove protruding surfaces and growth edges of teeth by a dental rasp or float.

FLORA   Various beneficial bacteria found in the intestinal contents.

FOALCHEK   A commercial test used to determine immune body levels in the foal's plasma.

FOAL HEAT   The first estral cycle experienced by the parturiant mare; usually occurs eight to 12 days following delivery of a foal.

FOAL-LAC   A commercial milk substitute. Contains a well-balanced formula but no antibodies.

FOAL HEAT SCOURS   Foal diarrhea occurring around nine days of age.

FORMULA A recipe or prescription giving method and proportions of ingredients for the preparation of some meal or medication.

FOUNDER Inflammation of the laminae of the feet (the vertical leaves or structures attaching the sensitive *os pedis* to the insensitive hoof wall); there are many degrees of laminitis, of which founder is the most severe.

FREE-CHOICE FEEDING To make food available at a rate to be selected by the individual animal.

GENES The elements by which hereditary characteristics are transmitted; such characteristics are of two kinds: dominant, the major and overriding characteristics, and recessive, those that appear in the absence of the dominant genes; the biologic unit of heredity, self-producing and located in a definite position on a particular chromosome.

GESTATION Period of pregnancy; 11 months in the mare, nine months in the cow and human.

GET Sire or stallion's progeny or offspring.

GLOTTIS The space between the vocal cords at the upper portion of the larynx; structures around the larynx.

GLUTEAL MUSCLES Large muscles of the buttocks ideally used for injections.

GOITER Enlargement of the thyroid gland; caused by deficiency or overabundance of iodine in soil or diet.

GONAD The sexual gland, either ovary or testicle.

GROSS Coarse or large; macroscopic.

GUTTURAL POUCH A large mucous, membranous sac; a diverticulum (or pouch) of the eustachian tube, peculiar to the equidae (horse, zebra, and ass; a single-hooved mammal); thought to be pressure regulators in the airway involving equilibrium.

HEAT LAMP Infrared heat lamp that is safe and indicated for use in a foal's stall. Avoid ultraviolet light.

HEMATOMA A localized swelling usually full of clotted blood from a ruptured blood vessel or vessels and confined within an organ or tissue space.

HEMOLYTIC ANEMIA Anemia caused by destruction of red blood cells, usually resulting in loss of hemoglobin.

HEREDITARY Inherited from parents; genetically transmitted from parent to offspring.

HERNIA Any protrusion of an organ or tissue through the connective tissue or the wall of the cavity in which it is normally enclosed.

HERPES VIRUS   The causal viral agent of herpes simplex; causes upper respiratory symptoms in young horses; responsible for rhinopneumonitis in mares, which results in abortion.

HUSBANDRY   A study of conservative and efficient methods relative to the control and management of horses, soil, and farming.

HYDROCEPHALIC   When abnormal accumulation of fluid causes enlargement of the cranial vault and subsequent compression and atrophy of brain tissue, with mental weakness and convulsions.

HYDROPS AMNION   Excessive fluid accumulation in the uterus from fetal failure to swallow, resulting in abortion.

HYPOGLYCEMIA   Abnormal decrease of sugar in the blood. Most foals suffer this state at birth prior to ingesting colostrum.

HYPOPLASIA   Defective formation; incomplete development.

HYPOTHERMIA   Reduced body temperature; first symptom of shock syndrome.

ICTERUS   See JAUNDICE.

ICU   Intensive care unit—found in modern equine hospitals.

IM   Abbreviation for intramuscular or injected within the substance of a muscle.

IMMUNODEFICIENCY   Inability of foal to either receive, absorb, or utilize antibodies present in the mare's colostrum.

IMMUNOGLOBULIN   Serum proteins capable of conferring immunity.

IMPACTION   Severe constipation; sluggish movement or stasis of intestinal contents.

INAPPETENCE   Lack of appetite.

INDUCTION AREA   That space in an equine hospital in which the patient is administered the drugs that induce surgical plane of an anesthesia.

INFECTIOUS   Cause of infection by microorganisms easily transmitted by actual contact.

INFLUENZA   Viral respiratory infection.

INFRARED LIGHT   Safe for use in foal stalls.

INGESTA   Food or substances taken into the body by mouth.

INGUINAL   Pertaining to the area of the groin.

INTERVENTRICULAR   Concerned with a small anatomical cavity, as of the brain or heart.

INTERVENTRICULAR SEPTAL DEFECT   A defect of the wall between the two ventricular cavities of the heart.

INTRANASAL   Within the nose.

INTRAUTERINE   Within the uterus; in utero.

INTRAVAGINAL   Within the canal leading from the vulva to the uterus.

INVOLUTED   The return of the uterus to normal size after enlargement by birth.

ISOERYTHROLYSIS   Destruction of the foal's erythrocytes by its own mother's colostrum loaded with lethal antibodies.

ISOIMMUNIZATION   The body's own development of defending antibodies against a mare's own pregnancy.

IV   Abbreviation for injection (intravenous) within a vein or veins.

JAUNDICE (ICTERUS)   A yellowish discoloration of tissues and body fluids; the results of hemoglobin destruction of the foal's red blood cells or erythrocytes. Commonly associated with neonatal isoerythrolysis.

JOINT ILL   Hot, swollen, painful joints most commonly caused by *Streptococcus equi* infection.

JUGULAR VEINS   The large blood vessels that pass down each side of the horse's neck; commonly used for injection purposes.

KERATITIS   Generalized inflammation of the cornea of the eye.

KILLED-VIRUS VACCINE   A dead virus capable of stimulating an antibody response in the horse's body.

KLEBSIELLA EQUUS   Encapsulated microorganism found in the respiratory or intestinal tract, frequently associated with diarrhea and pneumonia in foals.

LACTOBACILLUS   Beneficial bacteria that is often fed as an additive during ill health or disease to replenish or replace normal bacterial flora found in the healthy horse's gut.

LEGUME   Food plants that efficiently utilize nitrogen from the air; legume hay is alfalfa, clover, or soybean.

LESION   A pathological alteration of tissue; a wound or injury; loss of function of a part.

LEUCOCYTE   A white blood cell that helps fight infection.

LIGATE   To tie, or bind, a vessel or part by thread, gut, or wire.

LINSEED MEAL   Ground flaxseed, high in protein and selenium. Fed as an additive for improvement of skin and coat.

LITER   The basic unit of capacity in the metric system; it is equivalent to 1.0567 quarts liquid measure or 1,000cc.

LIVE-VIRAL VACCINE   A living microorganism contained within a laboratory preparation administered to produce antibodies against a specific virus or disease; a *killed vaccine* retains its antigenicity; an *attenuated* viral preparation has had its pathogenicity reduced in order to diminish its virulence and enhance safety of inoculation.

LOCKJAW   Lay term for the fatal disease tetanus; caused by *Clostridium tetani*.

LORDOSIS   Swayback.

LUMBOSACRAL   Pertaining to the lower back.

LYMPHOCYTE   A type of white blood cell formed in the lymphoid tissue throughout the body; associated with the immune system.

LYMPHOPENIA   Reduction of circulating white blood cells, specifically the lymphocytes, which are important to the formation of immune responses of the body.

MAIDEN MARE   A mare who has never produced a foal.

MALPRESENTATION   Faulty or abnormal fetal presentation at time of delivery.

MAMMARY (UDDER)   Pertaining to the milk-producing glands.

MANDIBLE   The bone of the lower jaw.

MASTITIS   Inflammation of the mammary gland and teats.

MAXILLARY   The bone of the upper jaw.

MECONIUM   An accumulation of semisolid material in the fetal intestinal tract during intrauterine life; thought to be associated with the embryonic ingestion of amniotic fluid.

MEDIAL CARPAL DEVIATION   Inward deflection of the forelegs at the level of the knee.

METACARPOPHALANGEAL   Having to do with that part of the leg from below the knee to and including the ankle joint.

MICROORGANISM   A minute living organism, usually microscopic. Those of equine medical interest are bacteria, Spirochete organisms, Rickettsial, viruses, molds, and yeasts.

MILK NOSE   The presence of milk on a weakened foal's face and nose; occurs and serves as a warning when a foal cannot manage to keep pace with the mare's milk flow while nursing.

MILKY NOSE SYNDROME   A condition characteristic of a weakened foal that is either becoming ill or recovering from an illness; it cannot keep pace with the mare's normal milk flow and consequently ends up with an excess of milk on its face and nose.

MONORCHIDISM   Lack of proper descent of one testicle.

MOTILE   The inherent power of motion; having the power to move spontaneously.

MUCOPURULENT   Containing both mucus and pus.

MULTIPARA   A mare that has had two or more foals, whether or not the foals were alive at birth.

NASOGASTRIC TUBE   A small hollow tube used to transport nourishment and medicine directly to the foal's stomach via the nasal passages; commonly called stomach tube.

NAVEL   Point of attachment of the umbilical cord to the body of the foal.

NAVEL ILL   Bacterial invasion with subsequent infection of the navel stump in young foals. Streptococcal microorganisms are commonly the causative agent.

NEMATODE   Any internal parasitic worm possessing a threadlike, unsegmented body (roundworms or bloodworms).

NEONATE   A newborn.

NEUROMUSCULAR   Pertaining to nerves and muscles.

NEUROTROPHIC   Having an affinity for nervous tissue or exerting its principal effect on the nervous system.

NICTITATING MEMBRANE   The inner or third eyelid.

NUTRITIONAL CONTRACTION   A crippling condition caused by over-nutrition during rapid growth months; the bony structures of the young horse out-pace the tendon growth; thus, the tendons become too short in relation to the bone length and crippling contraction occurs.

OCCLUSION   Blockage of a vessel, usually by thrombosis or emboli.

OMPHALITIS   Inflammation and abscesses in and around the navel cord stump.

ORGANOPHOSPHATES   A group of worm medicines that are considered somewhat unsafe for use in foals and adults; affect birds and the general environment.

ORIFICE   Any natural opening in the body.

OS PEDIS   Coffin bone in the foot or third phalanx.

OSTEOARTHRITIS   Chronic, multiple degenerative joint disease, usually of traumatic or physical origin in the equine.

OSTEOCHONDRITIS DISSECANS   Joint lesions in foals and young horses.

OSTEOMYELITIS   Inflammation and degeneration of bone tissue caused by a pathogenic microorganism.

PALPATE   To examine by hand; to feel.

PARESIS   Partial or incomplete paralysis.

PAROTID AREA   Below the ear and behind the curve of the jaw; jowl area.

PARTURITION   The act of giving birth.

PATELLA   A flat triangular bone located at the front of the stifle joint.

PATENT   Apparent, open, unobstructed.

PATHOGENS   Any disease-producing microorganisms or material.

PATHONOMONIC   The indisputable symptom or group of symptoms that are diagnostic.

PEN-STREP   Any combination of the antibiotics penicillin and dihydrostreptomycin.

PERINATAL   Immediately after birth.

PERINEAL AREA   The associated structures occupying the pelvic outlet.

PERISTALSIS   Involuntary movement that propels ingesta through the gastrointestinal tract.

PERITONEUM   A serous sac encasing the abdominal contents.

PERVIOUS URACHUS (LEAKY NAVEL CORD)   Occurs when the urachus, inside of the navel cord, fails to close after birth as it should, and continues to leak urine from the navel stump.

PHARYNGITIS   Inflammation of the pharynx.

PHENOTHIAZINE   A compound widely used to combat intestinal nematode parasitisms of the horse; popular for many years, it is presently being replaced by newer anthelmintics.

PHYSIS SYNDROME   A catch-all term for a group of limb and joint aberrations found in fast-growing young foals. Manifested by tendon contraction, crooked legs, epiphysitis, apple ankles, OCD and cervical deformities.

PHOTOPHOBIA   Increased sensitivity and intolerance to light.

PIPERAZINE SALTS (PIPERAZINE CITRATE)   An anthelmintic used for the removal of round worms (ascarids) in the foal.

PITUITARY GLAND   The endocrine gland which controls the other endocrine glands, influences growth, metabolism, maturation, and parturition as well as the entire reproductive cycle.

PLACENTA   The developed organ within the uterus which at conception establishes life-sustaining communication between the mare and embryo.

PLACENTA PREVIA   The premature detachment of a normally situated placenta; infection, hormonal, trauma, are among many other causes.

POLYDACTYLIA   A developmental anomaly characterized by the presence of more than the normal number of limbs (appendages).

POSTMORTEM   Autopsy; surgical exploration to determine the cause of death.

POSTPARTUM   Immediate period after birth.

PREDISPOSITION   Tendency or inclination; latent susceptibility to disease, which may be activated under certain conditions, as by stress.

PREFORMED ANTIBODIES   Manufactured biologic serums that confer passive immunity to an individual after injection of specific antibodies produced in another individual or other tissues that provide immediate protection to the recipient. Example: tetanus antitoxin.

PREPARTURIENT   Previous to delivery.

PREPPED   Prepared for medication or surgical procedure.

PREPUCE   A large tubular fold of skin covering the glans penis.

PROFOUND   Extreme, great.

PROGENY   Offspring, descendants.

PROGNATHIA (SOW MOUTH)   Over-growth of lower jaw in relation to the upper jaw.

PROGESTERONE   A hormone produced by the corpora lutea, thought to be responsible for preparation of the uterus for the reception and development of the fertilized ovum by glandular proliferation of the endometrium and maintenance of pregnancy.

PROPHYLAXIS   The prevention of disease.

PROSTIGLANDINS   An injectable hormone that possesses a strong luteolytic action upon the gonads of the mare.

PROVIDONE-IODINE   A disinfecting agent.

PSEUDOCYESIS   False or spurious pregnancy.

PSEUDOMONAS   A family of gram-negative bacteria capable of causing chronic infections in animals; associated with subfertile brood mares.

PURGING   Projectile diarrhea.

PYOGENOUS   Producing or caused by pus.

RECTOVAGINAL TEAR   Tearing of the tissues separating the vaginal (birth) canal from the rectum.

REDUCE   To restore to the normal place or relation of parts, as to reduce a fracture.

RESECT   Surgical removal of a considerable portion of intestine or structure such as bone.

RETICULOENDOTHELIAL   Pertaining to the tissues having both reticular (net-like) and endothelial (cells that line the cavities of the body) attributes concerned in blood cell formation and destruction that play a defensive role against inflammation and help in creating immunity.

RH DISEASE   A condition in which the mother produces antibodies to her fetus; counterpart of isoerythrolysis in the mare and foal; blood typing prior to breeding and compatibility tests during gestation and immediately after birth have been helpful in the recognition and prevention of this disease.

RHINOPNEUMONITIS   Viral infection of the upper respiratory tract in young horses; inevitable cause of abortion in mares by attacking the placental membranes and causing viremia in the fetus, followed by fetal death.

RHODOCOCCUS EQUUS   See CORYNEBACTERIUM EQUUS.

ROUNDED HOCK   To the lay person, any deviation from normal in the structure of the hock.

SACROSCIATIC LIGAMENTS   Ligaments attached to the sacrum and the ischium.

SCHISTOSOMUS REFLEXUS   A fetal monster; the abdominal contents lack skin covering.

SCOLIOSED or SCOLIOTIC   Lateral curvature of the spine with a secondary compensatory curve.

SCOURS   Diarrhea.

SCROTUM   The external pouch of skin enclosing the two testes and their accessory organs.

SELENIUM An essential trace element. Deficiencies cause white muscle disease in foals and alkali disease in adult horses.

SEPTAL Pertaining to a septum (a dividing wall or membranous partition) between two soft masses of tissue.

SEPTICEMIA Blood poisoning due to bacterial invasion of the circulatory system.

SEROLOGY The study of the blood serum.

SERUM TRANSFUSION Indicated when a foal requires preformed antibodies for protection against disease. Blood is drawn from an adult donor and prepared, separating the blood components and leaving the straw-colored serum needed for transfusion on the top of the vial. Concentrated antibody level.

SHAKER FOAL A usually fatal neuromuscular disease caused by *Clostridium botulinum* found in suckling foals of about eight weeks in age; the foal is weak, unable to stand, and suffers progressive shaking and profound muscular tremors. In adults *Clostridium botulinum* causes the deadly disease called botulism. Different symptoms, both lethal.

SHIGELLA EQUULI One of the microorganisms that causes foal septicemia.

SICKLE HOCKS Hocks shaped like a sickle; these hocks bend in a backward or posterior curve.

SILENT or SPEC MARE A mare that shows no outward sign of being sexually receptive.

SIMILAC A commercial milk substitute. Lacks essential antibodies.

SLEEPER FOAL A systemic infectious disease of newborn foals, caused by *Actinobacillus equuli*. Typically, the foal is weak, semi-comatose, unable to stand. Commonly called "dummy" or "wanderer" foal. *Shigella equuli* was the former name and cause of this syndrome.

STARY Dull or lusterless coat.

STASIS The cessation of a biological function.

STAZ-DRI Trade name for a commercially manufactured bedding material.

STENOSIS Narrowing or stricture of a duct or canal.

STIFLES The joint above the hock and below the hip. Comparable to the human knee.

STOCK UP Swelling of any of the lower legs because of interference with circulation or bruising of the tissues.

STOOL   Fecal material.

STRANGLES   An acute infectious disease caused by *Streptococcus equi*, characterized by enlargement and suppuration of the lymph glands of the head and jowl, associated with pneumonia.

STREPTOCOCCUS PYOGENES   Bacteria most commonly the cause of joint and navel ill.

STRONGYLES   Bloodworms.

SUBLUXATION   Faulty articular processes of a joint or joints; an incomplete or partial dislocation.

SUPERIOR CHECK LIGAMENT DESMOTOMY   Surgical procedure for relief of tendon inequity in the superficial digital flexor tendon.

SUPERNUMERARY DIGIT (POLYDACTYLISM)   Extra appendages; more than the usual number of limbs for the species. Considered a genetic throwback.

SUPPURATE   To fester or form pus.

SUPRAORBITAL RIDGE   The bony prominence above the cavity that contains the eyeball.

SWEET FEED or SWEET STOCK   Any of several concentrates (cereal grains) mixed with molasses to enhance palatability.

SYMPHYSIS   A site or line of union of bony surfaces by means of a plate of fibrocartilage.

SYNDROME   A group of signs or symptoms that collectively characterize a disease.

TERM   The end of a normal pregnancy.

TETANUS ANTITOXIN   Preformed tetanus antibodies; injected, it affords passive immunization to tetanus and should be given, instead of tetanus toxoid, to every newborn foal and repeated if foal under four months of age sustains a foot or lower leg wound.

TETANUS TOXOID   A killed preparation of tetanus microorganisms administered by injection to confer immunity to tetanus; contraindicated in a foal under four months of age. At four months, toxoid vaccination is indicated.

THORAX   Chest or lung and rib area.

THRIFTY   Growing vigorously; thriving.

TIBIA   The bone that extends from the stifle to the hock.

TOPICAL   Applicable to or pertaining to a particular part of the body.

TORSION   Twisting.

TORTICOLLIS   Wry or contorted neck muscles associated with unnatural position of the head.

TOXICITY   Poison.

TRACE MINERALS   Iodine, iron, copper, cobalt, sulfur, manganese, magnesium, selenium, and potassium are considered trace minerals as they are needed in small amounts for maintenance of life.

TRANQUILIZER   Any drug capable of reducing anxiety and tension states in people and animals. (A word of caution: When used in the equine, the drug will produce a sleepy horse without altering the pain threshold; any pain stimulus can quickly result in a dramatically awakened horse.)

TRANSECT   A cut across a long axis; a cross section.

TRANSFUSION   The transfer of blood, plasma, or serum intravenously.

TROCHLEA   A pulleylike structure, as the part of the distal end of the humerus that articulates with the ulna.

TUBE FEED   The delivery of food to the stomach through a naso-gastric tube.

TUBER ISCHII   A large elongated mass on the body of the ischium (part of the hip bone) to which several muscles are attached.

TYMPANY   Air-filled guttural pouch.

UDDER   Mammary gland.

ULNA   An incomplete bone in the foreleg; from the elbow to the knee.

ULTRASOUND   High-frequency sound waves, used for diagnostic and treatment purposes including pregnancy and progency diagnosis.

ULTRAVIOLET LIGHT   Light that emanates from wavelengths shorter than those of visible light and longer than those of X-rays; this light is bacteriocidal, but produces no warmth and may harm the foal's eyes. It is contraindicated in foal stalls. Infrared light is safe and strongly suggested.

UMBILICAL CORD   A fetal life-support system for receiving nutrients and carrying off waste products during embryonic development. One end of cord is attached to the fetal abdomen; it then spreads out into the allantois chorion placental tissue attached to the lining of the maternal uterus.

UREMIA   An excess of urine and its constituents in the blood and the toxic condition produced thereby.

URETHRA   The membranous canal through which urine is discharged from the urinary bladder.

VACCINE   A preparation that is administered to produce or increase immunity to a particular disease.

VECTOR   Commonly, a bloodsucking or biting insect; an organism that carries pathogens (infective agents) from one host to another.

VEE   Abbreviation for Venezuelan equine encephalomyelitis.

VENTRAL   Abdominal or lower surface of the body.

VERTEBRAL COLUMN   Backbone or spine.

VESICLE   Small bladder or sac containing liquid.

VIRAL   Caused by or pertaining to a virus.

VIREMIAS   The presence of viruses in the blood.

VISCERA   Internal organs of the body contained in the abdominal cavity.

VULVA   External entrance to the female reproductive tract.

WANDERER FOAL   A systemic infectious disease of newborn foals, caused by *Actinobacillus equuli* and *Shigella equuli*. Typically, the foal is weak, semi-comatose, unable to stand. Also called "dummy" or "sleeper" foal.

WATER-DRINKING SYNDROME   As no healthy foal either requires water or shows any interest in drinking it, water-drinking syndrome is a sign of impending illness.

WAX   A viscous, honey-colored substance that seals, and may or may not drip from the teats; the precursor of first milk or colostrum; almost always present prior to first labor, it is produced by the activated ducts and tubules of the milk glands.

WHIRLBONE   See TUBER ISCHII.

WHITE MUSCLE DISEASE   Fatal in perinatal foals; caused by a deficiency of the trace mineral selenium in the brood mare during gestation.

WOBBLES   Ataxia, with weakness of hindquarter motion initially, and characteristically pain-free lack of control of the hind legs. Many known causes, with feeble treatments.

WOLF TEETH   Little extra teeth in the upper jaw that interfere with the position of a bit and result in pain when the bit is forced backward against these fragmented, useless pre-molars; a functionless, rudimentary vestige of evolution. Extraction is indicated.

ZINC TURBIDITY TEST   A blood test administered to determine immune body levels in the newborn foal.

INDEX